WU STYLE TAIJIQUAN

— A DETAILED COURSE FOR HEALTH AND SELF-DEFENCE AND TEACHINGS OF THREE FAMOUS MASTERS IN BEIJING

Wang Peisheng & Zeng Weiqi

HAI FENG PUBLISHING CO. Hong Kong
and
ZHAOHUA PUBLISHING HOUSE Beijing, China

Editor: Zeng Weiqi

Authors: Wang Peisheng & Zeng Weiqi

Translators: Zeng Weiqi & Li Jiaqiao

Cover and Illustration: Li Shiji

ISBN 962-238-015-8

Published by
HAI FENG PUBLISHING CO.
Rm. 701, Chung Shang Bldg. 7/F.
9-10, Queen Victoria St.
Hong Kong

and

ZHAOHUA PUBLISHING HOUSE
Chegongzhuang Xilu 21
Beijing, China

Printed by
C & C JOINT PRINTING CO. (H.K.) LTD.
75, Pau Chung St.
Kowloon, Hong Kong

First Edition 1983

7.297-16E 00360 7-E-1680p

CONTENTS

FOREWORD

In the days of our ancestors, it was not unusual for a martial arts enthusiast to trudge over a thousand miles, scaling high mountains and fording rapid streams to seek a great master and some helpful friends, for it was common practice that any subtle technique, precious experience, and special knowledge were made esoteric and only to be handed down from father to son and master to selected disciple.

Today, with the advent of ultrasonic jets and other modernized means of transportation, travelling over thousands of miles presents no hardship, however, it is still not at all easy to find a great master who has the real stuff and is willing to hand it over to anyone who comes to his door.

But you will find in this book three of the old masters of Wu style *Taijiquan* in Beijing together with the crystallized teachings of their unique merits as presented by me, one who has the privilege of being their student.

Though *Taijiquan* is both a wonderful system of physical culture and a superior form of Chinese martial art, today, the ways of applying the art to practical self-defence is not known to many and is actually mastered only by a few.

Now master Wang Peisheng presents you in this book a course showing you, with detailed instructions and hundreds of specially drawn illustrations, how each movement of different *Taijiquan* postures can be made effective as a defensive and offensive move if executed correctly as instructed. Master Wang Peisheng's expertise in making actual applications of the martial art of *Taijiquan* is generally recognized and praised not only by people in the Taijiquan circle, but by many a master of other schools of Chinese martial arts as well.

It is hoped that the publishing of this book will render some service to thc *Taijiquan* enthusiasts, be they veterans or beginners, and will enhance the cultural interflow between the peoples of the People's Republic of China and the different countries of the world.

Editor

Publisher's Notes

1. The 37-Postures Taijiquan set presented in this book is a condensed yet complete set of Wu style Taijiquan rearranged by the famous Chinese martial art expert master Wang Peisheng after deleting almost all the duplicate postures and retaining all different postures contained in the much longer traditional set. The purpose is to shorten the time for learning and for daily practice without sacrificing any completeness or subtlety. At the same time, the posture "Grasp the Bird's Tail" which includes four movements originally (warding, pressing, rolling and pushing) has now been developed to include eight movements (warding, pressing, rolling, pushing, pulling, splitting, elbow-striking and shoulder-striking).
2. There are two sets of specially drawn illustrations accompanying the text of 37-Postures Wu style Taijiquan: one (comprised of 240 drawings) to show the form of the different movements of the thirty-seven postures constituting the solo sequence; another (comprised of 273 drawings) to demonstrate how each movement is applied to defence or/and offence in a supposed context of confrontations. Study the related drawings of the two sets of illustrations correspondingly will help to do and to use a certain movement correctly. However, in actual application, many of the movements are often not done in the exact manner as in solo practice, and it is also the case with the drawings.
3. At the end of the instructions given for each movement in the solo sequence, the reader will almost always find a phrase "The weight is now on right (or left) foot." which means that one's whole or a greater part of body weight is now borne by the right (or left) foot. To find a precise percentage of the body weight distributed on each foot, please refer to the footprints right below the relevant illustrations.
4. In reading the instructions, one will often come across an expression such as "the right shoulder seeks to meet the left hipbone, the right elbow seeks to meet the left knee", etc. Here "seeks to meet" denotes not the seeking of an actual meeting of the two parts, but is rather a thought to guide a certain part of the body to move toward a definite point to ensure a correct posture, to keep one's body in better balance or to shift one's centre of gravity in a way that will render one's defensive or offensive action more effective.

Outstanding Expert, Master Wang Peisheng

THE WAY TO MASTER THE MARTIAL ART OF TAIJIQUAN

— Teachings of the Outstanding Expert, Master Wang Peisheng

Following closely the fundamental Taijiquan principles in practical application, making careful analysis of every success and failure, then summing up one's experience to formulate one's own rules and testing them again and again in practical application.

Brief Introduction to the Master

Master Wang Peisheng, born in 1919 in Wuqing County of Hebei Province, has lived in Beijing most of the time since childhood, and has become a professional Taijiquan instructor since 18. Now 64, Wang is perhaps the youngest among the living old Taijiquan masters of Beijing, and has retained his super skill in the application of the art in self-defence up to the present. For this, he has not only won fame in the Taijiquan circle, but is also praised and respected by some masters of different schools of Chinese martial arts, who have witnessed the efficacy of his super skill.

Wang had ten years of very hard and varied training when young, and had thus built up a solid foundation necessary for the making of a real master. At 8, he was taught by some neighbours who were working in a circus to do all sorts of limbering and strengthening exercises for the waist and legs and was able to execute 36 somersaults in succession on a table top. He started to learn the Eight Trigrams Palm at 12, and the Springy Legs at 13, both from competent masters. Then at 14 he started to learn Taijiquan from a well known master Yang Yuting who was a student of Wang Maozhai. Wang had the fortune of being taught directly by Quan You, a Manchurian captain of the squad safeguarding a royal family, and who had inherited the art of Taijiquan directly from the founder of the Yang School Taijiquan, the great master Yang Lucan. Quan You later modified what he learned in some way and had his art evolved to be recognized as another style of Taijiquan which was later known as the Wu School Taijiquan since his son Wu Jianquan, an illustrious master of his father's style of Taijiquan in the early decades of this century, adopted a Han racial family name Wu. Hence Quan You was honoured as the father of the Wu School Taijiquan.

From 15-17, while receiving personal instructions from Master Yang Yuting and sometimes even directly from Yang's teacher, Master Wang Maozhai, Wang Peisheng also served as Yang's assistant in helping to coach three different groups of students. During those three years, he used to get up at 3 o'clock in the morning, then went to the woody area near the present site of Tiananmen Square and trained by himself for about two hours. His own training ranged from pilestance-keeping (a form of traditional Chinese isometric training system) to the solo practice of various forms of martial arts of Taiji school, the quan (bare-hand), the sword, the broad sword and the staff, with deep concentration on letting every movement be directed by a tranquil mind in accordance with Taijiquan principles. Then he devoted a portion of his early morning workout to repeated practice of a group of movements or a single movement for mastering a particular technique or correcting a certain weak point, after careful analysis of the success or failure in application. At 6 A.M. when the gate of the Grand Temple (now the Working People's Cultural Palace) was just open, he would go right to the "Taijiquan Study Society" inside the Temple, to assist Master Yang who was the chief instructor, in coaching the members. The first group of students, mostly clerks and small merchants, coming at 6 A.M. and leaving before 8 A.M., were given group lessons by Master Yang, with Wang Peisheng help correcting the students' postures. The second group, arriving after 8 A.M., mostly retired elders, the weak, the sick or the rich, came for individual instructions, and if Master Yang was occupied, Wang Peisheng would take his place. The third group, coming around 10 A.M., was composed mostly of Yang's advanced students who had already learned well solo sets and were in different stages of pushing-hands practice. Aside from receiving occasional instruction from Master Yang, they were met by Wang Peisheng as their trainer or sparring partner, one after another, till each sweating. As many as 20 people would be taught by Wang in a single morning, and that generally lasted till noontime! What a work-load of training and instructing for a day, and every day for three years!

After the founding of the People's Republic of China, during the fifties, Wang had been invited to teach Taijiquan at several colleges and institutes by their labour unions, and had also been contracted to teach Taijiquan and other forms of Chinese martial arts to the students majoring in Physical Culture and Sports at the Peking Normal University. Then he was away from Beijing until 1980. After about 18 years of absence, when he was seen again by the older and for the first time by the younger generations of Taijiquan enthusiasts as the winner of Taiji-broadsword at Beijing's Third Annual Taijiquan Contest for the Aged, with the highest points given in that contest, what surprise and praise were aroused! Since then, Wang has resumed teaching Taijiquan at different institutes, including the National Library of Beijing, Beijing Normal University, the Foreign Languages Institute in Beijing, etc.

Master Wang's Creative Interpretation and Application of Some Taijiquan Principles in Self-defence

Master Wang makes it a point of emphasis and has set an example to his students of how one should use one's mind and learn from experience of success and failure after having studied carefully the theories set in the Taijiquan classics, listened earnestly to his teacher's or anyone else's interpretations, and watched attentively their ways of applying these principles in practising or combating. The following are a few examples:

(1) There is a principle (a sentence of eight Chinese characters) set in the Taijiquan classics attributed to Wang Zongyue of Ming Dynasty, with a note that it had been handed down by Zhang Sanfeng, a Taoist on the Wudang Mountain in the Song Dynasty. The first half in four characters may be translated into English as "No excess, no insufficiency", and the generally accepted interpretation is — when doing Taijiquan, whether in solo practice or in pushing-hands exercise, or sparring with a partner, or in actual combating, you should use only the very necessary amount of force, not a bit more or less; and any movement you make should be just right in position. But the second half, also in four characters, are explainable in two ways: more generally as "stretch out as your opponent bends in", and some would also supply the natural reverse "and contract as your opponent expands"; and less generally as "follow the bending, adhere to (or follow) the stretching." Which is correct, or more adequate? What is Wang's opinion? Basically, Master Wang prefers the second one, but he would add something to it, as summed up from his long years of experience: "follow your opponent's bending without letting him have any chance to turn to stretching; and adhere to his stretching without giving him any opportunity to turn to bending, he will then be found in an awkward position ready to be handled easily."

(2) There is a sentence in a known Taijiquan treatise that may be rendered into English as: If you fail to catch a good opportunity or to gain an advantageous position, your body will be in a state of disorder and the cause of such a fault must be sought from the waist or legs.

Evidently this is a very important teaching, and as there is nothing abstruse with the language, we can just do according to the advice given. But why and how? The general view is that: to a human body the legs form the foundation of every posture taken and the waist acts like the axle of the moving parts, so if there is anything wrong, fundamentally there must first be something wrong with the waist or legs, or both, so the way to correct the fault is by adjusting the waist or legs. So far so good. But what if your waist itself senses some discomfort? Adjust the waist? And what if your legs sense some discomfort? Adjust the legs? Master Wang says no, and advises: if your waist senses some discomfort, forget the waist and adjust the legs; if your legs sense some discomfort, forget the legs and adjust the waist. Try it out yourself and see if it works.

(3) In the "Chant of Pushing-hands", there is a sentence with seven Chinese characters, the first four meaning — entice (your opponent) to advance and fall into emptiness (failing to reach his target); the last three, meaning — when all conditions are met, issue energy instantly. The principle is obviously sound and clear, but what are the necessary conditions, and how to catch that very moment instantly? To those who have had some basic knowledge and training in Taijiquan, the first part of the question is not difficult to answer, the following conditions are generally taken as the neccssary conditions: your opponent's slight loss of balance, the moment he gets into an awkward position, and his centre of gravity together with the most effective line through which to attack him all being sensed and located. But the second part presents real difficulty, many may have practised for years and have not yet found a sure way of catching that very right moment. If that is the case and energy is issued at the wrong moment, all the conditions may be instantly changed to your disadvantage. Now let me offer you Master Wang's simple and reliable way for your reference — The moment your opponent comes into contact with you, you should apply the Taijiquan principle and technique of "adhering, joining, sticking to, and following" to his every move, with no letting go and no resistance, while keeping an acute awareness of what is sensed from the point in touch with your opponent. Should he refrain from making an initiative, you could expose a point of weakness purposefully and entice him to take advantage of it. During the whole course of pushing-hands if a sense of heaviness is felt at the point of contact with your opponent, do not issue energy or restrain yourself instantly if you are about to issue; but at the moment when that sense of heaviness turns into lightness, lose no time to issue energy. Of course, to be able to catch the very right moment instantly, you must first have developed a keen sense of touch and a quick reaction through years of pushing-hands practice. Nevertheless, Master Wang's teaching offers a

simple to follow rule in judging whether the right moment is there or not. That surely is a thing of importance, and I hope Master Wang's advice will prove useful to you.

(4) As is generally known, the cardinal principle of Taijiquan is "using the mind (thought), not strength." Actually, in doing any physical movement, it is impossible not to use strength at all. Thus, in so saying, it is but to emphasize that the art of Taijiquan relies more on the use of one's mind than strength to overcome an opponent. Such a principle could be more easily apprehended and better appreciated today, for it is common sense now that whatever we do are controlled by our nerve system, with the cerebral cortax of our brain as the control centre. So the really important issue regarding this principle is not why it should be so, but how it should be done.

An answer seems to have been provided in another well known classic entitled "The Mental Elucidation of the Thirteen Postures". However, owing to the terseness and abstruseness of the original text in classical Chinese, it has been interpreted in different ways, such as:

1st — When the mind directs the qi, the mind must be calm, so the qi could permeate the bones. When the qi circulates through the body, the qi must flow freely and naturally, so the qi could be dictated easily and efficiently by the mind;

2nd — when the mind directs the qi, the qi must sink deep and steadily, so as to premeate the bones. When the qi moves the body, the body must be submissive, so as to be dictated easily and efficiently by the mind;

3rd — when the mind directs the qi, the directing must be calm and steady, so the qi could permeate the bones. When the qi circulates through the body, the circulating must be free and natural, so the body could be dictated easily and efficiently by the mind.

There might still be a 4th, 5th . . . From the above, we can see that in studying a Taijiquan doctrine, it is sometimes hard to catch its exact meaning by merely studying the wording in a classic; and in listening to the interpretations offered, there might be big differences of opinion that make it difficult to follow. So do not be disturbed if you find such difficulties and differences. Test what you have learned in your practice and application, sum up your experience of success and failure bit by bit, and form your own opinions one by one as Master Wang has done and advised.

Master Wang is highly praised for his subtle, varified, accurate, and effective movements employed in pushing-hands practice and in free sparring. He often cites a well known old saying: "How to use one's kungfu relies totally on one's mind-intent." I have particularly asked him about how he uses his mind to dircet his movements, and have finally focused on "What to concentrate his mind on and how to shift his points of attention in directing his movements so as to perform a certain posture or to execute a certain combative technique accurately, efficiently, and effortlessly." The following are the summerized points:

1 — Just before making any movement, think first of uplifting your head lightly and loosening the joints, especially the shoulder joint and the hip joint. This is a necessary prerequisite to make possible your facing the opponent with an attentive spirit and keeping the limbs in a fully relaxed state, so as to be able to respond quickly to any change and do the stretching or bending to the required extent.

2 — When you are doing Taijiquan in its solo form, you should have in mind a picture of meeting an opponent and that you should use a certain posture or Taijiquan technique that deemed fit to neutralize his attack or to set him off balance while he is in a certain imagined position. Thus you must first have the knowledge of the combative use of every movement of every posture as told by Master Wang in this book, or by other competent Taijiquan masters. Only by practising Taijiquan with such a picture in mind could you have the possibility of making actual use of it in combat.

3 — Whatever the form and number of movements used in a certain posture, there is a general principle, also a basic requirement, that your arms and legs should move coordinately, that the shoulder should come into unison with the hipjoint, the elbow with the knee, and the hand with the foot. To meet such a requirement, Master Wang's way is to think of letting the three vital points on your arm meet with or separate from the three corresponding vital points on the leg, those on the right arm in correspondence with those on the left leg and those on the left arm in correspondence with the right leg, one after another in succession in the course of the movement. Let them unite with each other when doing a "closing" movement, and separate from each other when doing an "opening" movement. All such uniting and separating should be led by the "insubstantial arm" and one's mind should chiefly be concentrated on it. The "insubstantial" arm is one on the same side of your "substantial" leg (one that bears the greater part of your bodyweight). Between the arms and legs, their "insubstantiality and "substantiality" coincide with the opposite party on the other side of the body, i.e. if the right leg is "substantial", the left arm is "substantial"; in this case the left leg is "insubstantial", as is the right arm. The three vital points on the arm are: the Jianjing point at the indented part of the shoulder girdle, near the neck; the Quchi point at the

outer side of the elbow; and the Laogong point at the centre of palm; the three vital points on the leg are: the Huantiao point at the outer side of the hipjoint; the Yangling point at the outer side of the knee; and the Yongquan point at the arch of foot. (See Appendix III: Diagram of Vital Points Mentioned in this Book)

Thinking (focusing and shifting your points of attention) in such a manner achieves two things: one is to let the mind direct the movement of the body via the movement of "qi", since the "qi" moves through a path along which are spread the vital points (as already known and made use of in acupuncture); another is to bring about a unison of the respective parts in a more precise and quicker manner, and to reach a stronger state, since a point on a limb is much finer than a part of the limb, a thought of unison comes quicker than the act of unison, and an external unison actuated by an attentive thought in the mind is stronger than a merely superficial external expression of unison.

4 — As the point of your opponent's weakness is shown, his being in a disadvantageous position or his slight loss of balance is sensed, and you are to send him off his feet, issue the energy from the bottom up by pressing the heel of your rear foot with a snap against the ground and at the same time think of the palm of the hand that is placed in the rear and is in line with the centre of gravity of your opponent. Do not place your focus of attention on the contacting point (or the fore contacting point, if there are two or more points contacted), nor on the object or the direction your eyes are looking at. Some may raise a question or have a doubt of whether this is in harmony with the general principle "at the instant the mind thinks of something, the eyes should be looking there, and the hands and feet should have reached there." Still some others may find that on this point Master Wang's way is even somewhat different from his teacher, Yang Yuting's. Yes, they are different as Master Wang has told me, and not without reason. According to Master Wang, in actual application, at the point of issuing energy, your eyes are looking at the direction toward which you are to issue your energy, and you yourself and your opponent should be linked together into one, so the contacting point should not be shifted at all, and therefore needs no more attention. But to enhance the effectiveness or to multiply the forcefulness of your energy sent out upon your opponent, no energy should be sent forth from the contacting point by you, but energy should be sent from bottom up and from the rear end to the foremost end, and that requires your full attention to ensure its being correctly done. And only when you and your opponent have been formed into one at the mo-

ment of operation, the energy you are sending out could then reach the target you have set on your opponent's body instantly.

Try out Master Wang's way, see if it works, at least he has offered us something that has made his art of Taijiquan outstanding in combative use.

37-POSTURES WU STYLE TAIJIQUAN

– A DETAILED COURSE

This sequence of 37-Postures is an abridged and rearranged version of the traditional Wu style sequence which is comprised of 81 postures. This abridged version has been in practice for 28 years now. The idea of abridgement and rearrangement occured to the author early in 1953 when teaching the traditional complete sequence at the Peking Polytechnical Institute, the Railway Sanatorium and a number of other institutes. Owing to the repetitiousness of the complete sequence, it takes too much time to learn or to practise. In order to meet the needs of his students, the author omitted most of the repetitious postures of the traditional sequence and retained 37 different postures which were properly arranged in order of physical intensity and degree of difficulty. The abridged and rearranged sequence takes no more than fifteen minutes to perform. The weak or the sick can select and repeat one or two postures which will benefit certain inner organs corresponding to their particular diseases. For instance, those suffering from gastrointestinal disorder or diabetes could repeatedly perform the Posture "Grasp Bird's Tail", while the sufferers of respiratory and circulatory diseases or neurasthenia could repeat the Posture "Wave Hands Like Clouds" for effective cure.

To help perform correctly, every movement under each of the 37 postures is provided in this book with the focal points of your attention, as well as your self-feeling during the performance, for you to check whether you are doing correctly or not. Failure to focus your attention as required, or to have the described self-feeling indicates some fault in your performance. You should try to find out the fault and make necessary corrections.

Besides, at the beginning of each posture an explanation of the posture name is given to help practioners understand the essence of that posture and thus do it properly and vividly.

Lastly, in order to help practioners to perform every movement of the solo sequence correctly and to be able to apply to self-defence, each of the solo movements is provided with explanation in words as well as with how-to drawings. Therefore, the thirty seven postures which are subdivided into 178 movements are provided with 240 drawings for solo sequence; and concurrently with 273 drawings for their application to self-defence.

List of 37-Postures Wu Style Taijiquan

Serial no.	*Name of posture*	*No. of movements*
	Preparation	
1	Beginning Form	4
2.	Grasp Bird's Tail	8
3.	Brush Knee and Twist Step	6
4.	Play the Lute	4
5.	Part the Wild Horse's Mane	4
6.	Fair Lady Works at Shuttles	20
7.	Watch with Fist Under Elbow	2
8.	Golden Cock Stands on One Leg	4
9.	Step Back and Repulse Monkey	10
10.	Diagonal Fly	4
11.	Lift Hand	4
12.	Stork Spreads Wings	4
13.	Insert Neddle to Sea Bottom	4
14.	Flash the Arms (Unfurl the Fan)	2
15.	Left and Right Separate Instep Kicks	12
16.	Turn and Strike with Heel	4
17.	Step Forward and Punch Down	6
18.	Turn Around and Cast Down with Fist and Palm	2
19.	Double Kick	6
20.	Left and Right Striking Tiger	4
21.	Two Fists Blow Ears	4
22.	Dodge and Kick	4
23.	Turn Around and Kick	4
24.	Press Face with Palm	4
25.	Cross-form Kick (Sweep Lotus with Single Hand)	4
26.	Brush Knee and Punch at Underbelly	4

27.	Front Single Whip	6
28.	Wave Hands Like Clouds	6
29.	Down-pushing Stance	2
30.	Step Forward to Form Seven Stars	2
31.	Step Back and Ride Tiger	2
32.	Turn Around and Press Face with Palm	2
33.	Turn and Kick Horizontally (Sweep Lotus with Both Hands)	4
34.	Bend Bow to Shoot Tiger	4
35.	Step Back, Deflect, Parry and Punch	4
36.	Seeming Close Up	2
37.	Embrace Tiger and Return to Mountain (Cross Hands Closing Form)	6

Detailed Instructions

This sequence of exercise consists of 37 postures made up by 178 movements. All movements composing a posture are in even numbers. The shortest posture is composed of 2 movements, whereas the longest one of 20 movements. However, the posture of Preparation, having no actual motion, is not counted in the 37 postures.

Posture of Preparation

Explanation of the posture name: Before doing the exercise, the physical body and the mind should enter into a state of preparedness.

Stand naturally, facing due south, feet together, arms hanging down in light contact with the outer sides of the thigh bones, tips of middle fingers tightly against Fengshi points (in the middle of the outer sides of thighs). Top of head erect, tip of tongue in touch with hard palate, eyes looking horizontally ahead. Distribute body weight evenly between two feet. Concentrate your mind on fingertips of both hands.

It is required that all sorts of distracting thoughts be expelled from the mind in order to maintain tranquility. Relax all joints, loosen all muscles. Once these are formed as a habit, the pleasure of doing movement lightly, nimbly, flowingly and effortlessly could be sensed. (Fig. 1)

Self-feeling: The body is relaxed and swings slightly back and forth, as if standing on a swaying boat. This indicates that you have expelled distracting

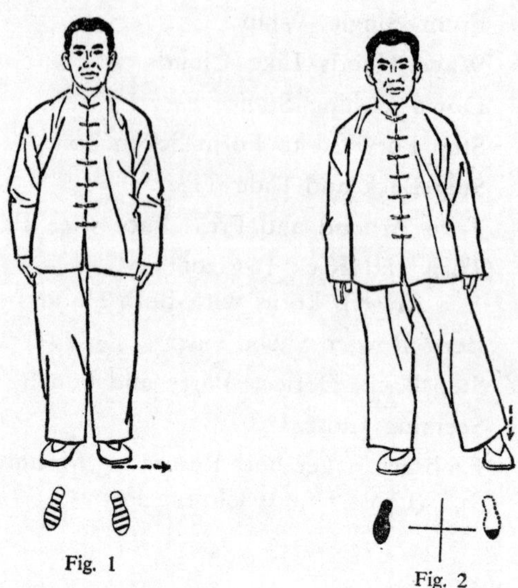
Fig. 1 Fig. 2

thoughts and entered into a state of tranquility. Then think first of your Mingmen point (in the middle of the small of the back), next think of your navel. Repeat thinking of these two points in this way for three times, your body will become steady. Now you can begin practising the following postures.

Posture I. Beginning Form (4 movements)

Explanation of posture name: The initial move of the entire sequence of postures.

1st movement: A lateral step by left foot

Keeping top of head and body plumb erect, eyes looking forward. Shift body slightly to right, and think for tip of nose to be vertical with right toe, and coccyx to be vertical with right heel. At this time left foot will move naturally sideways by shoulder-width, with left toe barely touching ground. Your weight is now on right foot; your mind concentrated on tip of right little finger. (Fig. 2)

Self-feeling: Right half of body tense, left half relaxed.

Practical application: When an opponent's right hand is on your left shoulder attempting a push at it to right, just think of your right shoulder, or of any portion on right half of your body,and the opponent will not be able to move you.

2nd movement: Standing with feet apart in parallel

Think in turn of tip of right little finger, ring finger, middle finger, forefinger, thumb, palm, and finally of the palm heel. Meanwhile set second toe of left foot onto ground, then its third toe, fourth toe, little toe, arch, and lastly its heel onto ground. Your weight is now evenly distributed on both feet; your mind is focused on tips of both forefingers; direction of your sight unchanged. (Fig. 3)

Self-feeling: As if you have just taken a deep and refreshing breath. Upper part of body is light and relaxed, the part below diaphragm sunken and steady, while feet planted firmly onto ground like a tree.

Practical application: This is a natural "pile-stance" in Taijiquan, which can help conserve health and guard against any of the offensive forces from six directions — the upper, lower, front, back, left and right. In the "Chant of Imparting the Secret Techniques" this stance was implied in the sentence "... to maintain the natural aspects of things ..."

3rd movement: Wrists forward ward

Think of all your fingertips, and direct joints of fingers to relax, for all fingers to extend naturally, then direct finger cushions to gather under each palm. At this instant, your fingers will feel an impetus that brings both arms to rise naturally forward and upward to shoulder level, and two arms apart by shoulder-width. Your sight and centre of gravity remain unchanged; your mind focused on both palms. (Fig. 4)

Fig. 3

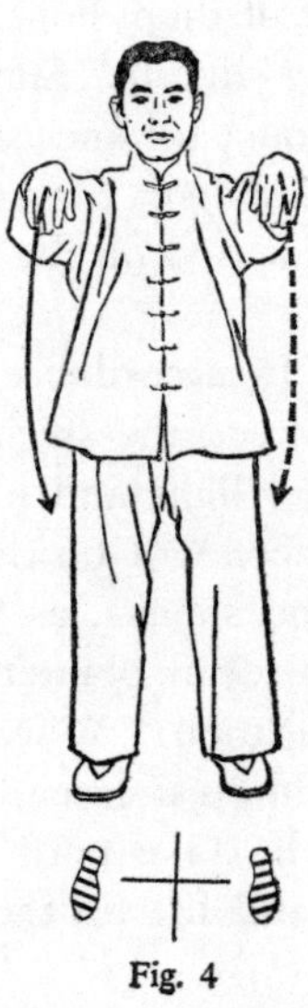

Fig. 4

Fig. 1/1

Fig. 1/2

Self-feeling: The chest comfortable.

Practical application: When your wrists are grasped by your opponent, gather your fingertips under both palms, so your wrists will protrude to hit the opponent's palms, setting him off balance and fall on back. (Fig. 1/1, 1/2)

4th movement: Hands down pull

Think of backs of both hands which will spontaneously fall down till thumbs stay at side of thigh bones, with palms down, fingers pointing forward and elbows bending slightly. Simultaneously relax knees and gradually lower torso to a quarter squat till kneecaps are perpendicular to toes. Draw in lower abdomen a little and look forward. Your body weight is still on two feet; your mind finally focused on the "outer Laogong" points at centre of back of hands. (Fig. 5)

Self-feeling: In accordance with the Taiji principle "When the lowest vertebra is plumb erect, the spirit of vitality will ascend to top of head, and entire body will feel light and nimble, as if top of head is being suspended from above", so there will be the feeling of distension, warmth and powerfulness in thighs and shanks, as well as the feeling of firmness in lower part of your body which seems planted onto the ground.

Practical application: When your opponent has grasped your wrists to draw you toward him, just extend your fingers and pull your hands downward and toward yourself (take note to slump your shoulders, sink your elbows, loosen your waist and lift up the top of your head), your opponent will fall forward. (Fig. 1/3, 1/4)

Fig. 1/3

Fig. 1/4

Posture II. Grasp Bird's Tail (8 movements)

Explanation of posture name: This is a figure of speech whereby the approaching arm of one's opponent is likened to a bird's tail, while one's own arm is likened to a rope turning up or down, forward or backward, left or right in close pursuit of the bird's tail, leaving no chance whatever of its getting away.

1st movement: Left hand up ward

Think of your Huiyin point (the perineum) moving downward and backward to right, so that coccyx will be perpendicular to right heel. Relax left shoulder, sink left elbow, and left hand will spontaneously rise forward and upward till its palm turned toward you, its thumb opposite to tip of your nose at a natural distance. At same time right hand will of its own accord rise to chest level till tip of its middle finger slightly touching inner side of left elbow, palm facing forward and downward. Then sink right elbow, relax right shoulder, and left foot will spontaneously move a step forward with heel resting on ground, and toes slanting upward (this is a right sitting stance). Now think for the Mingmen point (the point between two kidneys, at the small of back, an area supposed to be the source of vitality) to get to left hipjoint, your left foot will spontaneously rest flat on ground, and you are assuming a left archer stance. Meanwhile, left palm will spontaneously turn upward and forward till its thumb is opposite to your left nostril, though your right hand remains in the same place. Now look forward afar beyond left thumb; your weight is on your left leg; your mind is focused on Mingmen point. (Fig. 6, 7)

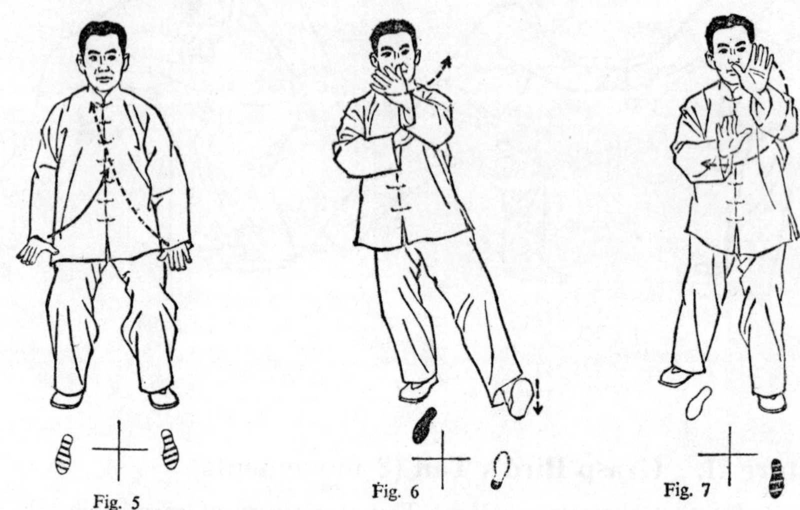
Fig. 5 Fig. 6 Fig. 7

Self-feeling: Slight wriggling in right palm and arch of left foot; and there is distension and warmth in left thigh and shank.

Practical application: If an opponent punches you with his right fist, just adhere to his right elbow with your left elbow, and also adhere to his right wrist with your own right wrist, so that his right arm will have to stretch out, not able to bend and withdraw. Your opponent is now being held up. Then move your left thumb to be aligned with his nose, and brush (at a natural distance) with your forefinger from the thick end of the opponent's right eyebrow to its thin tip. At same time adhere your right palm to his chest. (Take note not to detach this contact.) The opponent will be pushed off. (Fig. 2/1, 2/2, 2/3)

2nd movement: Right hand press

Let your mind direct your right shoulder to relax, right elbow to sink down, and your right hand will spontaneously move forward till palm adheres to inner side of left wrist. Now left arm will naturally bend, with forearm horizontal in front of chest, palm facing in, fingers pointing right. Right fingers now point upward, with forefinger opposite tip of your nose at natural distance. There being no change of step, your weight remains on left leg. Look forward over tip of right forefinger, concentrating your attention on the Jiaji point at the upper centre of your back. (Fig. 8)

Self-feeling: All your strength merged into an integrated whole. This strength is issued from your left foot, and travels through left leg, waist until

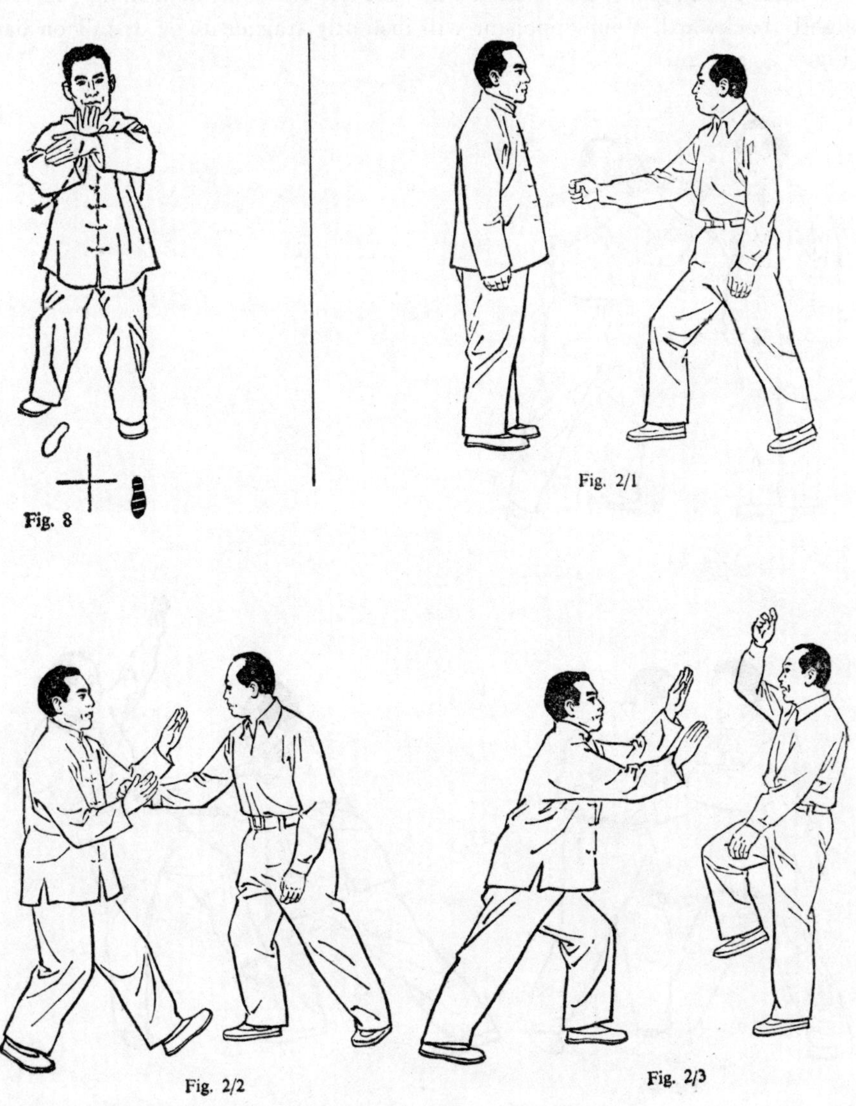

Fig. 8

Fig. 2/1

Fig. 2/2

Fig. 2/3

it reaches your back and delivered from your fingers. Thus you feel a powerful impetus.

Practical application: When your left arm is held by the opponent you can make use of the press (push-cut) energy to discard him. The way to do it is to hold your left forearm in front of your opponent's chest, then push your right palm against the innerside of your left elbow while leaning your back slightly backward. Your opponent will instantly stagger away or fall on back. (Fig. 2/4, 2/5, 2/6)

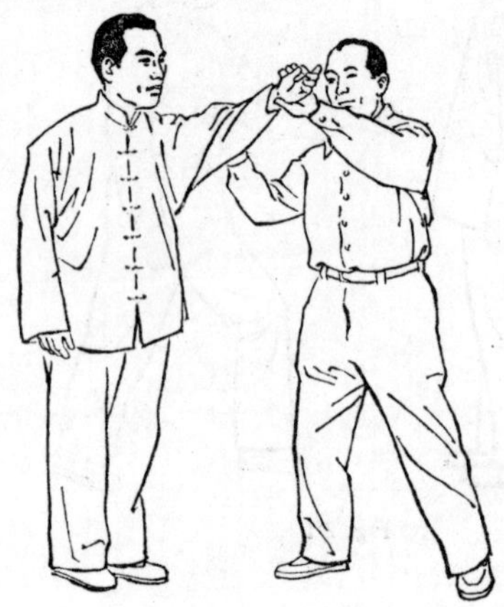

Fig. 2/4

Fig. 2/5

Fig. 2/6

3rd movement: Left hand down pull

Consciously direct left palm to get in touch with tip of right elbow, turn palm down, sink left elbow, relax left shoulder, and torso will spontaneously turn 90 degrees toward right, and your two feet also form a 90 degree angle. At same time turn right palm toward upper left, ends up, its thumb in line with tip of nose; correspondingly turn left palm downward and forward to get near to right elbow. Bend left knee so that kneecap is perpendicular to left toe, but right kneecap is perpendicular to right ankle. Both feet are now flat on ground. (This is a half riding stance whereby 70 percent of body weight is on left foot, 30 percent on right foot). Look at tip of left forefinger, with attention focused on left shoulder. (Fig. 9, 10)

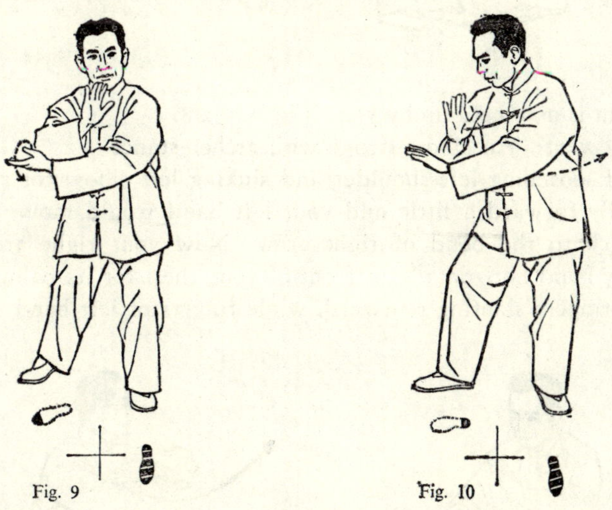

Fig. 9 Fig. 10

Self-feeling: Slight wriggling in left palm and right arch; distension and warmth in left thigh and shank.

Practical application: When your opponent strikes your right ribs or chest with his left elbow, adhere to his left wrist with your own left wrist; at same time turn torso toward left to adhere to his left elbow perpendicularly with your right forearm (to form a cross), then move slightly to upper rear left.

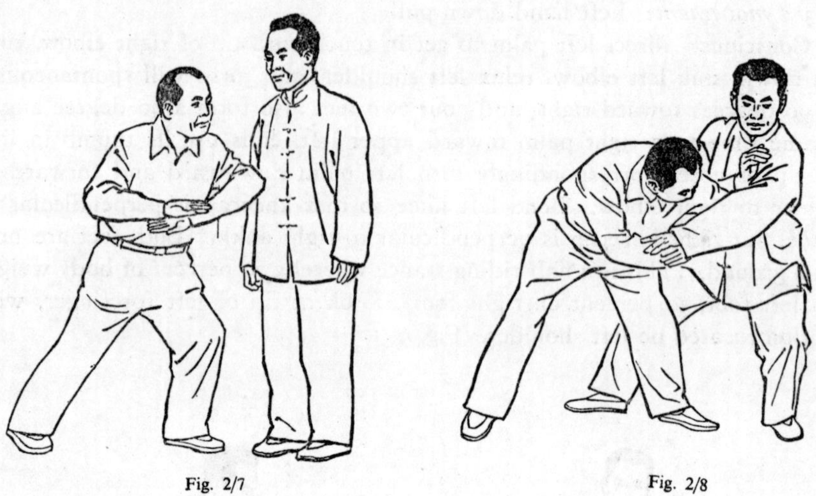

Fig. 2/7 Fig. 2/8

Your opponent is now held up by you. (Fig. 2/7, 2/8)

4th movement: An elbow-stroke with archer stance

Think of loosening left shoulder and sinking left elbow for right foot to move naturally forward a little and your left hand would move forward for palm to attach to the bend of right arm. Now your right arm will also spontaneously bend horizontally in front of your chest for its palm to get near its shoulder, fingers slanting rearward, while fingers of left hand are pointing

Fig. 11 Fig. 12

forward, thumb upward. Simultaneously rest right foot on ground, bend right knee and stretch hind leg to assume right archer stance. Your weight is now on right leg. Look beyond right elbow point. Focal point of your attention is on right palm. (Fig. 11, 12)

Self-feeling: All your strength integrated in a whole and with great impetus.

Practical application: Whatever hand techniques your opponent employs in attacking you, note his footwork first. If his left foot approaches first, you can take a right step forward to adhere the outer side of your right knee (Yanglingquan point) to the inner side of his left knee (Yinlingquan point). Meanwhile allow the point of your right elbow to contact your opponent's chest or ribs, push your left hand to the bend of your right elbow, and draw your right palm slightly close to your right shoulder, your opponent will be toppled or stagger away. Reversely, if his right foot is in the front, you may take a step forward with your left foot. Then repeat the movement, but reverse left and right. (Fig. 2/9, 2/10)

5th movement: Left shoulder-stroke

Imagine the nail of your right thumb to be contacting the sky horizontally; then imagine likewise in turn of other four fingernails, and right arm will naturally stretch out, palm down. Then let right arm fall with an arc from upper front right down to your rear right. During this fall relax the parts where your attention shifts to, e.g., first think and relax cushion of little finger, then think and relax in turn of other four finger cushions, then the palm, wrist, elbow, through to shoulder joint. At the instant your left shoulder

Fig. 2/9

Fig. 2/10

will have turned toward the front, and upper torso turned halfway to right, left heel turned outward slightly for two feet to be parallel. Bend both arms slightly, turn palms down, and the curve between thumb and forefinger of both hands form an oval with right hand slightly lower than the left one. This movement finishes with a right archer stance. Your weight is still on right leg. Look at your right forefinger; focus your attention on the Yuzhen point, (an indented point where the back of your head connects with the neck). (Fig. 13, 14a, 14b)

Fig. 13

Fig. 14a

Fig. 14b

Self-feeling: Wriggling in stomach and intestine. Together with the next movement, this movement affords good exercise for the pancreas and is an effective cure for diabetes.

Practical application: The outbreak of shoulder-stroke is as swift and violent as a thunderbolt. This stroke issues from the Yuzhen point, a key place which belongs to Danjin (vital energy passages). When issuing this stroke, lean sideway against your opponent with certain part of your body such as shoulder, elbow, back, hipbone, knee, etc., to cause your opponent devoid

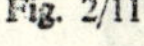

Fig. 2/11

Fig. 2/12

of strength. Use of this movement is continued from the preceeding elbow-stroke which has been neutralized by your opponent with an offensive pull, so you are again in the defensive and can cast a violent shoulder-stroke to his chest, at the same point where you have just dealt with your right elbow. (Fig. 2/11, 2/12, 2/13)

6th movement: Right hand up-split

Relax right shoulder, sink right elbow, and your body will spontaneously "sit" back on left leg, right toe slanting up. Right hand, relaxed, will of its own accord turn palm up and travel a course from right ribs to left ribs, then to left front, as right foot lands on ground. Now stretch out right arm to bring right palm in line with right shoulder, but a bit higher than it, with palm up, fingers pointing forward. At same time left hand has its palm turned

Fig. 2/13

down, middle and ring fingers lightly attached to inner side of right wrist. All through the travelling of both hands let your body turn spontaneously with the movement of your hands. Finally you are assuming right archer stance, your weight on right leg. Look ahead over right forefinger, and focus your attention on left foot. (Fig. 15, 16)

Self-feeling: The whole body experiences a comfortable feeling of full extension. There is wriggling and warmth in right palm and abdomen.

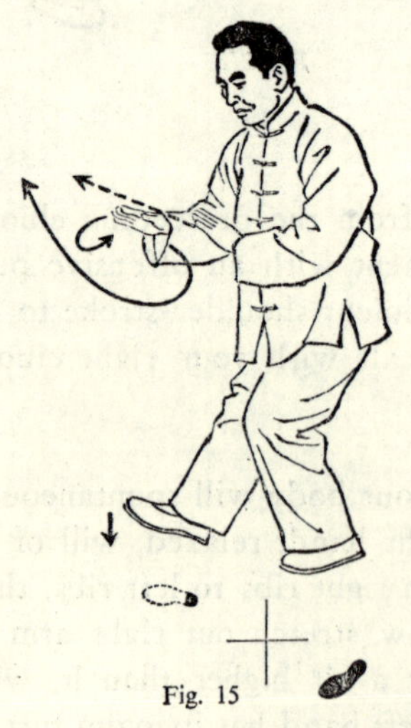

Fig. 15

Fig. 16

Fig. 2/14 Fig. 2/15

Practical application: The force of "split" is contrary to that of "pull". The former is a separating force. For example, to take hold of an opponent's arm and twist it is to "split". The split force is produced by the combining force of your hands and feet. When your right palm is up, turn outward your left heel with a snap, or when your left palm is up, turn outward your right heel with a snap, the opponent will be thrown away. (Fig. 2/14, 2/15, 2/16)

Fig. 2/16

7th movement: Two hands back roll

The force of roll involves extension and pliability. To perform this movement you should consciously direct cushion of your right forefinger to brush (not touching, but at a natural distance) from tip of your left brow to its thick end, then turn right palm out and direct the nail of your right forefinger to brush from the thick end of your right brow to its tip. During above process let your eyes follow your right forefinger and turn waist naturally. At same time left knee will bend spontaneously to a slight squat, and right leg extend forward with heel touching, toes slanting upward. Distance between two palms is about the size of your hand, right hand slightly higher, both palms facing outward and upward. Now your weight is transferred to left leg; your attention is focused on the Xuanguan point (a point between two eyebrows). (Fig. 17a, 17b)

Fig. 17a

Fig. 17b

Self-feeling: Distension and warmth in the left leg; warmth and wriggling in the right palm.

Practical Application: This is a movement to neutralize your opponent's warding movement. For example, if your opponent takes offensive by the warding movement (an oblique upward force), at the slightest feeling of his touch on you, you can adhere to his right wrist with your right hand, and also adhere to his right elbow with your left hand. Then roll your hands upward

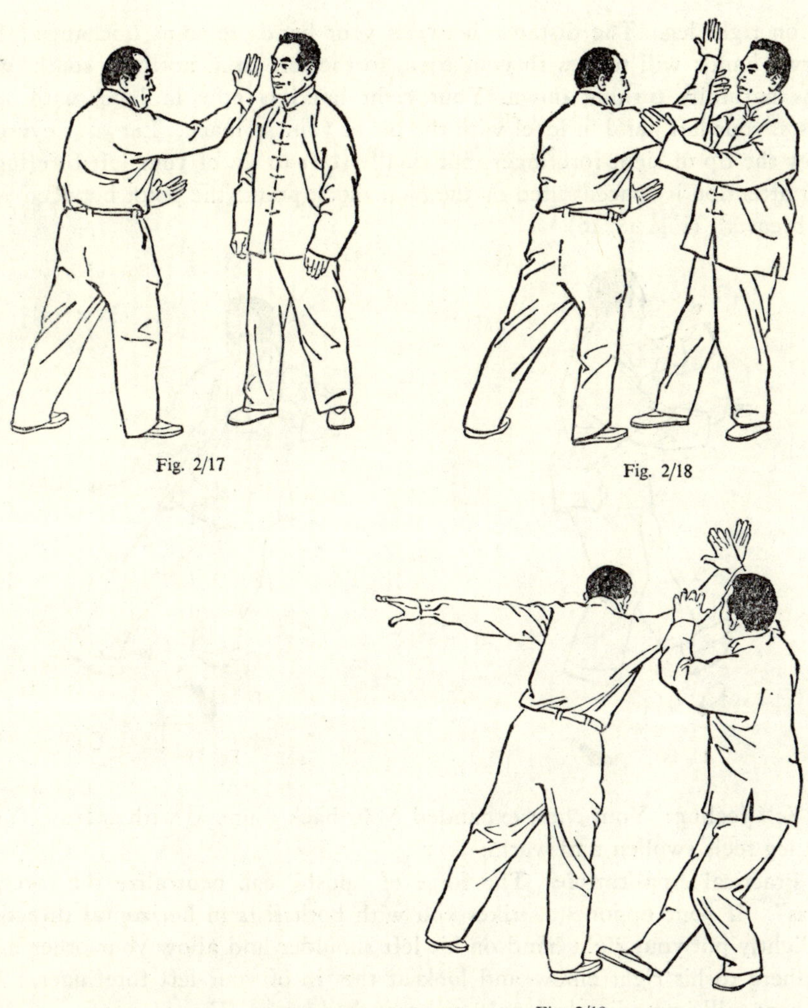

Fig. 2/17

Fig. 2/18

Fig. 2/19

to your right over your shoulder. Meanwhile turn torso slightly to right to cause the opponent's energy to fall on nothing so he will immediately topple. (Fig. 2/17, 2/18, 2/19)

8th movement: Two hands down push

Consciously relax your left wrist, your left elbow, and your shoulder, the tip of your right foot will turn left of its own accord to face south. Bend slightly your right knee. Stretch your left leg without moving left foot. The two feet will now form a half-perpendicular half-splay stance. Your weight is now on right leg. The distance between your hands remains unchanged, but the two hands will turn with your torso to the left from north to south, with palms naturally turning down. Your right hand is now in level with your breasts, your left hand in level with the pit of your stomach. Let your eyesight follow the tip of right forefinger, but finally shift to tip of your left forefinger. Your attention is concentrated on the Shanzhong point (the point between your two breasts). (Fig. 18, 19)

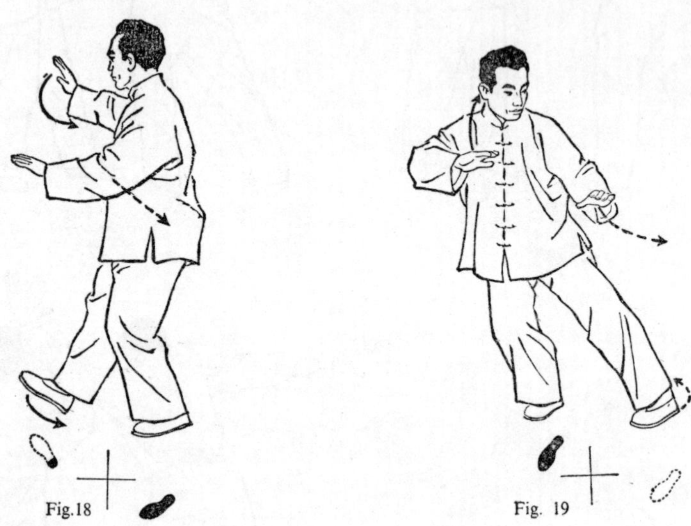

Fig.18 Fig. 19

Self-feeling: Your chest expanded, your back rounded with energy. Your right leg feels swollen and warm.

Practical Application: The force of "push" can neutralize the force of "press". If your opponent strikes you with both fists in horizontal direction, just lightly put your right hand on his left shoulder and allow your other hand to adhere to his right elbow and look at the tip of your left forefinger. The opponent will immediately topple or be pushed away. (Fig. 2/20, 2/21, 2/22)

The above-mentioned eight applications correspond to the eight movements of the Posture "Grasp the Bird's Tail." In actual application any outbreak of strength should depend on the ever-changing situation and be issued from the vital points in order to let out highly effective strength. All the eight applications here have to do with their respective vital points at different parts of the body. For instance, when you do the elbow-stroke, let out the strength from the Jianjing point which lies midway on each shoulder. This stroke is to be employed when you are on the verge of being rolled out of your centre of gravity. You may change suddenly from defensive to offensive with an elbow-stroke. This stroke is similar to the sudden cease-and-issue strength. When manoeuvered correctly this is a terrible stroke, and might cause accident, therefore special attention must be paid. There are altogether 16 varieties of elbow-strokes, e.g., one-knee stroke, two knee stroke, an under-elbow spear, explosion by elbow, pointing stroke, bump stroke, rolling in, rolling out, up-pointing elbow-stroke, twining, stroke against grasping, rocking, shaking, drilling, single whip press, and double whip press.

Fig 2/20

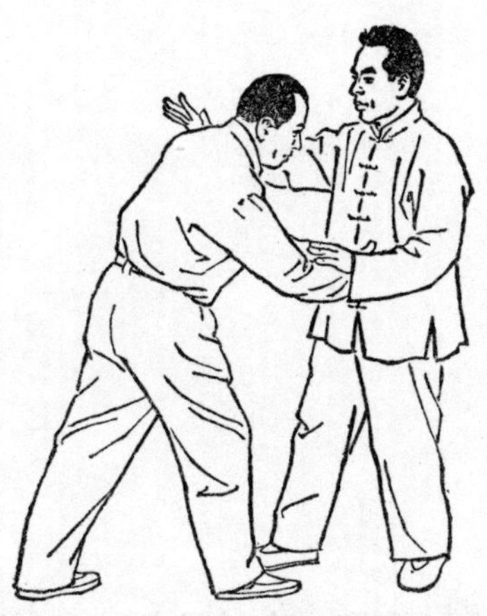

Fig. 2/21

Fig. 2/22

Posture III. Brush Knee and Twist Step (6 movements)

Explanation of posture name: "Twist step" is a technical term whereby the stepping forward of a foot (for instance, the left foot) is accompanied with the pushing forward of a hand of the opposite side of body (in this case, the right hand), or vice versa. "Brushing knee" is a technical term whereby one brushes aside or presses against the approaching part (fist, knee, foot) of the opponent with one hand at the height of one's knee, and leaves the other hand ready to make a counterattack. "Brush knee and twist step" is a method in Chinese pugilism to neutralize an attack aiming at one's own lower part, and simultaneously to deliver a counterattack aiming at any upper part of the opponent.

1st movement: Left hand down push

Loosen right wrist and lift right hand with its radial side close to right earhole. Sink right elbow and relax right shoulder, so left foot will automatically step sideways, with heel touching ground and toes slanting up. At same time your body and left arm will of their own accord turn left to face due east, with palm, facing down, perpendicular to left big toe. Your sight rests on left forefinger; your weight is on right leg; and your mind concentrated on right Jianjin point. (Fig. 20)

Fig. 20

Self-feeling: Right leg feels distended and warm; left palm feels a downward and forward pushing force.

Practical application: If the opponent strikes your face with his left hand and kicks at your abdomen with his right foot, just get hold of his left wrist with your right hand, and push down his kneecap with your left hand. At this juncture, if he withdraws the kick, it's all the better for him. Otherwise he is bound to stagger backward by his own force. (Fig. 3/1, 3/2)

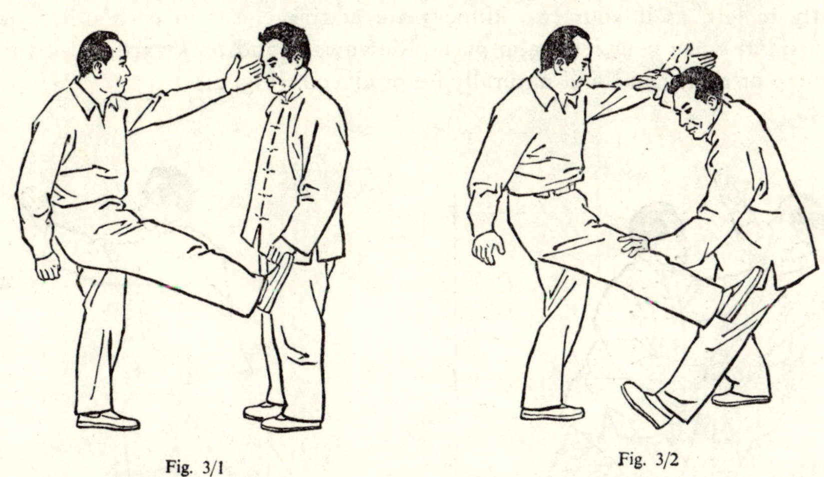

Fig. 3/1 Fig. 3/2

2nd movement: Right hand forward push

Gradually raise head and shift eyesight from left forefinger to distant front. Now let your mind direct right shoulder (Jianjing point) to seek left hipjoint (Huantiao point) (See note 1). Once you feel any heaviness on left heel, think for right elbow (right Quchi point) to seek left knee (left Yangling point). When your left foot rests wholly on ground, think for your right hand (right Laogong point) to seek to meet left foot (left Yongquan point). Now thrust right ring finger forward, as if it is a thread seeking the eye of a needle. When your weight has shifted from right leg to left leg, let middle finger lead and lift right hand by sinking right elbow and protruding the centre of palm for fingertips to point upward, though the wrist should not bend. Stretch right arm in a clockwise twist, its thumb pointing up and in level with the second knuckle of right forefinger. While right arm is thus doing, turn outward your right foot on its heel. Now shift attention to your left palm. Bend slightly left arm letting tip of left middle finger be aligned with tip of left elbow without any bending at the wrist. At same time, pull left hand rearward and downward until right foot could be lifted from ground without effort. When thrusting forward right hand, do not exert force, but let it move forward on its own accord. How is this done? Just look ahead over right thumb, let the thrusting hand follow the direction of your eyesight. Do not think of the thrusting but let right shoulder seek to meet left hipjoint, right elbow seek to meet left knee, right hand seek to meet left foot, then your right hand will naturally thrust forward, followed with a slight outward twist of right arm and the outward turn of right heel. Right side of your waist should now turn slightly to left, as if your two kidneys are getting closer to each other. At this instant, when your left palm pushes downward and backward, a forwarding force of right hand will naturally be produced. (Fig. 21)

Fig. 3/3

Fig. 21

(note 1) The expression "let right shoulder seek to meet left hipjoint" means in your mind your right shoulder seems to contact the left hipjoint. Similarly "right elbow seeks to meet left knee", and "right palm seeks left foot" carry the same implication.

Self-feeling: You should feel distension and warmth in your left thigh and shank. Your two palms should feel warm and slightly wriggling. Your kidneys feel expanded with strength.

Practical application: When the opponent failed in his attempt to kick you with his right foot, he is bound to drop down this foot. At this opportune moment thrust your left leg close to the inner side of his right leg. Simultaneously deliver a blow with your right hand at his chest or his face. The opponent will be blown a good distance off. (Fig. 3/3)

3rd movement: Right hand down push

Direct with your mind for left wrist to loosen and to rise to your left ear, the radial side of hand close to left earhole. Relax right knee, withdraw right foot and move a step forward, heel touching ground, toes slanting up, to form a left sitting stance, the body weight on left leg. At same time right hand, with palm down, will of its own accord push forward and downward, palm aligned with right toe. Your sight focuses on tip of right forefinger; your attention is concentrated on the centre of left palm. (Fig. 22, 23)

Fig. 22 Fig. 23

Self-feeling: Left leg feels distended and warm.

Practical application: If an opponent strikes your face and kicks your abdomen with his left foot, use your left hand to grasp his right wrist and your right hand to push down on his kneecap. If he now withholds the kick, it's better for him. If he keeps on kicking, he is bound to stagger back on his own force. (for illustration please refer to the application pictures of lst movement of this Posture: "Left hand down push", but reverse left and right).

4th movement: Left hand forward push

Detach eyesight from right forefinger and raise head to look forward to push forward left hand, and gradually land whole of right foot on ground. Bend forward right knee to assume right archer stance, and right hand will naturally rest beside right hipjoint. Look ahead over left thumb. Your weight now rests on right leg; your mind is concentrated on right palm. (Fig. 24)

Self-feeling: You should feel distension and warmth in your right thigh and shank; there is a feeling of warmth and slight wriggling in your palms; and there is expansion with strength in your kidneys.

Practical application: Now the opponent has failed to kick, the kicking foot is bound to fall forward. Losing no time you should thrust right foot to settle close against inner side of his left foot and deliver a blow with your left hand on his chest or his face. He will be blown a good distance off. (For

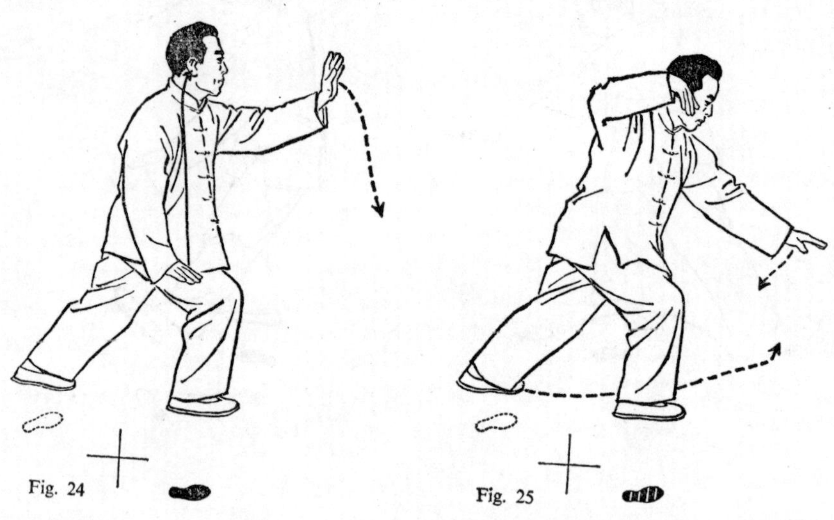

Fig. 24

Fig. 25

illustration please refer to the application pictures of 2nd movement "Right hand forward push" of this Posture, but reverse left and right.)

5th movement: Left hand down push

Repeat 3rd movement "Right hand down push" of this Posture, but reverse left and right. (Fig. 25, 26)

6th movement: Right hand forward push

Repeat 2nd movement "Right hand forward push" of this Posture. (Fig. 27)

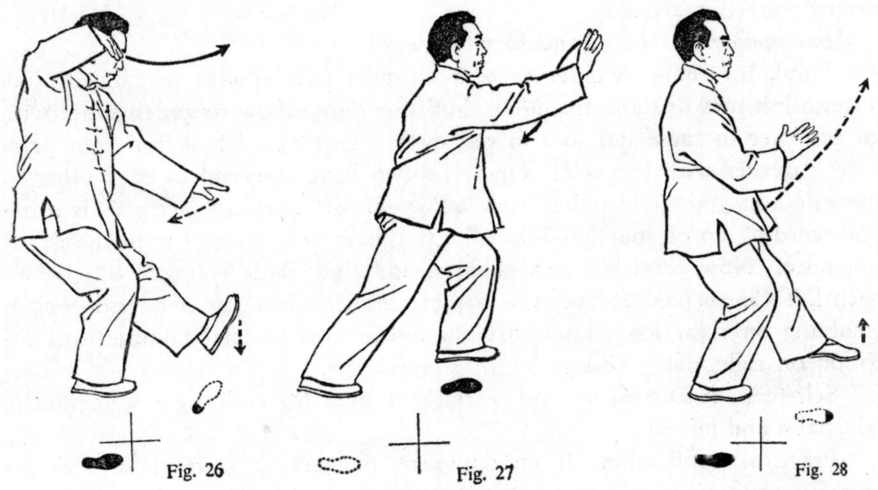

Fig. 26 Fig. 27 Fig. 28

Posture IV. Play the Lute (4 movements)

Explanation of posture name: This posture simulates playing a lute, whereby the two hands, one in the front the other in the rear, turn and move back and forth.

1st movement: Right hand back pull

Direct with your mind to loosen joints of left hand, then left elbow and left shoulder. Bend slightly right knee to sit automatically backward. Right hand will naturally draw backward till thumb is directly opposite the solar plexis, palm facing left; left hand is close to hipjoint, palm down. Now the tip of nose, right kneecap and right big toe should be in one plumbing line. Also, lowest vertebrae and right heel should fall in one straight line. Weight of your body is now on right leg. When you have just settled in this sitting stance and your left toes tended to slant up, let your left toes lightly touch the ground. Your right thumb will feel a sinking force. Look ahead and focus attention on left shoulder. (Fig. 28)

Self-feeling: Right thigh distended; shank rooted firmly onto ground.

Practical application: If your right wrist is held by your opponent and is being drawn toward him, let not the held wrist resist with force, but think for left shoulder to move rearward to seek your right hipjoint. The opponent can no longer draw you toward him, but on the contrary, he will be drawn over by you. (Fig. 4/1, 4/2)

2nd movement: Left hand forward ward

Think for right shoulder to seek to meet left hipjoint which will sink to cause left toes to slant up. Now think for right elbow to get together with the left knee to cause left toes to rise even higher up. Think for right palm to get together with left sole. Once the two have attached to each other in your mind let your right palm "suck up" your left sole. In fact, this is a natural warding up of your left arm till left thumb gets in level with the tip of your nose. Now bend left arm slightly, and right middle finger will lightly touch left Chitse point. You now assume a right sitting stance, with weight remaining on right leg. Look straight ahead beyond left thumb; focus attention on right palm. (Fig. 29)

Self-feeling: Distension and warmth of right leg and slight wriggling in right palm and left sole.

Practical application: If an opponent punches at your chest with his right fist, adhere to his right elbow with your left elbow, also adhere to his right wrist with your right wrist, so he can not bend his right arm any more. He is now off balance and is at your disposal. (Fig. 4/3)

3rd movement: Left hand forward push

Turn right palm up and stretch it forward to left, while thinking as if you are thrusting it beneath left sole to support it with your palm and to raise

Fig. 29

Fig. 4/1

it up. Once you have this idea in mind, your left toes will set down of their own accord, your centre of gravity will be shifted forward, and the left foot which has just laid down will feel as if it is treading on your right palm. The more the right palm tries to support upward, the heavier the palm will feel. This will weigh down the right elbow. Now let your right Quchi point (at bend of right arm) seek your left Yangling point (a spot at outer side of left knee), so these two points are in a vertical line, and your body will of its own accord turn slantingly right. Now let your right Jianjing point (at base of neck on right shoulder) seek your left Huantiao point (a spot at outer side of left hipjoint) until right foot could rise up from floor. Your left palm is by this time facing down with fingers pointing to front right, and a forward and downward push will naturally be produced. At the moment your right foot is devoid of weight, push down left hand. This is the socalled "close up", or "in place." Now the next move is to "open" which means to separate left shoulder from right hipjoint, left elbow from right knee, and left hand from right foot. Then move left hand to left. When your shoulder is loosened, the "qi" could then be transmitted to elbow; when your elbow is sunk, the "qi" could then be transmitted to the hand, and to tip of middle finger. When your mind is concentrated here, you will feel this part full of strength. The final part of this movement is to shift left hand from your front right to front left, with left forefinger taking the lead, left palm facing down, until right palm gets close to the bend of left arm. Now you have assumed left archer

Fig. 4/2

Fig. 4/3

Fig. 30
Fig. 31

stance; your weight rests on left leg; you are looking ahead over tip of left forefinger; your mind is concentrated on tip of left middle finger. (Fig. 30, 31)

Self-feeling: Whole body is at ease, a sense of comfort prevails all over. There is wriggling in left palm and right sole.

Practical application: When your right wrist is held by the opponent's two hands, just turn your right elbow inward clockwise. As he immediately topples forward, move your left hand toward your front right to weigh down

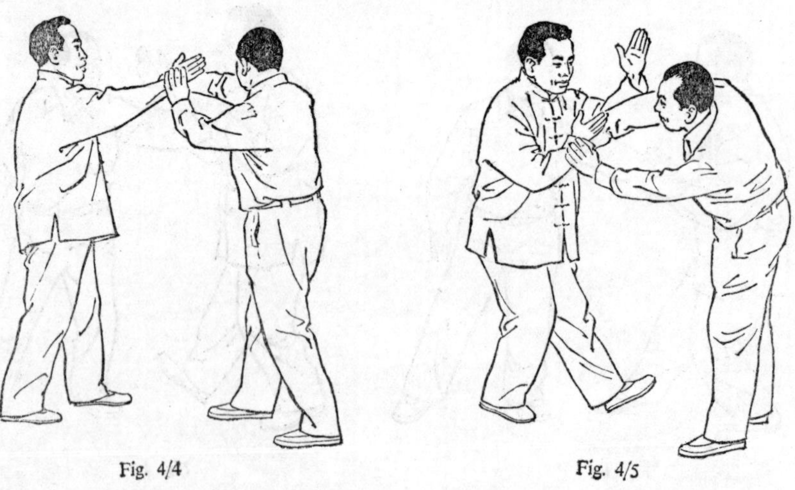
Fig. 4/4
Fig. 4/5

upon his right elbow. Then attach with tip of your left middle finger to his Yifeng point behind his left lobe, and also think of the Yifeng point behind his right lobe, as if there is a penetrated connection between these two points. This can make your opponent feel dizzy. (Fig. 4/4, 4/5, 4/6, 4/7)

4th movement: Left hand up ward

Pivoting on left thumb and led by little finger, left palm turns up, and right palm naturally turns down. Lift left palm as if supporting some weight, and stretch out the whole arm till you feel right heel has slightly detached from ground with only big toe touching. Continue with upward supporting motion of left hand, and then sink left elbow as if attached to ground, right foot will of its own accord draw next to left foot. (Take note not to interrupt the upward supporting motion, or right foot will be unable to move forward). Relax left shoulder to seek right hipjoint, you will feel right foot landing on ground, your weight falling onto both feet, and right hand will naturally descend, the wrist in level with navel, palm down. Lift your eyes to look ahead toward upper left. Meanwhile let left hand follow your sight till tip of middle finger is aligned with the thick end of left brow. Simultaneously, in keeping with the above motion, turn torso slightly to left for the pulsing point of right wrist to adhere to right ribs. Now bend slightly left arm and shift your

Fig. 4/6

Fig. 4/7

weight to left foot. Focus your mind on left palm. (Fig. 32)

Self-feeling: Left foot is rooted in ground like a tree. There is slight wriggling in left palm and right sole.

Practical application: When right arm of opponent is held straight by you, being in an inferior position, he will seek to escape. Continue with your up-supporting of his right elbow joint with your left palm. Simultaneously adhere you right palm to his right wrist. When both your hands exert force, draw your right foot next to your left foot to make it more forceful, you are jerking his bones toward opposite directions at the joint. As he is now in an awkward position, any struggle on his part will cause fracture. (Fig. 4/8, 4/9)

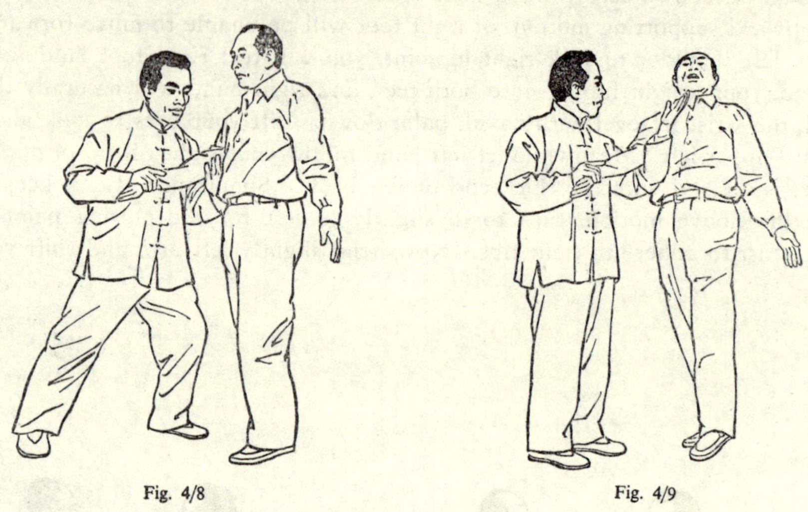

Fig. 4/8 Fig. 4/9

Posture V. Part the Wild Horse's Mane (4 movements)

Explanation of posture name: This posture simulates the tossing of the mane of a galloping horse. One's torso is likened to the horse head and limbs to horsemane. The sway of one's arms in correlation with the back and forth movement of the legs are likened to the tossing of the mane of a galloping wild horse.

lst movement: Left hand down pull

In continuation of the preceeding movement whereby you are facing the east, with weight on left leg, now loosen left shoulder, sink left elbow, with left little finger leading, and withdraw left hand to move downward and rightward till back of left hand rests at outer side of right knee, left fingers slanting downwards. During this process gradually assume a squatting stance

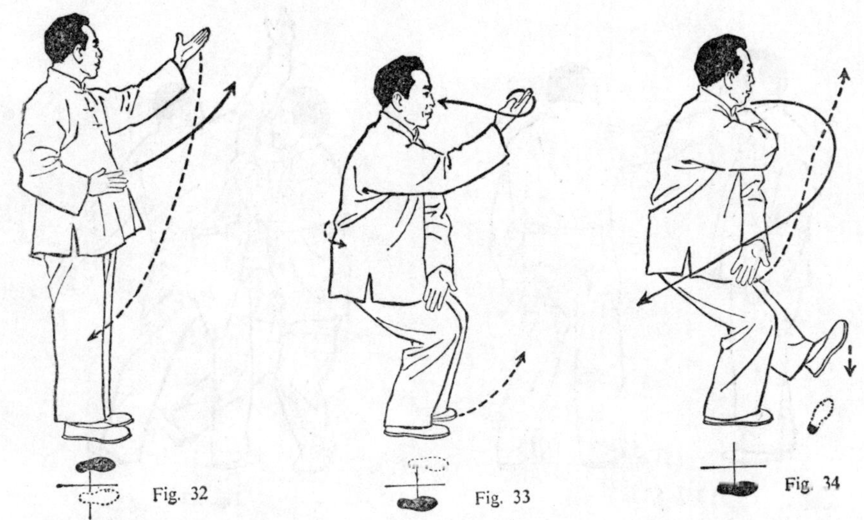

with torso kept erect. Shift your sight to front, and right hand will ascend naturally, palm up, as if upholding something. When right hand has ascended to eye level, direct right elbow to seek left knee, right hand will naturally push toward left. Now follow the direction of right elbow to look ahead toward left. Think for right shoulder to seek left hipjoint, your left foot will of its own accord take a step forward, with heel touching ground, toes slanting up. Your weight now rests on right leg; your mind's focal point is on right shoulder. (Fig. 33, 34)

Self-feeling: Right leg feels distended, warm and sore.

Practical application: This is an effective counteract against the slap on one's face. If the opponent attempts to slap your right face with his left hand, just lightly uphold his left elbow with your right hand, lightly push it to left and follow up with a step by your left foot to lock up both his feet. This movement being the first half of a complete action, is to make sure of locking one's opponent at a proper place, the other half of action is needed to topple an opponent. (Fig. 5/1. 5/2)

2nd movement: Left shoulder-strock

Relax right shoulder, sink right elbow, loosen right wrist, and extend forward right hand, palm turning down, fingertips forward, till your weight shifted to left foot and rear leg could be detached from floor. When your weight has rested on left foot, then you should move left hand by loosening left wrist to fully extend the curve between thumb and forefinger, and to

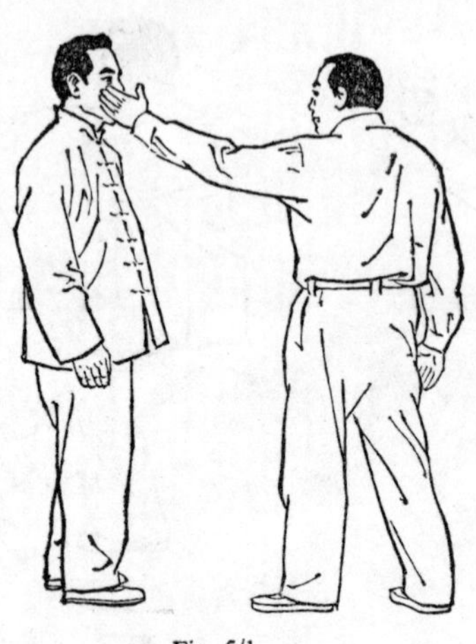

Fig. 5/1

Fig. 5/2

ascend, with palm up, along the bend of right arm for little finger to be in level with left ear. Lightly straighten left arm, turn torso toward right. Left hand should be "hooked" to right foot. That means in your mind your left hand and right foot seem to have been connected to form with your body a circle in which three lines due east and west are successively produced following the continued turning of torso to right. The first straight line is formed by left hand and right foot. With the continued turning of torso to right, your left elbow and right knee will form another straight line. Further turning of the torso will put left shoulder and right hipjoint into a straight line of the same direction. Only thus your strength will reach left shoulder. (Take note to incline outward your left knee, do not force it to incline inward. Let left kneecap be perpendicular to left toe.) Simultaneously descend right hand, palm down, naturally above the outer side of right ankle bone. Look at tip of right middle finger. Your attention is focused at the Yuzhen point, an indented point where the back of head connects the neck. (Fig. 35)

Self-feeling: Distension and warmth in left leg.

Practical application: If the opponent attempts to slap your right face with his left hand, uphold lightly his left elbow in your right hand giving it a little push to the left and take a forward step to lock his feet. Now the important procedure is to wedge and attach your left shoulder tightly against his left armpit, and then spread wide open your arms, one to the front, the other to the rear. Focus your sight on tip of middle finger of rear (right) hand. Now your left shoulder will gain vigorous impetus which tends to have it delivered

Fig 5/3 Fig. 35

from the leaning shoulder. The opponent will topple at a mere touch of this force and be thrown a good distance off. (Fig. 5/3)

3rd movement: Right hand down pull

Loosen left shoulder, sink left elbow, left hand will descend of its own accord. Simultaneously shift sight from right middle finger to forefinger,

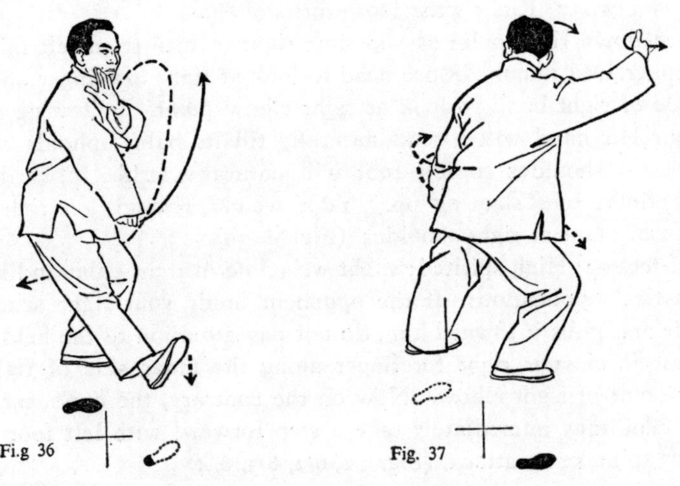
Fi.g 36 Fig. 37

thumb, and then detach from right thumb by raising head to look horizontally ahead. Right hand will naturally move to outer side of left knee with back of hand resting near the knee. Then sink left elbow, loosen left shoulder, shift sight horizontally toward right. At same time your right foot will naturally draw next to left foot and then take a forward step with heel touching ground, toes slanting up. Your weight is on left leg, back of your left hand close to right ear, your mind's focal point on left shoulder. (Fig. 36)

Self-feeling: Left leg feels distended, warm and sore.

Practical application: Same as that of lst movement "Left hand down pull" of this Posture, but reverse left and right.

4th movement: Right shoulder-stroke

Repeat 2nd movement "Left shoulder-stroke" of this Posture, but reverse left and right. (Fig. 37)

Self-feeling and Practical application: same as that of 2nd movement "Left shoulder-stroke", but reverse left and right.

Posture VI. Fair Lady Works at Shuttles (20 movements)

Explanation of posture name: This posture includes a number of back and forth, to and fro movements which are inter-woven and recurrent at the four corners. If performed properly they reveal the inherent pliability and exquisite nimbleness of Taijiquan. This posture is therefore likened to a fair lady working at shuttles.

lst movement: Right wrist loose turn

Turn down right palm as you shift sight in turn from left middle finger to forefinger, and thumb. Raise head to look at right forefinger and along the ulnar side of right hand to look at right elbow point. Following the shift of sight your left hand will ascend naturally till its palm upholds right elbow. Loosen right shoulder so left foot will naturally stride forward with heel touching floor, toes slanting up. Your weight remains on right leg; your mind's focal point at right shoulder. (Fig. 38, 39)

Self-feeling: High spirited; slight wriggling in right palm and left sole.

Practical application: If the opponent holds your right arm with both his hands and pulls it toward him, do not pay attention to the held arm. Just shift sight from your right forefinger along the ulnar side of right hand to settle at point of right elbow. Now on the contrary, the opponent is held up by you. You may immediately take a step forward with left foot to lock his feet ready to make an attack. (Fig. 6/1, 6/2, 6/3, 6/4)

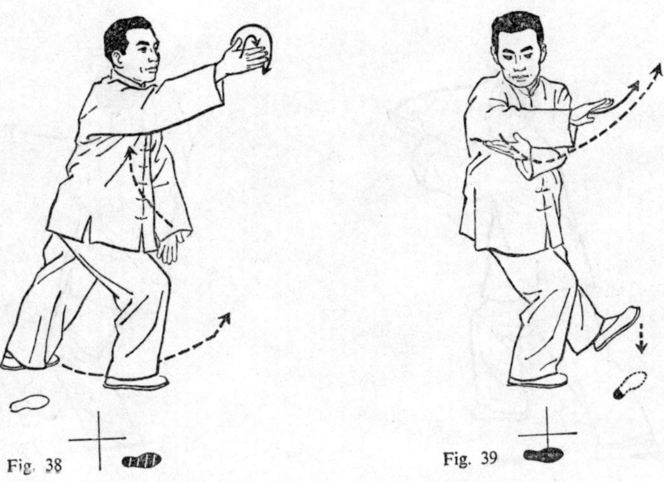

Fig. 38 Fig. 39

2nd movement: Left hand oblique ward

After your left heel has touched ground, relax right shoulder and sink right elbow. When you feel in right palm an impulse to move, protrude the palm and extend it toward front left. Now relax right wrist to "seek" left knee. When your weight has been shifted to left leg, let right shoulder "seek"

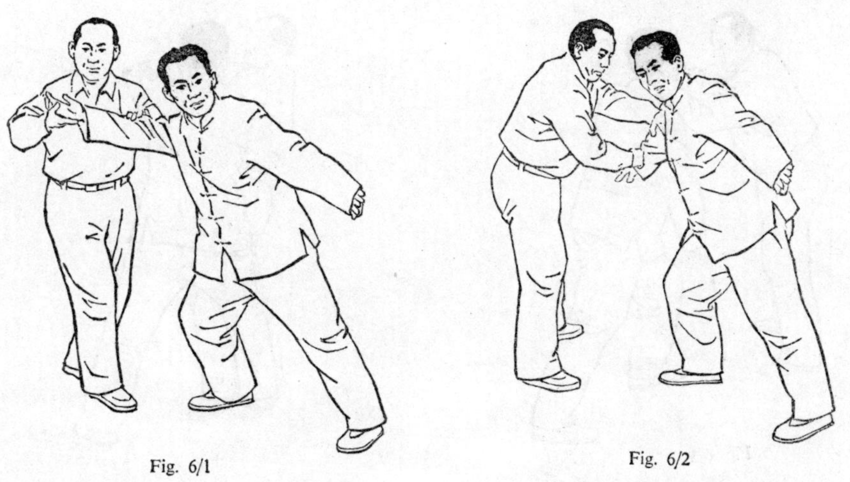

Fig. 6/1 Fig. 6/2

Fig. 40

Fig. 41

left hipjoint. The right leg should now feel devoid of weight, right heel will be able to turn slightly outward by pivoting on itself. Now think in turn of relaxing left shoulder, left elbow, left wrist, so you can easily rotate up left palm and extend to your front left till wrist (the part where one's pulse is taken) gets together with right middle finger and ring finger, and think in mind as if the nail of left thumb is attached to ground, then think in turn of

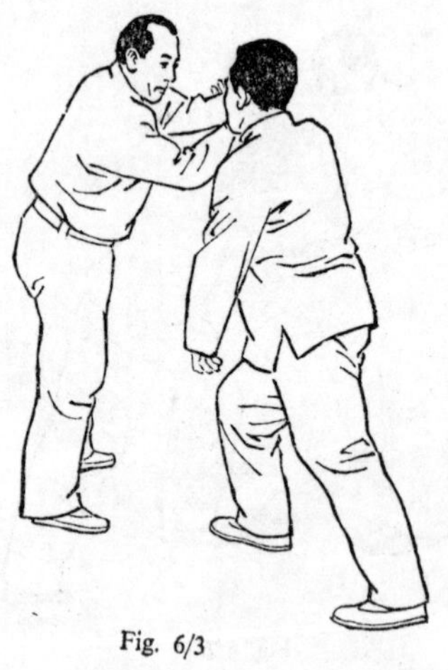
Fig. 6/3

Fig. 6/4

the nail of left forefinger, middle finger, ring finger, and little finger. When all left fingers seem to be attached to ground, your right foot will be devoid of weight, and should be able to be detached from ground without effort. Now you are assuming a left archer stance, with weight on left leg. Look far ahead over left forefinger. Your attention finally rests on nail of left little finger. (Fig. 40)

Self-feeling: Distension and warmth in left thigh and shank.

Practical application: If an opponent attempts to strike at your chest with his right hand, lightly adhere your right palm to his right wrist and rotate your torso slightly toward left. But suddenly turn your torso toward right, take a step forward with left foot to lock his hind leg, and stretch left palm toward his left ribs. Immediately ward up your left hand slantingly to your front left. This is an effective counteract against front horizontal attack. (Fig. 6/5, 6/6)

3rd movement: Left hand backward pull

Led by left forefinger, rotate left hand up toward your rear left, (south west corner) while right thumb attaches to the bend of left arm and follows the turn. Simultaneously relax right knee to "sit" toward rear right and stretch left leg with heel touching, toes slanting up to assume a right sitting stance. Your weight is now shifted onto right leg. Follow with your eyes the left forefinger, your attention is focused on left shoulder. (Fig. 41)

Self-feeling: Right leg feels distended and warm. Left palm warm and wriggles.

Fig. 6/5 Fig. 6/6

Practical application: If the opponent attempts to strike at your head with his right hand, attach your left palm beneath his right forearm and turn your left wrist to make an outward arc, while upholding your left palm and setting upper torso slightly down to rear. The opponent is held up by you. (Fig. 6/7)

4th movement: Right hand forward push

Place left foot gradually down on ground, bend left knee, slightly lower upper torso, and stretch rear leg. Your weight is now shifted onto left leg to assume a left archer stance. Simultaneously detach right hand from left arm to push at your front left (northeast corner) while turning up left palm for radial side of both hands to face each other at a natural distance. Look directly ahead over right thumb, with attention focused on left palm. (Fig. 42)

Self-feeling: There is wriggling in both palms. You should feel extension and warmth in left leg.

Practical application: This movement is closely connected with the preceeding one. By turning your left palm you have held up the opponent. Now you can push with your right palm at his chest. This is the way to neutralize an attack from above. (Fig. 6/8)

5th movement: Left hand right turn

Relax right arm, gradually turn its palm up to get near to left rib cage. With forefinger taking the lead turn left hand toward your rear right, and when it has reached due south your left toes should have turned due south too, (left heel carrying most of your weight, remaining in the same place

Fig. 6/7

Fig. 6/8

Fig. 42 Fig. 43 Fig. 44

while turning on it) your torso following the turn of feet. Continue with the turning of left hand till you face due west, and lift right heel slightly. Your weight is still on left leg. Your sight follows tip of left forefinger to front right (northwest corner). Your attention is focused on left palm. (Fig. 43, 44)

Self-feeling: You will feel the whole body wound up in spiral form like a driven screw. You should particularly sense the "rounded and powerful"

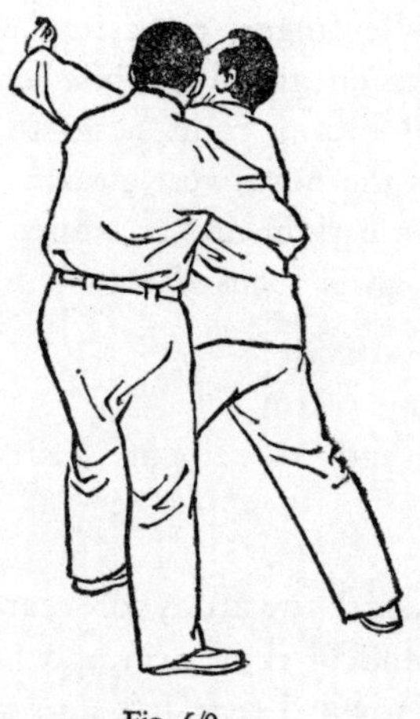

Fig. 6/9

Fig. 6/10

Fig. 45

Fig. 46

or distended feeling in your back. This movement is primarily done by turning the waist.

Practical application: If you are embraced by an opponent, wait for the juncture he has just exerted strength, then rotate your body, the opponent can no longer hold you but he himself will be thrown away. (Fig. 6/9, 6/10)

6th movement: Right hand oblique ward

Move right foot laterally toward rear right, toes touching first (toward northwest corner); at same time let left hand extend, palm down, to front left. Slide right palm along outer side of left arm toward your front right. When inner side of right wrist touches tip of left middle finger, right foot should turn on toes to point at west and whole foot rests on ground, while left foot also should turn on toes toward west. Continue sliding right hand to front right and stretch it as far as you can till it reaches the northwest corner. Now your weight is transferred onto right leg to assume a right archer stance. Your sight follows tip of right forefinger. Your attention is focused on right palm. (Fig. 45, 46)

Self-feeling: Whole of right leg distended and warm.

Practical application: Same as that of the 2nd Movement "Left hand oblique ward" except to reverse left and right.

7th movement: Right hand backward pull

Led by right forefinger turn right hand upward toward your rear right (northeast corner), while left thumb attaches to bend of right arm and follows the turn. Simultaneously relax left knee to "sit" toward rear left and stretch

Fig. 47 Fig. 48 Fig. 49

right leg forward, with heel touching ground, toes slanting up to form a left sitting stance. Your weight is now transferred to left leg. Let your eyes follow right forefinger. Focus your mind on right shoulder. (Fig. 47)

Self-feeling: Left leg distended and warm. Right palm feels warm and wriggling.

Practical application: If the opponent has grasped your right wrist with his left hand, turn up your right wrist to make an external rotation toward

Fig. 6/11 Fig. 6/12

your rear right while setting upper torso slightly down to rear. The opponent will be held up by you. The point is to keep the opponent's centre of gravity unstable. (Fig. 6/11, 6/12)

8th movement: Left hand forward push

Place right foot gradually down on ground, bend right knee, slightly lower your upper torso, and stretch rear leg. Your weight will now shift to right leg to assume a right archer stance. Simultaneously detach left hand from right arm to push at your front right (northwest corner). Turn up right palm while right arm makes an external rotation, so the side of both hands face each other at a natural distance. Look directly ahead over your left thumb, with attention focused on right palm. (Fig. 48)

Self-feeling: There is wriggling in both palms. You should feel distension and warmth in right leg.

Practical application: Continuing, by turning your right palm you have held up the opponent. Now push your left palm on his chest. This is the way to neutralize an attack from above. (Fig. 6/13)

9th movement: Palms diagonally facing

Relax two arms. Extend right hand forward to slide down to shoulder level; at same time slide left hand obliquely downward till left thumb touches right arm bend, and turn upper torso toward left (facing due west). Now loosen left knee, "sit" back, and slant up right toes, assuming a left sitting stance. Simultaneously move two hands toward front left, and turn right

Fig. 50

Fig. 6/13

palm in to face diagonally left palm. Your weight is now on left leg. Look forward beyond right thumb. Concentrate your attention on right Jianjin point. (Fig. 49)

Self-feeling: You feel the chest comfortable and at ease; left leg warm and distended.

Practical application: By making use of adherence and lifting this is a hidden strength. If the opponent punches your chest with left fist, adhere to his left elbow with your right elbow and also adhere to his left wrist with your left wrist. Simultaneously give a slight "lift" toward your rear left to take control of him. (Fig. 6/14, 6/15)

10th movement: Right hand down pull

Let left forefinger lead left hand to move diagonally toward upper right to rest beside right ear, with palm facing right and fingers pointing up. Meanwhile let right little finger lead right hand to move diagonally toward lower left to rest in front of left knee, with palm facing left and fingers pointing down. At same time move right foot slightly toward left for right knee to get near left knee, with heel touching ground, toes slanting up. Your weight remains on left leg. Your sight is directed horizontally ahead (due west). Your attention is focused on left palm. (Fig. 50)

Self-feeling: Distension and warmth in left leg.

Practical application: If your right wrist is firmly held by an opponent, raise your left hand toward upper right to rest near your right ear, and your

Fig. 6/14

Fig. 6/15

right arm will naturally gather an impetus for a down pull which will cause the opponent's inclining forward or fall. (Fig. 6/16, 6/17)

11th movement: Right foot lateral step

Move right foot laterally a half step to right, with heel touching, toes slanting up. Your hands remain without moving; your weight remains unshifted; your sight turned to front right (northwest); your attention focused on left shoulder. (Fig. 51)

Self-feeling: Left foot is like a tree rooted in ground. Left leg feels warm and sore. Right fingertips distended.

Fig. 6/16

Fig. 51

Fig. 6/17

Fig. 6/18

Practical application: The purpose for your right foot to take a half step toward right is to lock the opponent's hind leg, thus ready to make an attack at opportune time. (Fig. 6/18)

12th movement: Right shoulder leans rightward

Relax right elbow, let right forefinger lead right hand to extend to front right; while relaxing left elbow, letting left forefinger lead left hand to extend to front left. Bend right knee forward. As right foot has just landed, two palms should meet in your front and again separate. Allow left hand to continue its diagonal sliding toward rear left till its palm is perpendicular to outer side of ankle bone of left foot, while right hand continues its diagonal uprising to utmost point. Your weight is on right foot which is in position of a right archer stance. Your sight follows left forefinger; your mind concentrated on right Jianjing point. (Fig. 52)

Self-feeling: Right leg feels distended, warm, and sore. All your energy is transmitted to right shoulder.

Practical application: With your left hand brushing aside any obstacle in your front, adhere your right shoulder to the opponent's chest and/or rib cage. Then immediately turn back your head to look at your rear hand. Your right shoulder will naturally produce a great impetus. At a touch of this leaning force, the opponent will be over-thrown. (Fig. 6/19, 6/20)

13th movement: Right wrist loose turn

Repeat lst movement "Right wrist loose turn" of this Posture. (Fig. 53, 54)

Fig. 6/19

Fig. 6/20

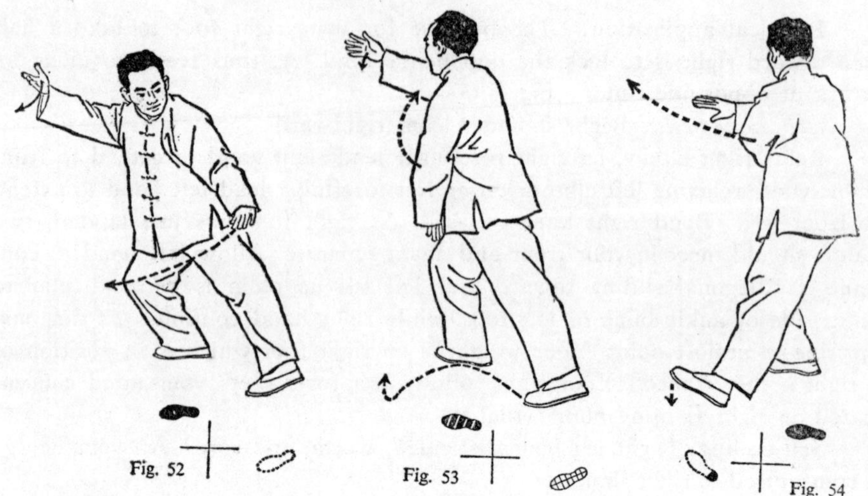
Fig. 52 Fig. 53 Fig. 54

14th movement: Left hand oblique ward

Repeat 2nd movement "Left hand oblique ward" of this Posture. (Fig. 55)

15th movement: Left hand backward pull

Repeat 3rd movement "Left hand backward pull" of this Posture. (Fig. 56)

16th movement: Right hand forward push

Repeat 4th movement "Right hand forward push" of this Posture. (Fig. 57)

Fig. 55 Fig. 56

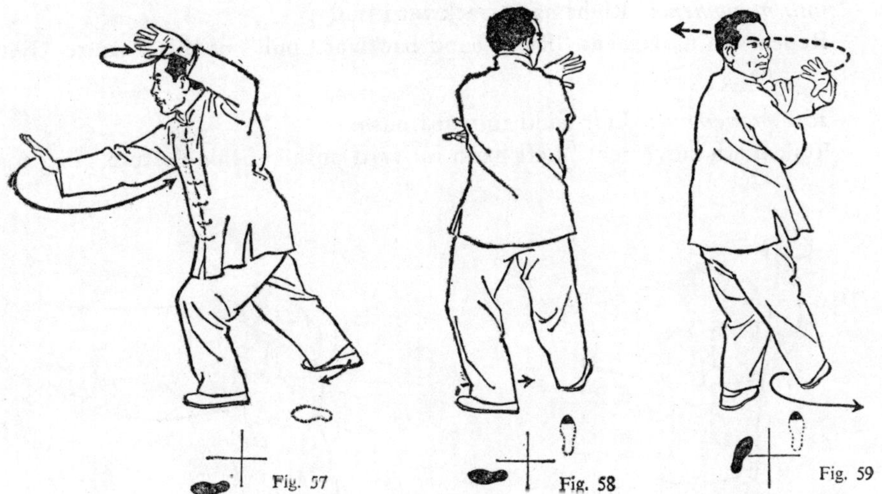
Fig. 57 Fig. 58 Fig. 59

17th movement: Left hand right turn

Repeat 5th movement "Left hand right turn" of this Posture. (Fig. 58. 59)

18th movement: Right hand oblique ward

Repeat 6th movement "Right hand oblique ward" of this Posture. (Fig. 60, 61)

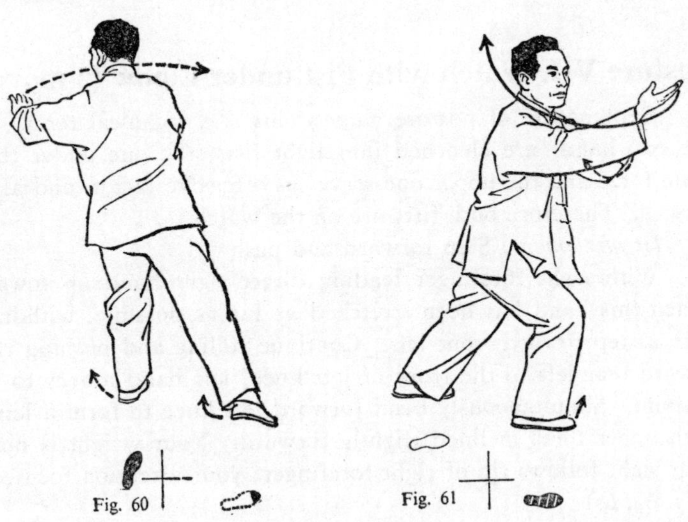
Fig. 60 Fig. 61

19th movement: Right hand backward pull

Repeat 7th movement "Right hand backward pull" of this Posture. (Fig. 62)

20th movement: Left hand forward push

Repeat 8th movement "Left hand forward push" of this Posture. (Fig. 63)

Fig. 62

Fig. 63

Posture VII. Watch with Fist under Elbow (2 movements)

Explanation of posture name: This is a technical term. In this posture the two hands are clenched into light fists, the one under the elbow is the main force and the upper one serves as offensive factor, and as advance guard as well. Therefore both fists are on the watch.

1st movement: Step forward and push

With right forefinger leading direct right hand up toward front right. When this hand has been stretched as far as possible, withdraw left foot to take a step toward front left. Continue rolling and pushing right hand, now toward rear left to the front of left knee; left hand moves to the side of left hipjoint. Simultaneously bend forward left knee to form a left archer stance, with upper torso inclined slightly forward. Your weight is now on left foot; your sight follows tip of right forefinger; your attention focused on left palm. (Fig. 64, 65)

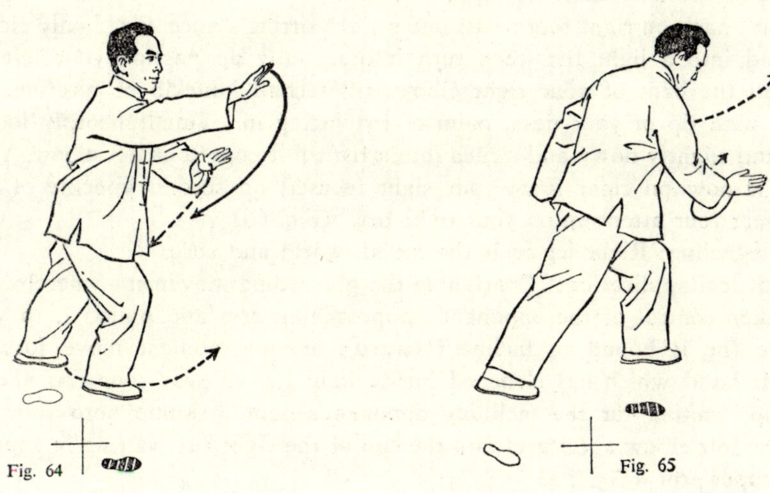
Fig. 64 Fig. 65

Self-feeling: Wriggling in right palm and left arch of foot.

Practical application: When an opponent launches a punch with left fist on your chest, grab his left wrist with your left hand and attach your right hand to his approaching elbow to take control of it. Incline your upper torso slightly forward while pushing and rolling his left arm to your left side. He will topple forward. (Fig. 7/1, 7/2, 7/3)

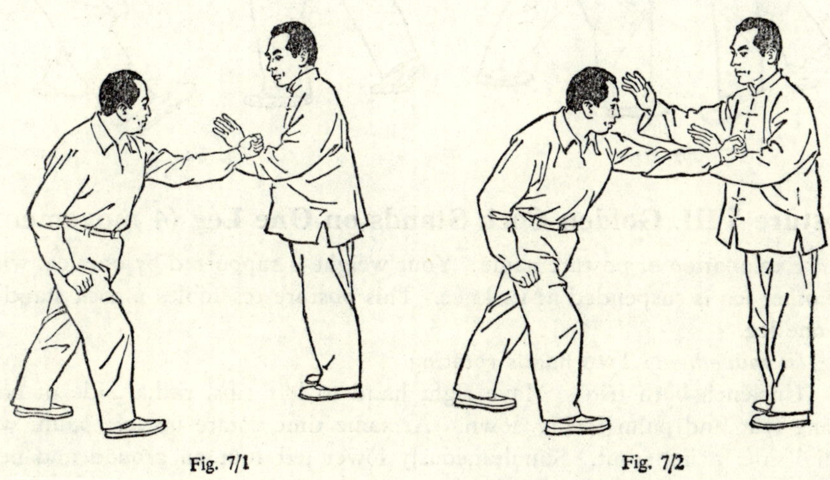
Fig. 7/1 Fig. 7/2

2nd movement: Left fist uplift

"Sit" back on right foot to assume a right sitting stance. Gradually clench left hand into a light fist, then turn it diagonally up passing your left rib cage and the bent of your right elbow, till second knuckle of forefinger is aligned with tip of your nose, palm of fist facing in. Simultaneously loosen right hand slightly down and clench into a fist till it cups your left elbow. Your weight is now on right foot; your sight focused on second knuckle of left forefinger; your attention on your right fist. (Fig. 66)

Self-feeling: Right leg feels distended, warm and sore.

Practical application: Continuing the preceeding movement whereby you have taken control of the opponent's approaching arm and pulled it to your left side (he is bound to incline forward), at this moment move forward your left hand which has clenched into a light fist to pass your ribs and to move up, waiting for the inclining opponent's chin to bump onto your fist while the left elbow aptly gets into the cup of the right fist waiting in support of the upper arm. (Fig. 7/4)

Fig. 7/3 Fig. 7/4

Posture VIII. Golden Cock Stands on One Leg (4 movements)

Explanation of posture name: Your weight is supported by one leg, while the other leg is suspended at its knee. This posture resembles a cock standing on one leg.

lst movement: Two hands rotating

Unclench both fists. Move right hand to left ribs, radial side of hand facing rear and palm facing down. At same time rotate up left palm, with radial side facing front. Simultaneously lower left foot on ground and bend

Fig. 66

Fig. 67

left knee to assume a left archer stance. Shift your weight onto left foot; look at tip of right forefinger, and focus your attention on left palm. (Fig. 67)

Self-feeling: Distension and warmth in left leg. Wriggling in two palms.

Practical application: When the opponent punches on your chest with his left fist, block his wrist with the backward lock of your right hand (the radial side of your hand rearward, palm down), and press with your right elbow on his left elbow, at same time grip his throat with your left hand (the radial side toward him, palm facing up). (Fig. 8/1)

Fig. 8/1

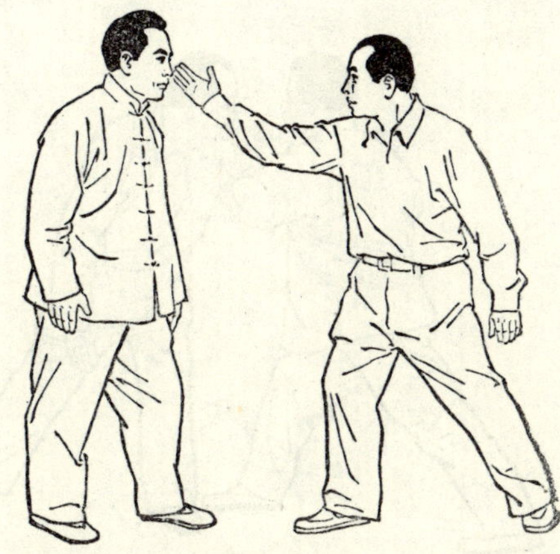

Fig. 8/2

2nd movement: Right hand up ward

Rotate both hands to turn left palm down, right palm up. With right forefinger leading, lift right hand along the underside of left arm toward front left, and stretch your waist and body during this process. When right arm bend reaches left palm, lift right knee, point up right fingertips, while continuing the turn toward right. When the torso has turned due east, raise high your right hand, palm to left, its ends up, as left palm descends naturally till left fingertips close to the upholding right heel. Now you are facing due east; your left leg supports all your weight; your sight directed far ahead; your attention focused on right kneecap. (Fig. 68, 69)

Self-feeling: Your waist feels warm, left leg sore and warm. The right knee feels powerful.

Practical application: If the opponent strikes with his right hand at your face, take hold of his right wrist with your left hand and attach with your right arm to outer side of his right arm and lift upward. Meanwhile lift up your right knee to strike at his lower abdomen. Care must be taken in employing this strike. Better know how to do it, yet try not to do it. (Fig. 8/2, 8/3, 8/4, 8/5)

3rd movement: Two hands rotating

Loosen right knee and squat slightly for right foot to fall down, heel touching first. Bend right knee to assume right archer stance. Meanwhile, with the lowering of torso, right hand also lowers a little, radial side facing forward, palm up. At same time, left hand gets close to underside of right elbow, radial side of hand facing rear, palm down. Your weight is now on

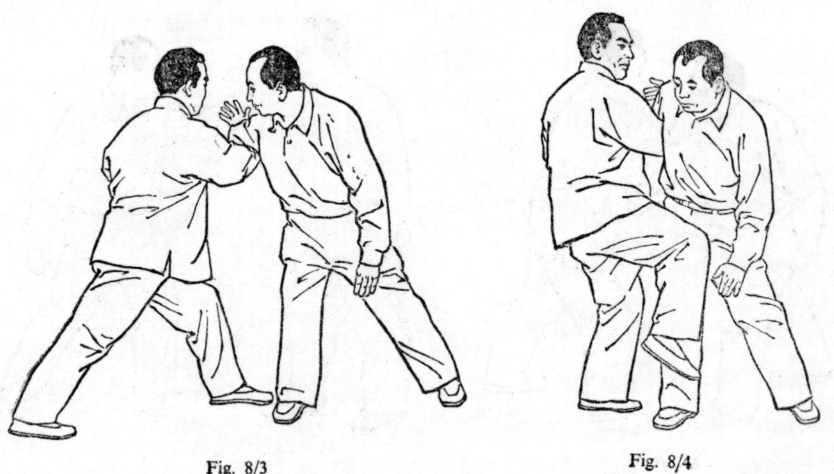

Fig. 8/3

Fig. 8/4

Fig. 68

Fig. 69

right foot; your sight focused on tip of left forefinger; your mind concentrated on right palm. (Fig. 70)

Self-feeling: Right leg distended and warm. Two palms wriggling.

Practical application: Same as that of the lst movement "Two hands rotating" of this Posture, but reverse left and right.

4th movement: Left hand up ward

Fig. 8/5

Fig. 70

Repeat 2nd movement "Right hand up ward" of this Posture, but reverse left and right. (Fig. 71, 72)

Fig. 71 Fig. 72 Fig. 73

Posture IX. Step Back and Repulse Monkey (10 movements)

Explanation of posture name: This is to advance in form of retreat. The opponent's straight forward offensive force is neutralized by setting it sideways or wavering and thus be repulsed. And you could be the pursuing party.

1st movement: Right hand reverse push

Lower left elbow for its tip to be aligned with left knee, and for left hand to reach left ear, palm facing right. At same time let right thumb lead right hand to move up to the front of right knee to give a reverse push, that is, to push with palm up, fingers obliquely down. Your sight is focused on right palm heel; your right leg still supports your weight, left leg still suspended; your attention concentrated on right palm. (Fig. 73)

Self-feeling: Warmth around your waist; wriggling in right palm.

Practical application: If an opponent strikes your chest with his right palm, attach your right forearm to his forearm to move up along a circular arc for the upgoing right palm to thrust to the front with your fingers pointing down, palm up, striking with an outburst of force at the opponent's lower abdomen. Take note to keep your forearm attached to his right arm. (Fig. 9/1, 9/2, 9/3, 9/4)

2nd movement: Left hand forward push

With right thumb leading, turn right hand toward left to brush the uprised left knee, better include the instep and slide to the side of right hipbone, palm down, fingers pointing forward. Simultaneously relax right knee to bring torso slightly lower. Now with left ring finger leading, thrust left hand to a forward push to rest above and beyond right knee, while the uprised left leg

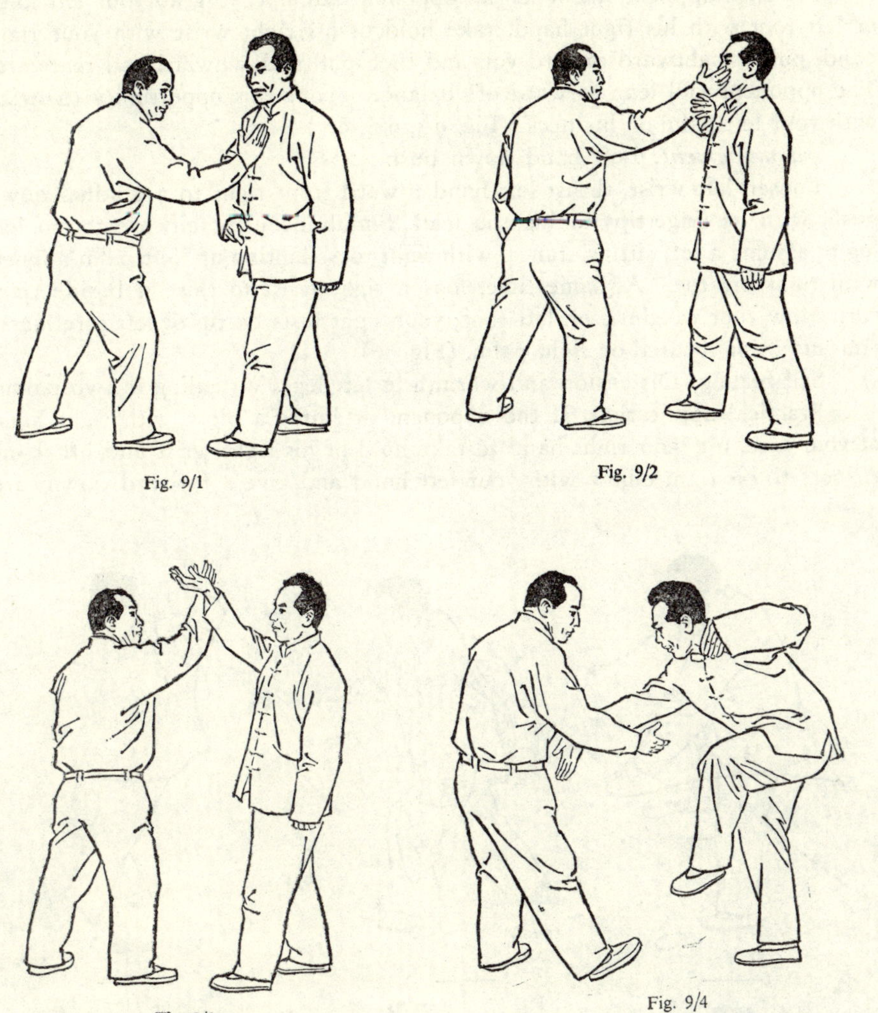

Fig. 9/1

Fig. 9/2

Fig. 9/3

Fig. 9/4

stretches as far as possible to rear with toes touching first (facing due east). When its heel gradually rests on floor and turns out slightly, right knee will naturally bend to a right archer stance. Your weight is now on right foot; your sight on left forefinger; your attention focused on right palm. (All through this Posture special attention should be paid to acquire coordination and integrity of torso and limbs in turning leftward and rightward.) (Fig. 74, 75)

Self-feeling: Right leg distended and warm; wriggling in palms.

Practical application: When an opponent attempts to grab your left knee or left foot with his right hand, take hold of his right wrist with your right hand, pull it rightward toward you and then pull it downward and rearward. The opponent will lean forward off balance. Take this opportunity to strike with your left palm on his neck. (Fig. 9/5, 9/6, 9/7)

3rd movement: Left hand down push

Loosen left wrist, thrust left hand toward front right to a gradual down push, with its fingertips taking the lead. Simultaneously shift weight to left leg to assume a left sitting stance, with right toes slanting up, left palm aligned with right big toe. At same time, loosen right wrist to raise it beside right ear. Now your weight is on left foot; your sight rests on tip of left forefinger; your attention focused on right palm. (Fig. 76)

Self-feeling: Distension and warmth in left leg. Wriggling in two palms.

Practical application: If the opponent attempts a blow with right hand at your face, use your right hand to take hold of his right wrist and lift it up. Adhere to his right elbow with your left hand and give a forward downward

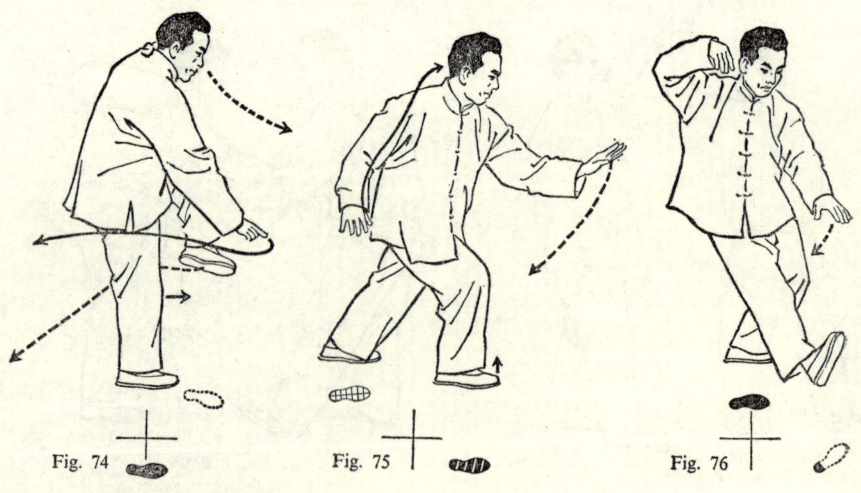

Fig. 74 Fig. 75 Fig. 76

Fig. 9/5

Fig. 9/6

Fig. 9/7

Fig. 9/8

push while shifting torso slightly backward to left leg. The opponent could be thrown away a good distance or tumble down. (Fig. 9/8)

4th movement: Right hand forward push

Let right ring finger lead right hand to extend forward while shifting sight from tip of left forefinger to upper left. When right hand reaches the direct front, straighten torso and shoulder, loosen right knee for right leg to stretch rearward with big toe barely touching ground. Simultaneously roll left hand backward to outer side of left knee, palm down. Now right foot will have stepped flat on ground and left knee bent to form a left archer stance.

Fig. 77
Fig. 78

Concurrently, slide right hand above and beyond left foot, palm down, ends forward. Now your weight is on left foot; your sight rests on tip of right forefinger; your mind concentrated on left palm. (Fig 77, 78)

Self-feeling: Distension and warmth in left leg. Wriggling in two palms.

Practical application: If the opponent attempts a blow with his left hand at your face, use your left hand to take hold of his left wrist to pull it toward your right knee, then quickly to your rear left. When this has pulled him off balance and inclined toward you, strike with your right palm at his neck. (Fig. 9/9, 9/10, 9/11)

Fig. 9/9
Fig. 9/10

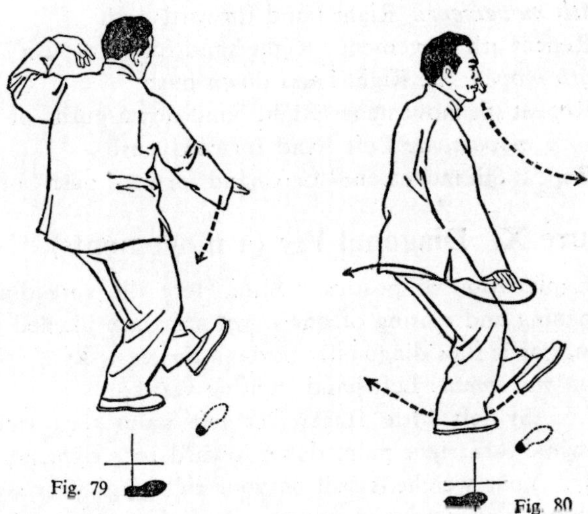
Fig. 79 Fig. 80

5th movement: Right hand down push

Repeat 3rd movement "Left hand down push" of this Posture, except to reverse left and right. (Fig. 79)

6th movement: Left hand forward push

Repeat 4th movement "Right hand forward push" of this Posture except to reverse left and right. (Fig. 80, 81)

7th movement: Left hand down push

Repeat 3rd movement "Left hand down push" of this Posture.

Fig. 9/11 Fig. 81

8th movement: Right hand forward push

Repeat 4th movement "Right hand forward push" of this Posture.

9th movement: Right hand down push

Repeat 5th movement "Right hand down push" of this Posture.

10th movement: Left hand forward push

Repeat 6th movement "Left hand forward push" of this Posture.

Posture X. Diagonal Fly (4 movements)

Explanation of posture name: Here the spreading and contracting, or the opening and closing of one's two arms are likened to a big roc spreading its wings as it flies diagonally through the vast sky.

1st movement: Left hand slanting ward

Led by left little finger, let left palm turn slanting up toward left. Meanwhile turn right palm down toward rear right, and loosen waist to sink slightly. Your weight is still on your right leg; your sight rests on tip of left forefinger; your attention focused on right palm. (Fig. 82)

Self-feeling: Distension and warmth in right leg.

Practical application: If an opponent attempts to box your left ear with his right hand, intercept by adhering your left palm at the bend of his right arm. Care must be taken not to apply an outward pushing force, but let your mind direct your right palm to exert force diagonally down toward rear right (imagine supported on ground) and this hand forms a triangle with your two feet. (Fig. 10/1, 10/2)

Fig. 82 Fig. 83 Fig. 84

Fig. 10/1

Fig. 10/2

2nd movement: Left hand down roll

With left little finger taking the lead, turn left hand in a downward arc at your outer left side till it stops above your right knee, palm toward right, ends downward. At same time, right hand, led by its forefinger, moves in an upward arc toward left till it gets beside left ear, palm out, ends up. Your weight remains on right foot; your sight horizontally ahead; your attention focused on right palm. (Fig. 83, 84, 85)

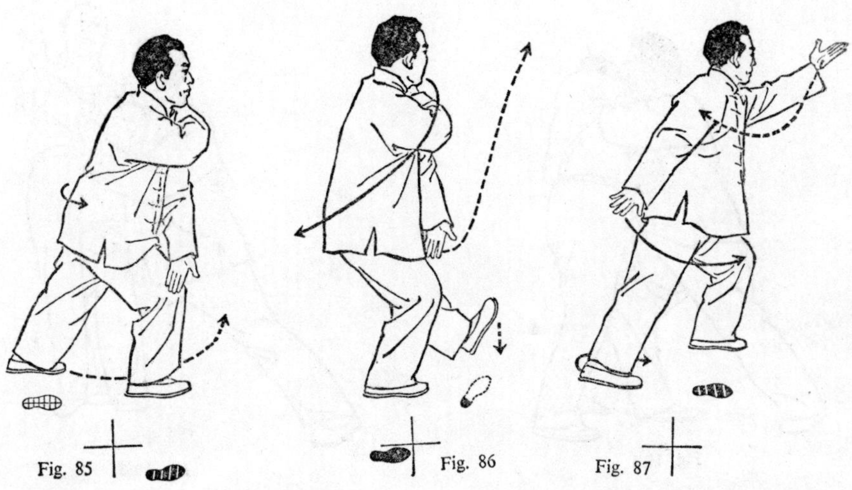

Fig. 85

Fig. 86

Fig. 87

Fig. 10/3

Fig. 10/4

Self-feeling: Right leg feels distended, warm and sore. There is wriggling in two palms.

Practical application: Succeeding the previous movement, the opponent now tries to box your right ear with his left hand. Allow your right hand to support and raise up his left elbow to left till back of your hand nearly adheres to your left ear. Meanwhile let your left palm adhere to his right arm and to move down to your rear right, till back of your hand gets close to outer side of your right knee. His torso being twisted, he is off balance. (Fig. 10/3, 10/4)

Fig. 10/5

Fig. 10/6

3rd movement: Left leg forward step

Relax left knee to move left foot a step to front left with the heel touching, thus assuming a right sitting stance. Your weight is still on right leg; your sight directed forward to left; your attention still focused on right palm. (Fig. 86)

Self-feeling: Right leg increasingly warm and distended.

Practical application: Succeeding the previous movement, now move your left foot a step to front left, just in place to lock his hind leg. (Fig. 10/5)

4th movement: Left shoulder stroke

Relax both elbows. Guided by little finger, drop right hand toward rear right. Meantime lift up left hand toward front left, guided by its forefinger. Put down left toes also on floor just in time when two palms meet at natural distance on each other's course of motion. Then bend left knee just in time when two palms leave each other to continue their own move. Left hand moves up toward front left till its wrist reaches shoulder level, palm slanting in; right hand pulls down toward rear right till palm is aligned with right external ankle bone. Your weight is now on your left leg, you are assuming left archer stance; your sight concentrated on left forefinger; your mind focused on right palm. (Fig. 87)

Self-feeling: Left leg feels distended and warm. The two palms feel wriggling.

Practical application: Succeeding the previous movement when the opponent's limbs are all locked up and can not stir at all, now spread your arms respectively toward front left and rear right while bending your left knee to assume a left archer stance. This is the posture of diagonal fly. Your opponent will immediately fall backward. (Fig. 10/6, 10/7, 10/8)

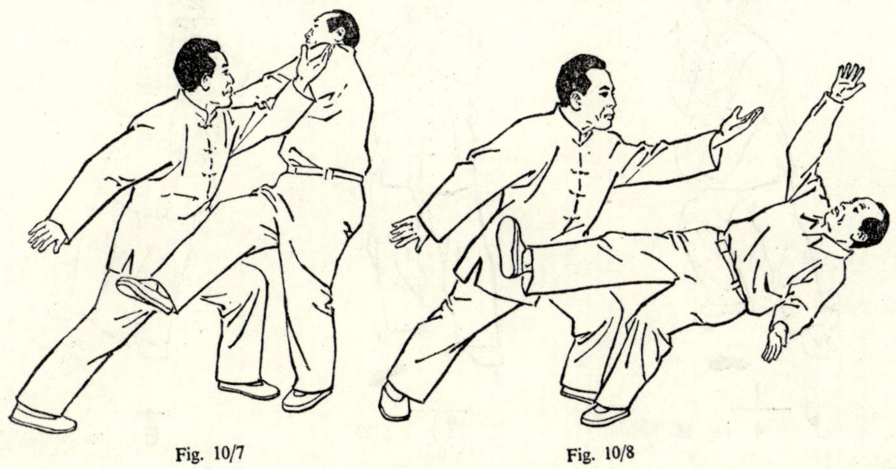

Fig. 10/7 Fig. 10/8

Posture XI. Lift Hand (4 movements)

Explanation of posture name: A hand is raised as if lifting some object.

1st movement: Turn halfway rightward

Detach sight from left forefinger to look toward front right for upper torso to turn to right till you face due south. At same time, lift slightly right heel to turn left on its toes (for the toes to point south by west), and sit back to assume a left sitting stance. Simultaneously move left hand for its thumb to rest beside right armpit, and carry right hand to left knee. Then, while you continue with the sitting stance, let left toes move slightly toward south, for right foot to rest naturally on its heel, its toes pointing at southwest. Meanwhile move up right hand toward left till its thumb be aligned with tip of your nose. Your two palms now diagonally face each other; your weight is still on left foot; your sight passes over right thumb to aim ahead; and your attention is focused on left palm. (Fig. 88, 89)

Self-feeling: Left leg feels distended and warm. Two palms sense the wriggling feeling.

Practical application: If an opponent punches at your right rib cage with his left fist, adhere to his left wrist with your left palm and adhere to his left elbow with your own right elbow. Now turn upper torso slightly to right, while sucking in your stomach to move torso slightly backward. The opponent will be lifted up by you. (Fig. 11/1, 11/2, 11/3)

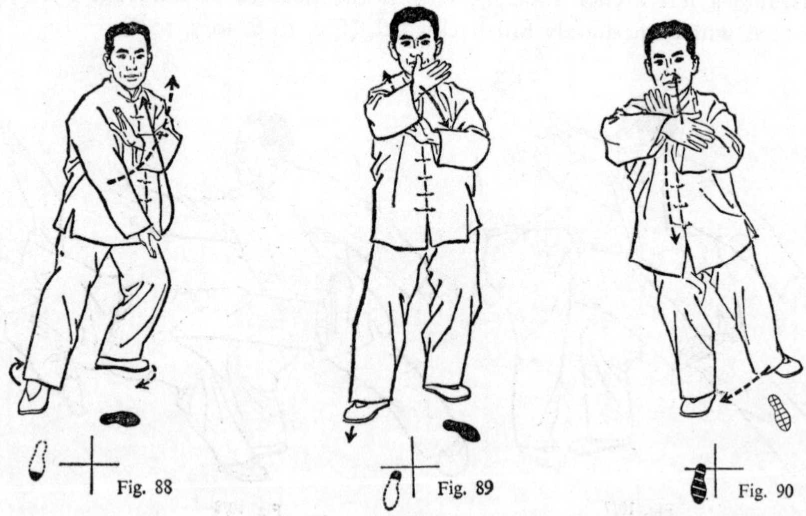

Fig. 88 Fig. 89 Fig. 90

Fig. 11/1

2nd movement: Left hand press

Gradually place whole right foot on ground, bend right knee and stretch left leg behind to assume an archer stance. Simultaneously relax right hand, led by its little finger, to descend to shoulder level while its elbow naturally ascends till elbow and fingertips are all horizontal at shoulder level, palm in. Now press left palm against inner part of your right wrist, palm facing out, fingertips upward, with tip of forefinger and tip of nose aligned. Look horizontally away from tip of left forefinger; your weight is now on right leg; your attention is focused on left palm. (Fig. 90)

Fig. 11/2

Fig. 11/3

Fig. 11/4

Self-feeling: All your energy issued from your feet passes through your legs, your waist, finally reaches your back and moves up to your fingers. You may sense an integrated energy in you.

Practical application: Continuing, bend your right arm at 90 degree angle, so the back of your right hand gets in touch with the opponent's chest. Immediately attach your left hand to inner side of your right wrist, and deliver energy with both hands pressing together, while your back leans slightly rearward, your eyes look horizontally far away. The opponent will be pressed away a good distance. (Fig. 11/4, 11/5)

Fig. 11/5

Fig. 11/6

3rd movement: Right hand turns hook

Bring up right hand slightly to right while gathering its fingertips to form a hook hand, ends down. Simultaneously accompanying the rise of right wrist stretch up your torso while shifting body weight completely to right foot. The weightless left foot will naturally draw next to right foot. At same time lower left hand till its thumb rests just below your navel, palm down, fingers pointing right. Your sight rests on right wrist; your attention focused on right palm. (Fig. 91)

Self-feeling: When right fingers gather together, right shank feels tense, centre of right palm wriggling.

Practical application: If the opponent attempts a blow with his right fist on your chest, attach your left hand, palm down, to his right forearm and then turn up your palm to pull down his forearm. Meanwhile, slightly loosen your right fingers to form a loose hook to strike the opponent's chin with your up-lifting right wrist. (Fig. 11/6)

4th movement: Open right hook-hand

Lift right hook hand with its little finger leading. Gradually open hook till right hand finally ceases above head, palm up, fingers slanting toward left. Your torso follows right hand to finally stretch up. Now look out from under your right forefinger. Your weight is still on right foot with left toe barely touching ground; your attention focused on right palm. (Fig. 92)

Self-feeling: Chest comfortable and at ease; both palms warm and wriggling.

Fig. 91

Fig. 92

Practical application: Continuing, when you have dealt an upward blow at the opponent's chin, but now the opponent has neutralized your blow by a slight backward evasion of his head, you may open the hooked right hand and turn up the palm to pursue his chin with an up warding stroke. (Fig. 11/7)

Fig. 93

Fig. 11/7

Posture XII. Stork Spreads Wings (4 movements)

Explanation of posture name: This posture imitates the stork spreading its wings in joy, thus to function in promoting health as well as in combating an opponent.

1st movement: Bend and push

With sight fixed on right forefinger, gradually bend forward, palm facing out. Just as right hand descends to shoulder level, shift sight to left forefinger and fully push down left palm, but without further bending. Keep knees straight during bending your torso. Now draw left foot slightly forward to set the whole foot on ground, but most of your weight on right foot. Your attention is focused on right palm. (Fig. 93)

Self-feeling: The tendons at the hollow of both knees feel sore due to stretch. Both palms feel warm.

Practical application: Continuing, If you missed the opponent's chin with your up warding, you may bend upper torso slightly forward in order to push on his face with an upward, forward and then downward curve by your right palm. At same time, bring left foot slightly forward. The opponent will be blown away. (Fig. 12/1)

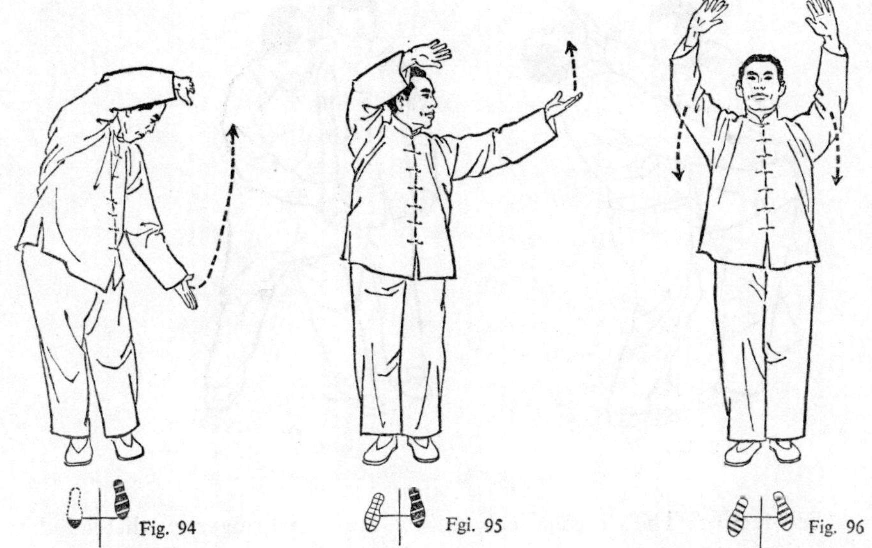

Fig. 94 Fgi. 95 Fig. 96

2nd movement: Twist body leftward

Relax left knee, drop left fingers down (your sight still on left forefinger), and let left thumb lead palm to face left, then gradually outward, till it reaches due east at outer side of left foot. Transfer your sight to tip of left middle finger, while right palm follows the turn to face east too. (Actually your upper torso does the turning, or the twist.) Your weight is shifted onto left foot; your attention is focused on left palm. (Fig. 94)

Self-feeling: Your rib cage extended. There is wriggling in palms. The hollow behind your left knee feels warm, distended and sore.

Practical application: If the opponent strikes at your face from your left with his right palm, or grabs your neck, you can twist your upper torso toward left, simultaneously work up your right palm from under his right arm for your right hand to grab, or for your right wrist to attach to, his wrist. Attention should be paid not to detach from his wrist. (Fig. 12/2, 12/3, 12/4)

3rd movement: Left hand up ward

With left middle finger guiding left hand to stretch outward as far as possible, your left arm will ascend of its own accord to the position above head, palm facing front (still due south). Simultaneously right hand moves also above head, palm facing front. Now both hands have their fingers up. Look out upward and forward from between two hands. Your weight has finally shifted from left foot to an equal distribution between two feet; your attention is focused on two palms. (Fig. 95, 96)

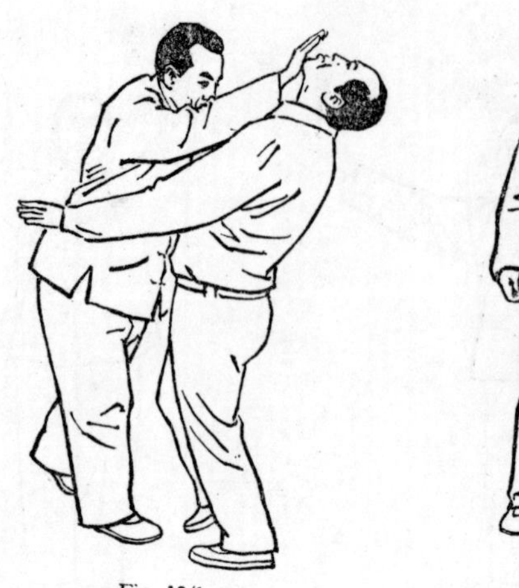
Fig. 12/1

Fig. 12/2

Self-feeling: The rib cage feels fully at ease. All fingertips distended and warm.

Practical application: Continuing, keep your right hand grabbed at his right wrist, or your right wrist attached to his right wrist, but meanwhile let your left arm closely adhere to the outer side of his right arm and lift it up till

Fig. 12/3

Fig. 12/4

Fig. 97 Fig. 98

your left elbow is a little higher than his right elbow. (Fig. 12/5)

4th movement: Elbows sink down

Relax knee joints and gradually squat, then relax shoulders, elbows, waist and hipjoints. Following the squat, sink the points of elbows and turn palms in till your wrists descend to shoulder level. Your weight is equally supported by both feet. Look out from two palms. Your attention is concentrated on all fingertips. (Fig. 97)

Fig. 12/5

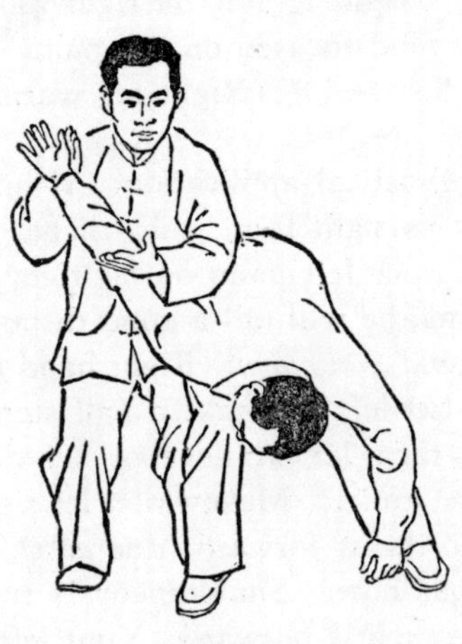
Fig. 12/6

Self-feeling: Whole body light and comfortable. Both palms warm and fingertips distended.

Practical application: Continuing, when your left elbow has attached to his right elbow, turn immediately inward your left forearm for the palm to face in. At same moment adhere your right hand to his right wrist, with the rotation of your right palm press down your wrist and then extend it up. Simultaneously sink your left elbow, your palm will face rear. During the above process, bend your knees to a squat. Because the opponent's right elbow has been surpressed by your rolling elbow, he has to fall with face down. (Fig. 12/6)

Posture XIII. Insert Needle to Sea Bottom (4 movements)

Explanation of posture name: One's fingers are simulated to a needle which pricks the opponent's sensitive point under armpit, a vital point called Sea Bottom point. However, the present day practice usually omits this quick as flash movement but simulates the down thrust of right hand as the insertion of a needle to sea bottom. In the movements illustrated here, the author has followed the usual practice, but in the practical application of the 4th movement of this Posture, the pricking of armpit point is retained.

lst movement: Left hand down push

Left hand, led by its little finger, pushes down toward front left till left arm is fully extended as if left hand is placed on some object. Simultaneously relax right wrist to rest beside right ear, palm down, ends pointing forward; your upper torso turns left to follow your sight which follows left finger. Your weight is now on right foot; your sight is still fixed on left forefinger; your mind focused on left palm. (Fig. 98)

Self-feeling: Right leg warm and distended. There is wriggling in both palms.

Practical application: If an opponent attempts to kick at your left leg with his right foot, wait till he has just lifted his knee, and you may lightly place your left palm on his right knee, exerting no force. If he insists on the kicking, he will fall a good distance backward. (Fig. 13/1)

2nd movement: Right hand forward push

Let left foot take a half step toward left (facing due east), heel touching first, then let whole foot set down and bend left knee to assume a left archer stance. Meanwhile, let right ring finger lead right hand to leave right ear to thrust forward (due east), palm facing out, its thumb aligned with tip of your nose. Simultaneously turn on the ball of right foot for the heel to move slightly outward. Your left hand rests at outer side of left knee. Your weight rests onto left foot. Look out over your right thumb; your attention

Fig. 99 Fig. 100

on your right palm. (Fig. 99, 100)

Self-feeling: Left leg distended and warm. There is wriggling in both palms.

Practical application: Watch for the moment when the opponent failed in his kick at you and just dropped his foot on ground. Take an immediate left step forward for your left knee to be attached to the inner side of his right knee. Thrust your right hand at his face, or push at his chest. He will fall away a good distance. (Fig. 13/2)

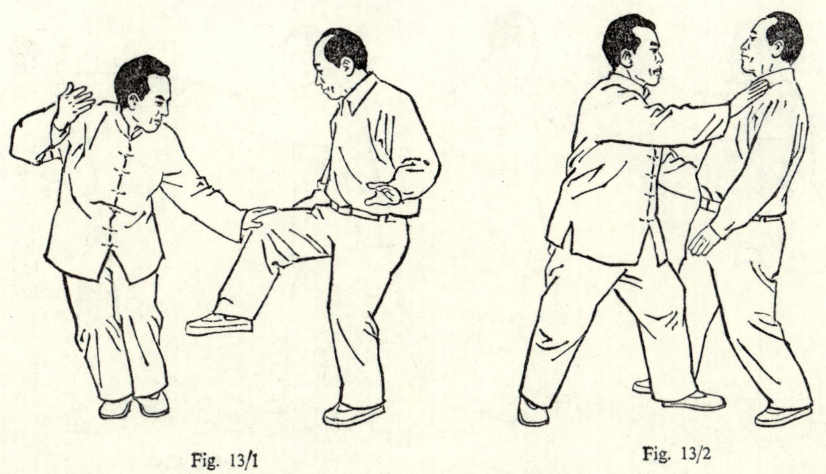
Fig. 13/1 Fig. 13/2

Fig. 101

Fig. 102

3rd movement: Right hand forward extend

"Sit" back to shift your weight to right leg to assume a right sitting stance. At same time relax right wrist for its fingers to point forward, palm facing left. Look ahead over right thumb. Your mind is concentrated on right palm. (Fig. 101)

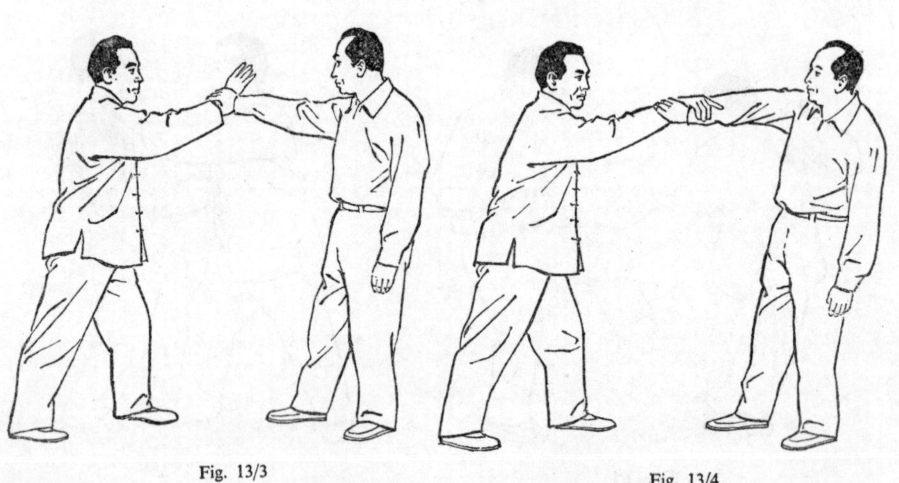

Fig. 13/3

Fig. 13/4

Self-feeling: Right foot firmly rooted in ground. There is wriggling in right palm and left sole.

Practical application: If your right wrist is held and pulled away from you, follow this pull, relax your right arm and wrist, and extend your fingertips while slightly lean your upper torso backward for your coccyx to be perpendicular to your right heel, and then "sit" down. As a result, the one being pulled over is the opponent. (Fig. 13/3, 13/4, 13/5)

4th movement: Right hand down point

Relax waist and right wrist. Descend right hand in between knees, palm facing left, fingertips pointing down. At same time left hand, led by its forefinger, moves to upper front to shoulder level, then sink its elbow to bring left hand up to right ear, palm out, fingers up. Simultaneously relax left knee to withdraw left foot next to right foot, with toe lightly touching ground. Your weight remains on right foot. Look horizontally afar. Your attention is focused on right palm. (Fig. 102)

Self-feeling: Right leg distended, warm and sore.

Practical application: Continuing, when your right wrist is grabbed by the opponent, just thrust forward your left hand to prick his sensitive point near his armpit, and then insert right hand downward as if to penetrate through the ground, while left hand moves up to right ear, palm out. At same time, bend knees to a squat. The opponent will fall forward on knees. (Fig. 13/6)

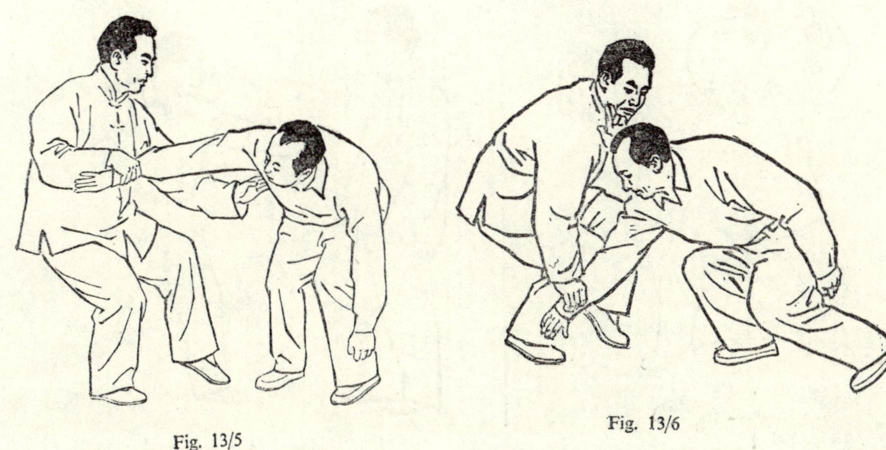

Fig. 13/5

Fig. 13/6

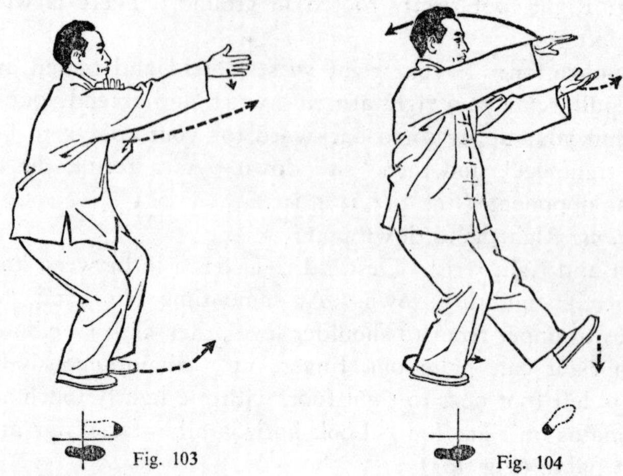

Fig. 103 Fig. 104

Posture XIV. Flash the Arms (Unfurl the Fan, 2 movements)

Explanation of posture name: This posture derived its name from the fan-like correlated movement of waist and arms. The waist is likened to the mount of a folding fan and the two arms its covering. Rotation of the waist, which brings about the extension of two arms, resembles the sudden extending of a fan from folded form. Another name for this posture is "Flash Arms Through Back" because it functions as a good exercise for the arm-stretching muscles connecting with one's back.

1st movement: Hands forward thrust

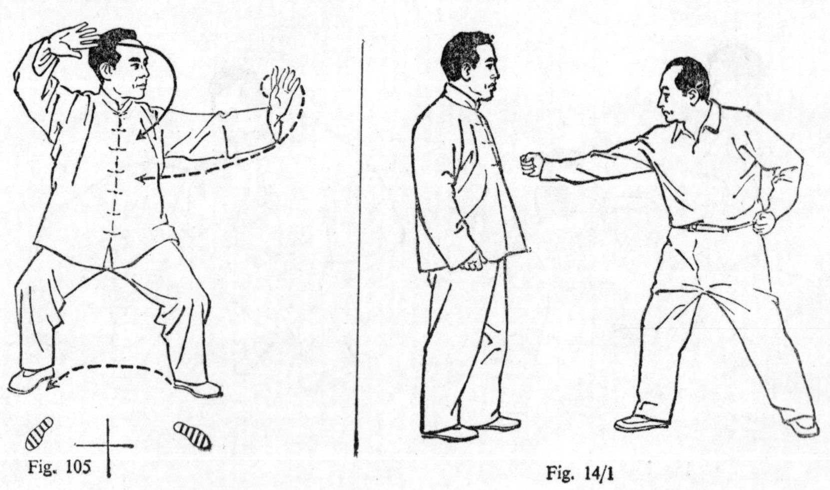

Fig. 105 Fig. 14/1

Without transfer of your weight, move up right hand to shoulder level, forefinger leading, palm to left, while left hand descends, palm up, from right ear to the underside of right arm, and thrusts forward along the underside of right arm to a full extent. At same time right palm also has turned down to face left palm at a natural distance (about 10 cm.). Simultaneously draw left foot forward with heel touching, toes slanting up. Look at right forefinger; focus attention on right palm. (Fig. 103, 104)

Self-feeling: Right leg distended and sore.

Practical application: If an opponent punches with his right fist on your chest, attach your right palm to outer side of his elbow to raise it up. At same time, turn upper torso slightly to right and draw left foot forward to let your left thigh contact with his right thigh. The opponent would lose his balance. (Fig. 14/1, 14/2)

2nd movement: Left hand forward push

Turn raised left toe to right and set down whole foot, while separating two hands. Push left hand to front left, forefinger leading, palm out, ends up. Ward up right hand to rear right, little finger leading, elbow bending, forefinger pointing to end of right brow. At same time, lower upper torso by relaxing waist, and turn right heel to left to assume horse-riding stance. Your weight is equally distributed between two legs. Look out over tip of your left forefinger, your attention focused on left palm. (Fig. 105)

Self-feeling: Chest feels comfortable; feet planted into ground and full of energy.

Practical application: Continuing the preceeding application, now squat to a horse-riding stance and take offensive by pushing forward your left hand at his right armpit or rib cage. (Fig. 14/3)

Fig. 14/2 Fig. 14/3

Posture XV. Left and Right Separate Instep Kicks (12 movements)

Explanation of posture name: It is so named because in execution one tenses the instep of left foot in separating left foot to a leftward kick, and then tenses the right instep in separating right foot to a rightward kick. This movement is also likened to the spreading of a bird's wings, and is also named wing foot.

1st movement: Palms loosely facing

Withdraw left hand to chest, little finger leading, palm up. Turn right toes in. At same time loosen right hand to descend in your front to shoulder level, palm down to loosely face left palm (about 20 cm. apart). Meanwhile, stretch waist, draw in left foot (its heel about $3^1/_2$ cm. from right foot), with toes barely touching ground, forming a T-shape with right foot. Your weight is now on right foot; your sight on right forefinger; your mind concentrated on right palm. (Fig. 106)

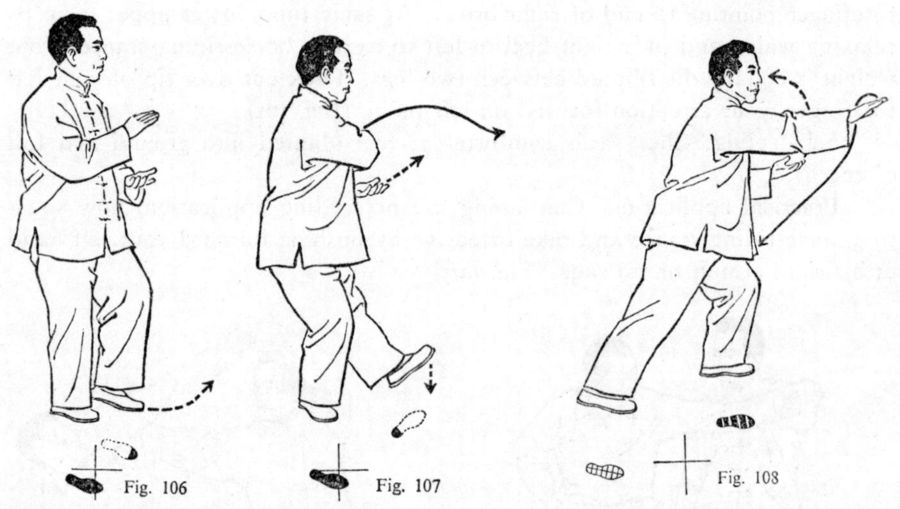

Fig. 106 Fig. 107 Fig. 108

Self-feeling: Right leg warm; palms warm and wriggling.

Practical application: If the opponent punches on your chest or abdomen with his right fist, you may receive his approaching wrist with the curve between your left thumb and forefinger. In your mind simulate his right arm as the reins of a horse, this will help you maintain your own stability and detect any change on his part. (Fig. 15/1, 15/2)

Fig. 15/1

Fig. 15/2

2nd movement: Hands rightward thrust

Relax right knee and "sit" back on it as low as possible, so you can easily draw left foot a step forward, heel touching first, rest of the foot follows on. With the forward shift of your weight, and the slight leftward rotation of upper torso, thrust right hand toward left as far as possible. Then, accompanying the slight rightward rotation of upper torso, move right hand along an outward arc to reach your front right. Now right hand is farther away from you, palm down; left hand naturally moves forward and rightward to the bend of right arm, palm up. Your weight is now on left foot; your sight rests on right forefinger; your attention focused on left palm. (Fig. 107, 108)

Self-feeling: Left leg feels distended and warm. There is wriggling in left palm and arch of right sole.

Practical application: Continuing, when you have adhered to his approaching wrist with your upward left palm, now draw left foot to front left and lightly touch his neck near his right shoulder with your right hand (palm down). The opponent will topple as he is already out of balance. (Fig. 15/3)

3rd movement: Right hand back roll

Lower right hand toward left, little finger leading, till its back rests outside left knee; simultaneously at the start of right little finger let left forefinger lead left hand to ascend toward upper right till its back rests beside right ear. But before right hand reaches its destination beside left knee, when it passes the midpoint between two knees, your upper torso will naturally rotate leftward, and your sight should shift to pursue right forefinger, causing your head to bend and turn slightly to left. At same time turn out right heel by pressing against ground, thus your legs form the left archer stance. Your weight

Fig. 15/3

Fig. 15/4

is still on left foot; your sight passing over right forefinger to rest on inner side of right heel; your attention focused on left palm. (Fig 109)

Self-feeling: Left leg distended, warm and sore. The muscles at back of your right knee feel sore from stretch.

Practical application: Continuing, when you have lightly touched the opponent's right shoulder, now your right hand could pass over the back of his neck to touch lightly on his left shoulder and roll backward for the back

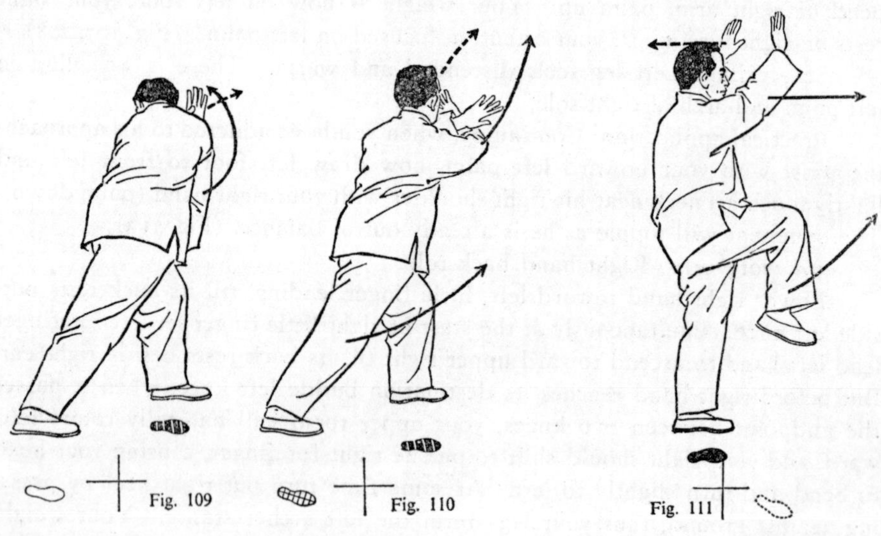

Fig. 109

Fig. 110

Fig. 111

Fig. 15/5

Fig. 15/6

of this hand to move toward the outer side of your left knee. At same time when you raise your left hand to upper right to uphold and adhere to his right wrist till your left hand rests beside your right ear, the opponent will tumble up-side-down or be thrown on ground. (Fig. 15/4)

4th movement: Cross hands

Rotate right palm toward you, thumb leading, then raise right hand along an outward arc to front left, while continung with the rotation of wrist till it reaches shoulder level, palm facing out. At same time, raise left hand slightly toward front left, forefinger leading, till it crosses right wrist from within, both palms now facing out. Your weight remains on left foot. Look out over the crossed hands. Focus your mind on left palm. (Fig. 110)

Self-feeling: Both sides of the chest are comfortably at ease; all fingertips warm and distended.

Practical application: If an opponent attempts to strike at your head with his right hand, take hold of his right wrist with your left hand. Then attach your right hand to his right arm from its outside and underneath, thus blocking and upholding his fowarding arm with the cross formed by your hands. (Fig. 15/5)

5th movement: Hands uprise

With two little fingers leading, raise both hands overhead toward upper left, while uplifting upper torso in correlation, and lifting right knee to hip level, right foot hanging naturally. Now you are standing on left foot. Look out from beneath your upraised wrists. Focus your mind on left palm. (Fig. 111)

Fig. 15/7

Self-feeling: As if left foot is firmly rooted in the ground. All fingertips are warm and distended.

Practical application: Continuing, now uplift your hands which have blocked his right arm. At same moment lift your right knee, ready for delivering a kick. (Fig. 15/6)

6th movement: Separate hands

Led by fingertips, separate two hands to form an angle of about 135 degrees, right hand toward front right, left hand toward rear left, till they are at shoulder level. Right palm now faces left, fingers pointing forward; left palm faces front, fingers pointing sideward. Simultaneously let right foot kick toward front right, instep tensed, toes pointing forward, and right leg is parallel with right arm. Your weight remains on left foot; your sight focused on right thumb; your mind concentrated on left palm. (Fig. 112)

Self-feeling: Toes of left foot grabbed onto the ground. Energy of right leg is transmitted to tip of toes. Both palms feel warm.

Practical application; Continuing, you have blocked the opponent's right arm from withdrawing, now with the thrusting rearward of your left hand, your right foot will automatically kick forward at the opponent's front or right chest. (Fig. 15/7)

7th movement: Palms loosely facing

Relax left knee to loosen waist to lower upper torso, right heel will descend to form left sitting stance, at same time relax both elbows. Roll down right hand toward rear right, little finger leading, till back of hand gets close to right knee, palm up, ends toward left; push left hand toward front right,

Fig. 112

Fig. 113

forefinger leading, till it reaches above right hand, simultaneously turn upper torso slightly to right. Now left palm faces down, ends toward right, two palms loosely and diagonally facing. Your weight is now on left foot; your sight on left forefinger; your attention on left palm. (Fig. 113)

Self-feeling: Left leg distended and warm; palms warm and wriggling.

Practical application: If the opponent punches on your chest with his left fist, adhere with your right hand, palm up, in reverse direction, to his

Fig. 114

Fig. 115

Fig. 116

wrist. You are regarding his left arm as the reins of a horse. (For figures, refer to movements 1 & 2 of this Posture, except to reverse left and right.)

8th movement: Hands leftward thrust

Repeat 2nd movement "Hands rightward thrust" of this Posture, except to reverse left and right. (Fig. 114)

9th movement: Left hand back roll

Repeat 3rd movement "Right hand back roll" of this Posture, except to reverse left and right. (Fig. 115)

10th movement: Cross hands

Repeat 4th movement "Cross hands" of this Posture, except to reverse left and right. (Fig. 116)

11th movement: Hands uprise

Repeat 5th movement "Hands uprise" of this Posture, except to reverse left and right. (Fig. 117)

12th movement: Separate hands

Repeat 6th movement "Separate hands" of this Posture, except to reverse left and right. (Fig. 118)

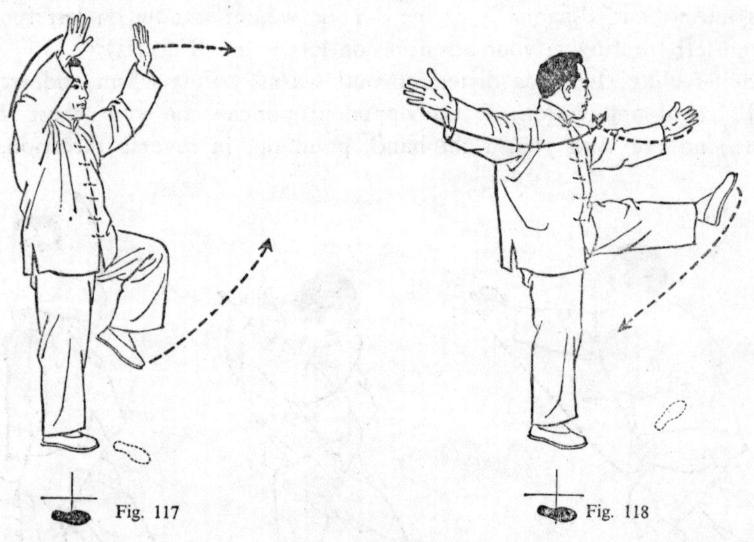

Fig. 117 Fig. 118

Posture XVI. Turn and Strike with Heel (4 movements)

Explanation of posture name: This is named after the 180 degree body rotation on single leg and heel kicking.

Fig. 16/1

1st movement: Cross fists

Loosen left knee for its foreleg to hang from knee; lossen both arms for two little fingers to lead both hands to clench into loose fists; and cross wrists to form an X in front of chest, left fist over right fist, both palms facing in. All through this movement your weight remains on right foot. Look out from between crossed fists. Focus your attention on right fist. (Fig. 119)

Self-feeling: Right shank tense and makes you feel more energetic; rib cage fully at ease.

Practical application: Continuing, if the opponent grabs your left wrist or strikes on your face with his right hand, clench your hands into fists, bend your arm and sink your elbows. At same time rotate inward your arms and form an X in front of your chest, left foreleg hanging. The opponent will be held up by you. (Fig. 16/1, 16/2)

2nd movement: Lift knee rotate torso

Lift left knee toward rear left (to hipjoint level); pivoting on right heel, rotate torso 180 degrees toward rear left (due west) while right toes rotate 180 degrees toward left (pointing north west), without changing the crossed fists. Your weight is still on right foot; you are still looking out from the crossed fists; your attention still focused on right fist. (Fig. 120)

Self-feeling: Your rib cage fully at ease; back and waist energetic; whole body feels lightened.

Practical application: Should an opponent punches from rear on your head with right fist, rotate your torso quickly toward left and block his fist with

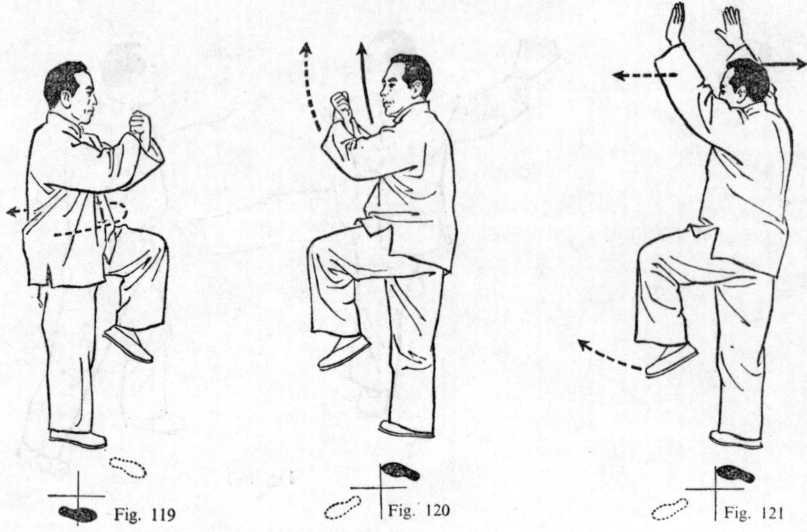
Fig. 119
Fig. 120
Fig. 121

your crossed fists. Take note in mind to maintain your own balance thus to easily change your movement. (Fig. 16/3, 16/4)

3rd movement: Hands uprise

Relax both arms, upraise both fists to front, while rotating palms out and unclench fists, ends up. Your weight remains on right foot; look straight ahead; focus attention on right palm. (Fig. 121)

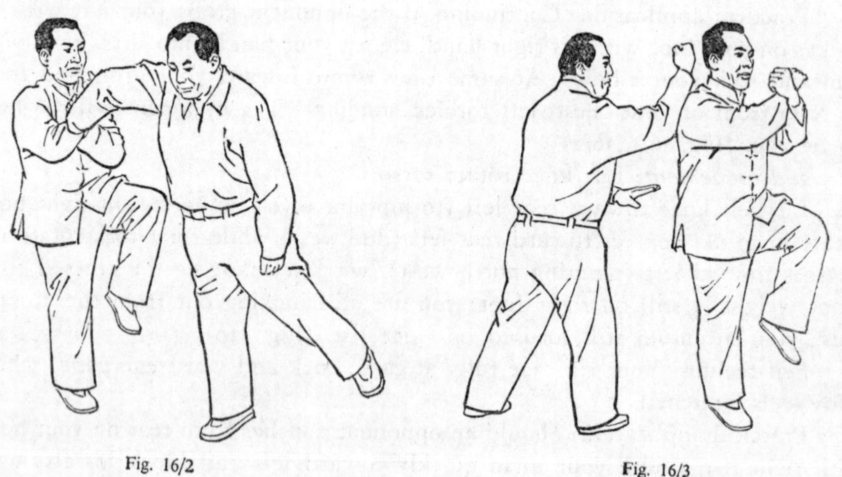
Fig. 16/2
Fig. 16/3

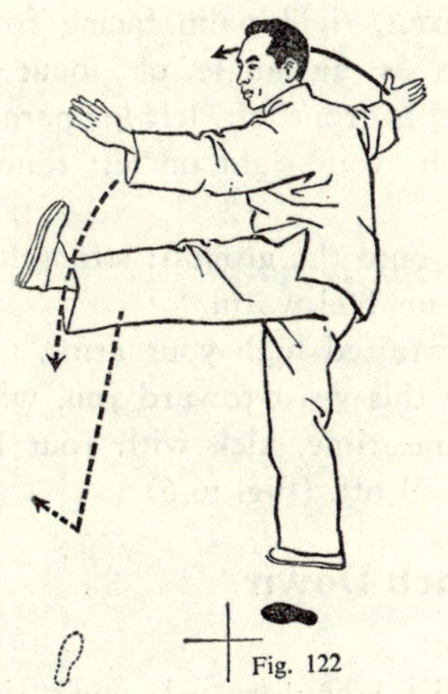
Fig. 122

Fig. 123

Self-feeling: Right leg distended and warm; all fingers distended and warm.

Practical application: Continuing, you have rotated torso, now attach firmly your right hand to his right wrist immediately, and upraise both arms, blocking his right arm with both your hands, ready to attack. (Fig 16/5)

4th movement: Separate hands

Fig. 16/4

Fig. 16/5

Separate hands, little fingers leading, upward and outward to shoulder level, left palm facing right, fingers pointing front, right palm facing front, fingers pointing sideward, between two arms is an angle of about 135 degrees. At same time left foot kicks with its heel to front left, left leg parallel with left arm. Your weight is still on right foot; your sight on left thumb; your attention focused on right palm. (Fig. 122)

Self-feeling: The toes of right foot grabbed onto the ground; strength of your right leg transmitted to your heel. Both palms feel warm.

Practical application: Continuing, you have raised high your arms, now attach your right hand to his right wrist to drag this wrist toward you, while delivering a chopping palm at his face. At same time, kick with your left heel aiming at his hipjoint. He will be kicked well off. (Fig. 16/6)

Posture XVII. Step Forward and Punch Down (6 movements)

Explanation of posture name: With a twist step forward, one's right fist punches down as if holding a sapling and planting it into an imagined hole in front of your left foot.

1st movement: Left hand down push

Relax right knee and waist to lower torso. Set down left foot, heel touching, toes slanting up to assume right sitting stance. Following the fall of left foot, push down left hand, its palm aligned with left toe vertically. At same time relax right wrist to lift it to right ear. Your weight still on right leg; your sight follows left forefinger; your attention focused on right palm. (Fig. 123)

Fig. 16/6

Self-feeling: Right leg distended and warm; there is wriggling in right palm and arch of left sole.

Practical application: If the opponent punches on your chest with his right fist and steps up with his right foot, chop the mid-section of his right forearm with your left palm. At same time, move forward your left foot in between the opponent's feet, heel touching ground, toes slanting up, with your weight remaining on right leg, lift your right wrist to your right ear, ready to deliver a blow. (Fig. 17/1)

2nd movement: Right hand forward push

Gradually set left toes on ground and bend left knee forward to assume left archer stance. At same time, detach right hand from right ear to push forward (due west), ring finger leading, palm facing out, thumb aligned with tip of nose. Simultaneously slightly turn out right heel. Now left hand rests at outer side of left knee, palm down, fingers forward. Your weight is on left foot; look out over right thumb; focus attention on left palm. (Fig. 124)

Self-feeling: Left leg distended, sore and warm; wriggling in both palms.

Practical application: Continuing, when you are pulling down the opponent's bend of right arm with your left hand, you can push on his face with your right hand. At this moment, set down left foot, bend left knee and stretch hind leg to assume left archer stance. The opponent will topple. (Fig. 17/2)

3rd movement: Right hand down push

Push right hand downward and forward, tip of forefinger leading, to the front of left knee, while loosening left wrist to raise it near left ear. At same

Fig. 17/1

Fig. 17/2

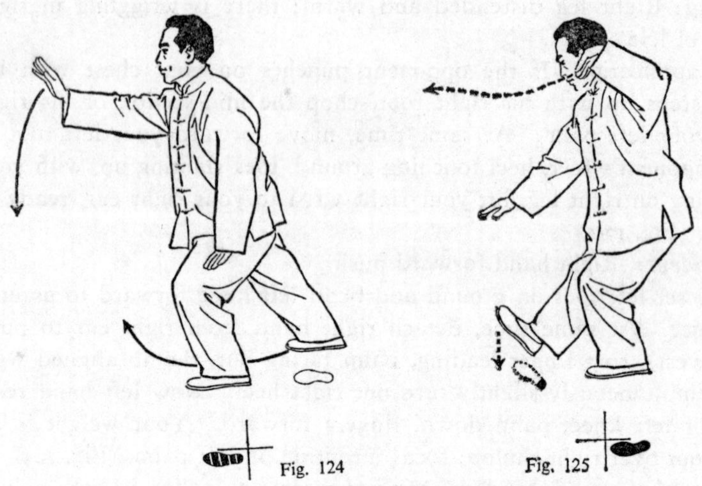

Fig. 124 Fig. 125

time, relax right knee, and draw right foot forward, heel touching, toes slanting, to assume left sitting stance. Right palm is vertical to right toe. Your weight remains on left leg; look at right forefinger; focus attention on left palm. (Fig. 125)

Self-feeling: Left leg warm and distended.

Practical application: If the opponent employs his left hand to strike at your face with his left foot at the front, push at the bend of his left arm while drawing forward your right foot to lock up his left leg. Lift up left hand to left ear, ready to deliver a blow. (Fig. 17/3, 17/4)

Fig. 17/3 Fig. 17/4

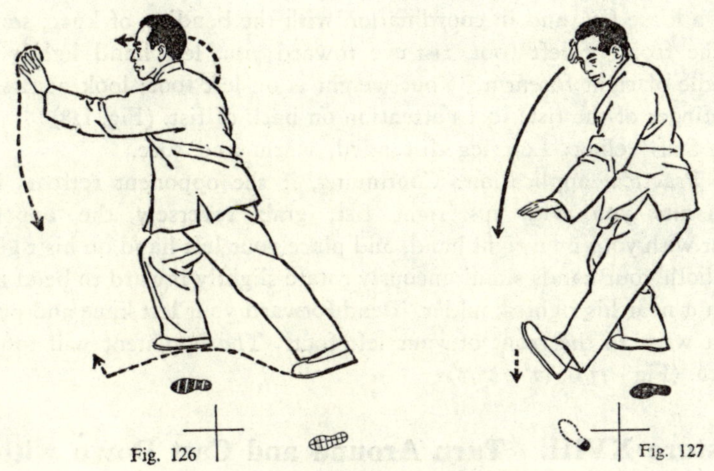

Fig. 126 Fig. 127

4th movement: Left hand forward push

Lifting head to gradually look forward, raise top of head, upstretch waist, and set down right foot to assume right archer stance. At same time, push left hand forward, palm out, thumb aligned with tip of nose. Turn left heel slightly out, and lower right hand slightly to rear, to rest at outer side of right knee, palm down, fingers forward. Your weight is on right foot; look ahead over left thumb; focus attention on right palm. (Fig. 126)

Self-feeling: Right leg warm, sore and distended; palms wriggling.

Practical application: Continuing, when you have pulled the opponent's left arm, you may now thrust left hand onto his face. At same time, set down right foot, bend forward right knee and stretch out rear leg to assume right archer stance. The opponent will be off balance. (Fig. 17/5)

5th movement: Left hand down push

Push left hand downward and forward, tip of forefinger leading, to the front of right knee, while loosening right wrist to raise it to right ear. At same time, draw left foot forward, heel touching, toes slanting, to assume right sitting stance, left palm vertical to left toe. Your weight remains on right foot; look at tip of left forefinger; focus attention on right palm. (Fig. 127)

Self-feeling: Right leg warm and distended.

Practical application: Same as that of the lst movement "Left hand down push" of this Posture.

6th movement: Right fist down push

Lifting head to look gradually forward, raise top of head, upstretch waist, and set down left foot, bend forward left knee to assume left archer stance. At same time, when left hand has brushed left knee, clench right hand into a loose fist, and in coordination with the bending of knee, send fist down to the front of left foot, fist-eye toward you, left hand lightly attached to middle of right forearm. Your weight is on left foot; look at first knuckle of forefinger of the fist; focus attention on back of fist. (Fig. 128)

Self-feeling: Left leg distended, warm and sore.

Practical application: Continuing, if the opponent retreats his left foot and hits you with his right fist, grab reversely the opponent's right wrist with your own right hand, and place your left hand on his right arm bend. Let both your hands simultaneously rotate slightly inward to bend his wrist and push it near his right shoulder. Bend forward your left knee and push down his right wrist to the front of your left foot. The opponent will topple and fall down. (Fig. 17/6, 17/7, 17/8)

Posture XVIII. Turn Around and Cast Down with Fist and Palm (2 movements)

Explanation of posture name: The 180 degree rotation of torso in coordination with flinging of fist and palm gives rise to this name.

1st movement: Lift right fist and turn around

Extend right arm forward and upward and rotate wrist to turn eye of fist down. When right fist reaches eye level, turn left toes rightward to point to due north, pivoting on its heel. Relax and turn right elbow toward rear right, with tip of elbow leading; torso follows arm to turn to due east. Keep

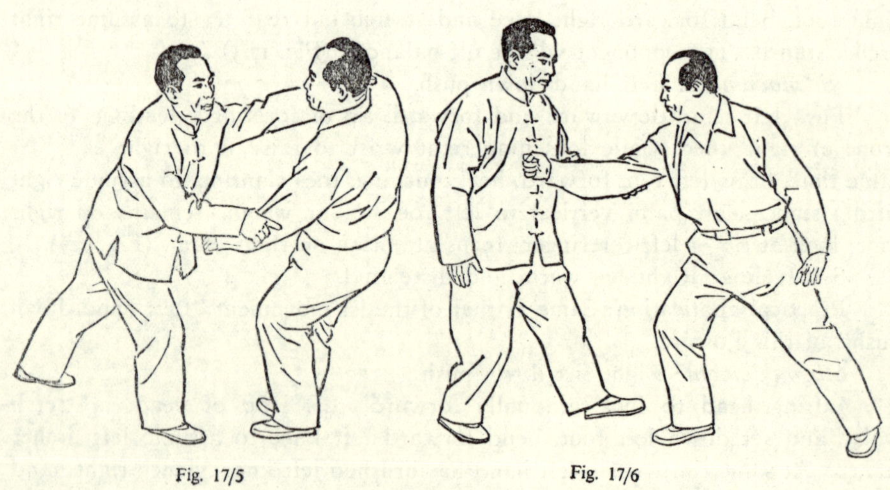

Fig. 17/5 Fig. 17/6

Fig. 128 Fig. 129 Fig. 130

weight on left foot, right heel detached slightly from ground. When left hand followed right fist to due north place left hand on bend of right elbow. During the rotating process, let your sight follow right fist at first, then follow right elbow when right elbow turned due north. Focus your attention on Wai Laogong point on right fist. (Fig. 129, 130)

Self-feeling: Left leg distended, warm and sore; tip of right elbow full of energy; warmth in back.

Fig. 17/7 Fig. 17/8

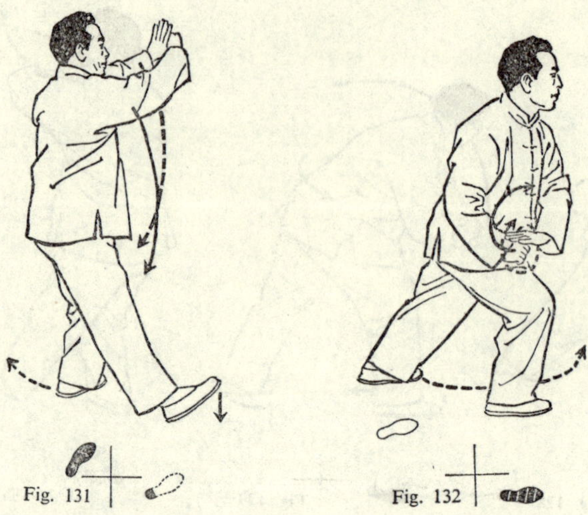

Fig. 131 Fig. 132

Practical application: If an opponent falls on you from your rear, rotate body immediately and bend arm to strike on his chest with your elbow point. (Fig. 18/1, 18/2)

2nd movement: Sideward down pull

Draw in right heel slightly to move right foot a lateral step to right, heel touching first, and bend forward right knee to assume a right archer stance. Concurrently lower right fist to reach its position above right knee at the same instant the right knee bends forward in position, eye of fist up, left palm

Fig. 18/1 Fig. 18/2

covering the eye. Your weight is now on right foot. When right foot has set down and right knee bent forward shift your sight from left forefinger to raise head and look horizontally ahead; your attention is focused on right fist. (Fig. 131, 132)

Self-feeling: Right leg distended and warm; back of left knee sore due to stretch of muscles and tendons.

Practical application: Continuing, move your right foot laterally when you pull down the opponent's right wrist toward you with both your hands and transfer your weight to right leg. Because the opponent's arm is now in awkward position, he has to follow the down pull to fall down, or any counter force will break his arm. (Fig. 18/3, 18/4)

Posture XIX. Double Kick (6 movements)

Explanation of posture name: The traditional jumping up and high kick with each foot in prompt succession gave rise to this name. But in recent years, only one kick is usually done, in order to render easier the execution.

1st movement: Turn over palm and step forward

Turn left palm, little finger leading, along outer side of right fist, so the palm is up when it gets below the fist. At same time, turn right fist to let its eye face you, then open fist into palm and raise to breast level to face left palm (with a distance about 20 cm.) Turn upper torso slightly to right, and relax left knee for left foot to step forward, heel touching, toes slanting up, forming a right sitting stance. Your weight is shifted onto right foot; your sight on se-

Fig. 18/3

Fig. 18/4

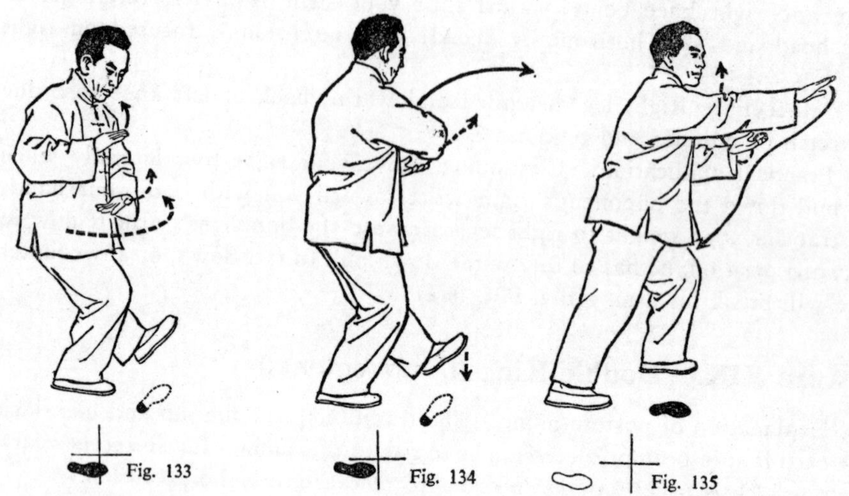

Fig. 133 Fig. 134 Fig. 135

cond knuckle of right hand; your attention on right palm. (Fig. 133, 134)

Self-feeling: Right leg distended and warm; wriggling in right palm and left sole.

Practical application: If your right wrist is held by your opponent, press your left hand on back of his hand and pull down with inward rotation. At same time open your right fist, adhere to his fingers to ward up with outward rotation. Simultaneously step left foot forward, intending to tread on his shin bone. (Fig. 19/1, 19/2, 19/3, 19/4)

Fig. 19/1

2nd movement: Hands rightward thrust

Set down left foot, bend forward left knee to assume a left archer stance. At same time thrust right hand naturally to left and then with an outward arc thrust to front right, palm down; left hand, following the thrust of right hand, moves forward and rightward to the bend of right arm, palm up. Your weight is now on left foot; your sight on tip of right forefinger; your attention on left palm. (Fig. 135)

Self-feeling: Left leg feels distended and warm; there is wriggling in left palm and arch of right sole.

Fig. 19/2

Fig. 19/3

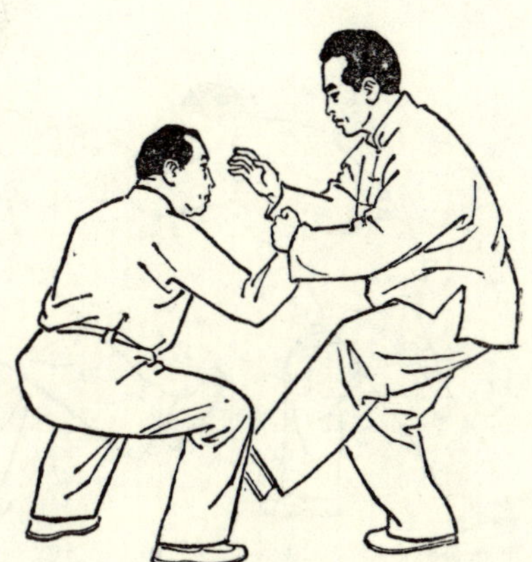

Fig. 19/4

Practical application: Continuing,if the opponent steps back and has evaded your kick, draw forward your left foot, let your left hand adhere to his right wrist and pull it down, while striking his face with your right hand. (Fig. 19/5, 19/6)

3rd movement: Right hand back roll

Lower right hand toward left, little finger leading, till its back rests outside of left knee; simultaneously at the start of right little finger let left forefinger lead left hand to ascend toward upper right till its back rests beside right ear. But before right hand reaches its destination beside left knee, when it passes the midpoint between two knees, your upper torso will naturally rotate leftward, and your sight should shift to pursue right forefinger, causing your head to bend slightly down. At same time turn out right heel by pressing against ground, thus your legs form the left archer stance. Your weight is still on left foot; your sight passing over right forefinger to rest on inner side of right heel; your attention focused on left palm. (Fig 136)

Self-feeling: Left foot distended, warm and sore. The muscles and tendons at back of your right knee feel sore from stretch.

Practical application: Continuing, if the opponent retreats, allow your left hand to grab reversely his right forearm, for his little finger to point up and thumb down. At same time, carry down your right arm from front right to rear left till it rests in front of your left knee. Your opponent will be off balance or be thrown on ground. (Fig. 19/7)

4th movement: Cross hands

Rotate right palm toward you, thumb leading, then raise right hand along an outward arc to front left, while continuing with the rotation of wrist till it

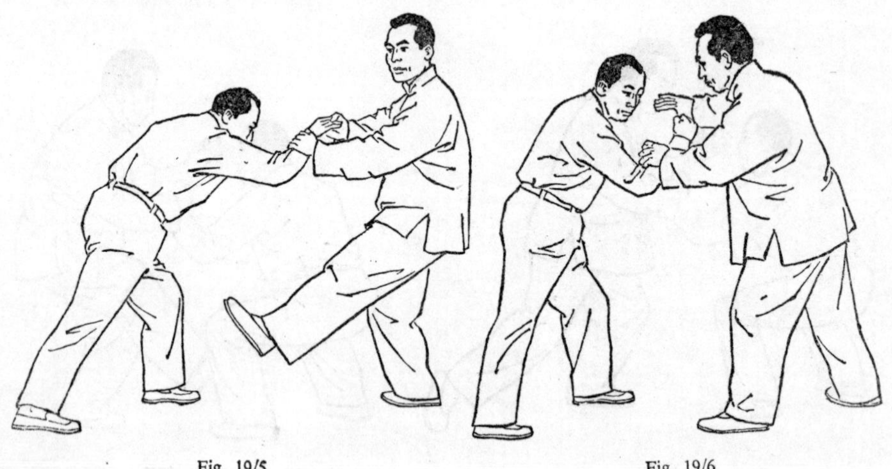

Fig. 19/5 Fig. 19/6

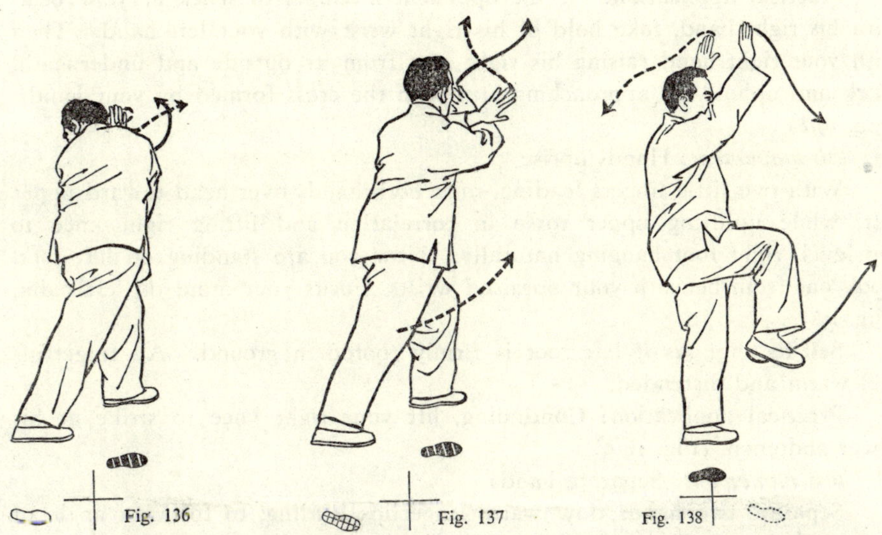

Fig. 136 Fig. 137 Fig. 138

reaches shoulder level, palm facing out. At same time, raise left hand slightly toward front left, forefinger leading, till it crosses right hand from within, both palms now facing out. Your weight remains on left foot. Look out over the crossed hands. Focus your mind on left palm. (Fig. 137)

Self-feeling: Both sides of the chest are comfortably extended; all fingertips warm and distended.

Fig. 19/7 Fig. 19/8

Practical application: If the opponent attempts to strick at your head with his right hand, take hold of his right wrist with your left hand. Then with your right hand raising his right arm from its outside and underneath, block and uphold his approaching arm with the cross formed by your hands. (Fig. 19/8)

5th movement: Hands uprise

With two little fingers leading, raise both hands over head toward upper left, while uplifting upper torso in correlation and lifting right knee to hip level, right foot hanging naturally. Now you are standing on left foot. Look out from beneath your upraised wrists. Focus your mind on left palm. (Fig. 138)

Self-feeling: As if left foot is firmly rooted in ground. All fingertips feel warm and distended.

Practical application: Continuing, lift your right knee to strike at his lower abdomen. (Fig. 19/9)

6th movement: Separate hands

Separate two hands downward, fingertips leading, to form an angle of about 135 degrees between them, right hand toward front right, left hand toward rear left, till they are at shoulder level. Right palm now faces left, fingers pointing forward; left palm faces front, fingers pointing sideward. At same time right foot kicks with its heel to front right, right leg parallel with right arm. Your weight remains on left foot; your sight focused on right thumb; your mind concentrated on left palm. (Fig. 139)

Fig. 19/9

Fig. 19/10

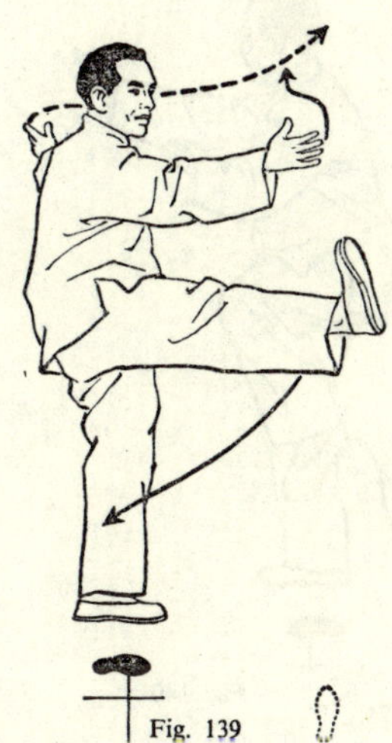

Fig. 139

Self-feeling: The toes of left foot grabbed onto the ground; strength of right foot transmitted to heel; both palms feel warm.

Practical application: Continuing, your knee-stroke having been evaded by the opponent, you may follow on with a kick on his chest. In execution, separate your hands to front and rear; the front hand strikes at his face, simultaneously kick by straightening your leg. The opponent will immediately be overthrown. (Fig. 19/10, 19/11)

Fig. 19/11

Fig. 140 Fig. 141

Posture XX. Left and Right Striking Tiger (4 movements)

Explanation of posture name: When one withdraws aside to evade an attack by extending arms to raise both fists, he is immediately on the offensive. This posture simulates the traditional image of striking an tiger.

1st movement: hands downward pull

Relax and bend right knee for foreleg to hang from knee. At same time turn down left palm, its forefinger leading, to move rightward to meet the concurrently descending right hand, also with its forefinger leading, palm turned down. Thrust both hands to front left (northeast corner), left hand at the front, right hand in the rear with its thumb attached to bend of left arm (at its inner side). Now relax left knee to lower upper torso as much as possible, thus enabling right foot to stretch to rear right (southwest corner), heel touching. Your weight remains on left foot; your sight rests on left forefinger; your attention on left palm. (Fig. 140, 141)

Self-feeling: Your rib cage loosened and comfortable; there is wriggling in left palm and right sole.

Practical application: Continuing, if the opponent withdraws and punches with his right fist on your chest, grab his right wrist with your right hand, and with your left hand pull down his right elbow toward rear right. At same time, lift your right foot to stretch to rear right. The opponent is now off balance. (Fig. 20/1, 20/2, 20/3)

2nd movement: Fists uprise

Pull both hands rightward, turn and set down the upslanting right toe to point to south when hands pass over left knee. As hands travelled to mid-point between two knees, set your weight equally on two feet to assume a horse-riding stance. Then as hands roll over right knee, bend right knee forward, and turn left toe rightward to point to south. At same time clench both hands into loose fists to thrust to front right, right fist ahead, its eye facing front left (due east), left fist has its eye upward, attached under right elbow. Your weight is now on right foot; your eyes look out to front left, (southeast corner); your attention is focused on right fist. (Fig. 142, 143)

Fig. 142

Fig. 20/1

Fig. 143

Fig. 20/2

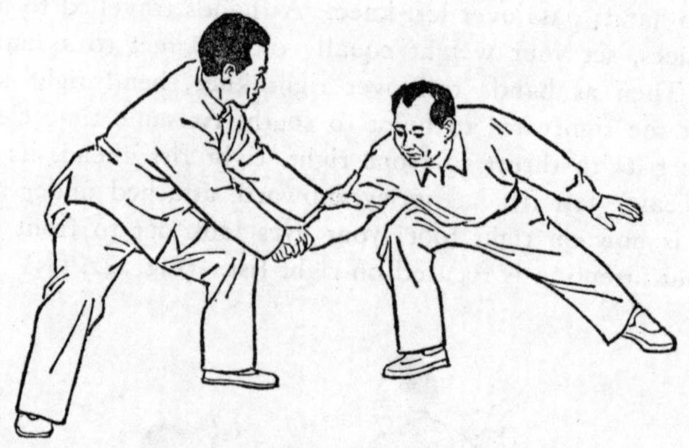

Fig. 20/3

Self-feeling: Right leg distended, warm and sore; rib cage relaxed and comfortable.

Practical application: Continuing, turn to right just as your right heel landed on ground (the roll and pull of hands should coordinate with footwork and torso rotation). The opponent will topple off a good distance. Then raise both fists, assume a sideward acher stance, ready for either an offensive or a defensive move. (Fig. 20/4)

3rd movement: Hands back roll

Turn right toe leftward (facing due east), torso follows to face southeast. Extend two fists to front right (southeast) while opening fists into palms; right

Fig. 20/4

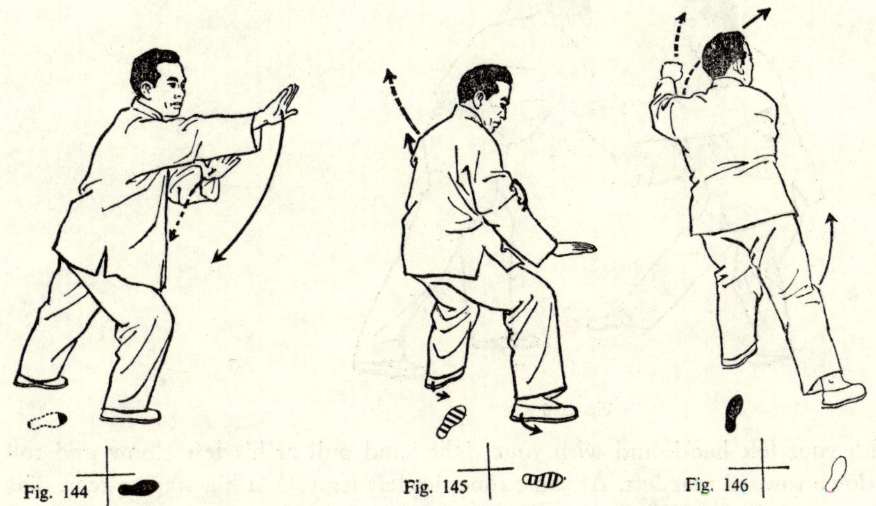

Fig. 144 Fig. 145 Fig. 146

hand ahead, left hand in the rear with thumb attached to left side of right arm bend, both palms facing down. Loosen right knee to lower torso as much as possible, left foot will naturally withdraw to rear left (northwest corner), toes barely touching. Your weight remains on right foot. Your sight shifts from right fist to tip of right forefinger, after fist has opened into palm. Your attention is on right palm. (Fig. 144)

Self-feeling: Right leg distended, sore, and warm; there is wriggling in right palm and arch of left sole.

Practical application: Continuing, if the opponent has not been thrown away by you, and is pushing your chest with two hands, grab his left wrist

Fig. 20/5

Fig. 20/6

with your left hand, and with your right hand pull at his left elbow and roll it down toward rear left. At same time, let left leg take a big step to rear. The opponent will be off balance. (Fig. 20/5, 20/6 20/7)

4th movement: Fists uprise

Pull both hands leftward, turn in left heel and set down whole foot to point to north when hands passes over left knee. As hands travelled to mid-point between two knees, set your weight equally on two feet to assume a horse-riding stance. Then as hands roll over left knee, bend left knee forward, and turn out right heel for right toe to point to north. At same time clench both hands into loose fists to thrust to front left, left fist ahead, its eye facing front right (due east), right fist has its eye upward, attached under left elbow. Your weight is now on left foot; your eyes look out to front right (northeast corner); your attention focused on left fist. (Fig. 145, 146)

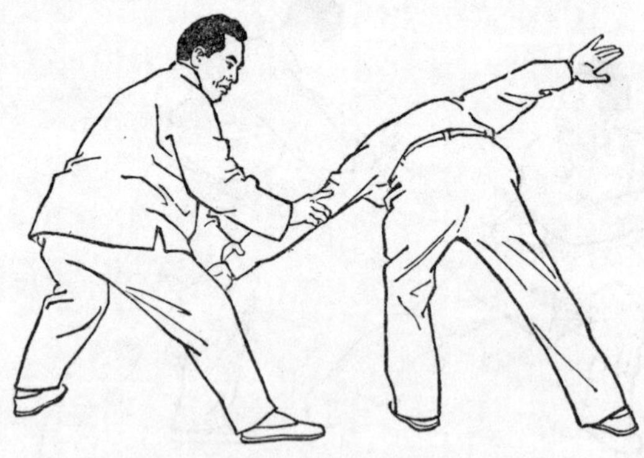

Fig. 20/7

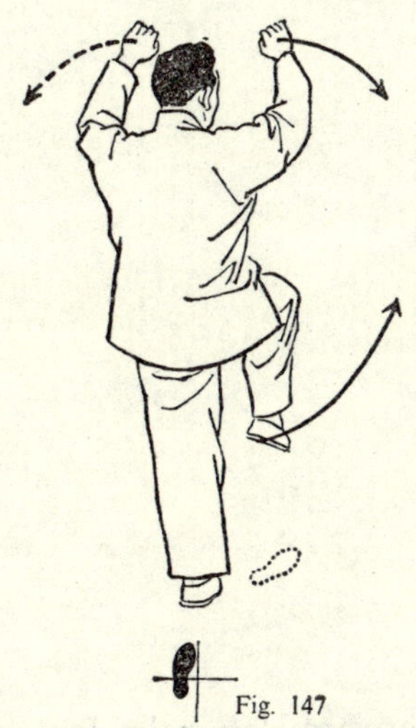
Fig. 147

Fig. 148

Self-feeling: Left leg distended, warm and sore; rib cage relaxed and comfortable.

Practical application: Repeat that of 2nd movement "Fists uprise" of this Posture, except to reverse left and right.

Posture XXI. Two Fists Blow Ears (4 movements)

Explanation of posture name: Unclench two fists and separate them to either side of body, then to back of body. Finally clench hands into fists again with a long arc to strike at the opponent's ears.

1st movement: Fists uprise

Detach right fist from left elbow and extend right arm as far as possible to front left (your torso rises following the arm) to naturally lift right knee, foreleg hanging. Raise both fists overhead, palm of fists facing out: look out along the direction of right elbow. Your weight is solely on left foot; your attention is on left fist. (Fig. 147)

Self-feeling: Your left foot planted onto the ground; your back warm.

Practical application: If the opponent treads with his right foot on your right leg, raise your fists high overhead, your right leg will easily rise to evade the kick, and you have now turned to be the attacker ready to deliver a kick. (Fig. 21/1, 21/2)

2nd movement: Separate hands

Unclench fists, separate them, little fingers leading, one to front right, the other to rear left to form an angle about 135 degrees. At same time, right foot kicks with its heel to front right, right leg parallel with right arm. Right

Fig. 21/1

palm now faces left, fingers pointing forward; left palm faces front, fingers fully extended. Your weight is still on left foot; your sight on tip of right thumb; your attention focused on left palm. (Fig. 148)

Self-feeling: Toes of left foot grabbed onto the ground; strength of your right leg transmitted to your right heel; both palms feel warm.

Practical application: Continuing, by lifting right leg you have evaded the opponent's treading, his treading foot will eventually drop on ground. Then, with hands separating, your right foot will naturally hit on opponent's right hipjoint. He will fall at the contact. (Fig. 21/3, 21/4)

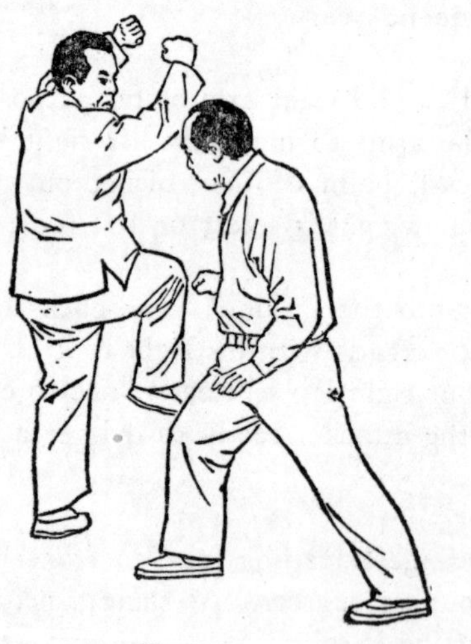

Fig. 21/2

Fig. 21/3

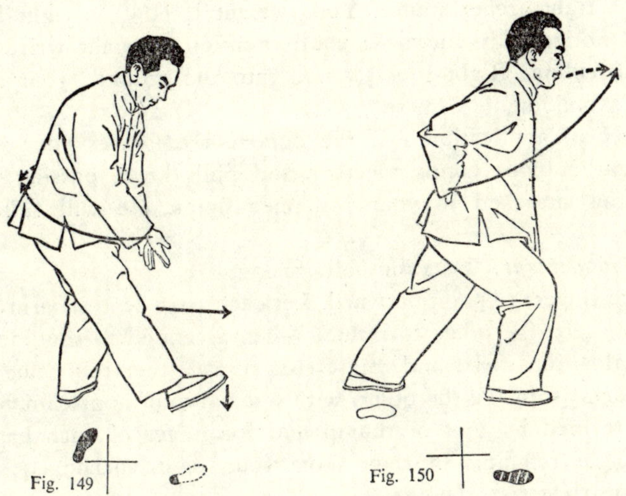
Fig. 149 Fig. 150

3rd movement: Hands down pull

Relax left knee to lower torso; and with right heel barely touching ground, assume the left sitting stance. Relax both arms. Move left hand, little finger leading, to the front of right knee; concurrently move right hand gradually downward; and gather fingers of each hand to form a forward-pointing hook hand. In coordination of relaxation and lowering of left knee, bend both wrists and let them lead both hook hands downward and rearward to Mingmen point (midway at small of your back). At this instant loosen hooks to resume extended hands while setting the rest of right foot on ground to

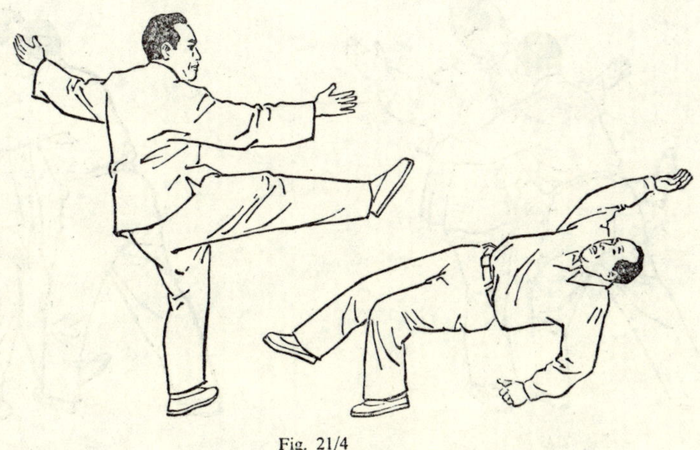
Fig. 21/4

assume a right archer stance. Your weight is now on right foot; your sight directed horizontally forward; your attention on right wrist. (Fig 149, 150)

Self-feeling: Right foot planted into the ground; your arms and chest loosely expanding.

Practical application: If the opponent embraces your waist with both hands, gather your hands together and pull down, passing his chest, until your palms attached to your Mingmen point. He will fall forward. (Fig 21/5, 21/6)

4th movement: Fists mutually facing

Turn fingers to point outward. Let each wrist lead its arm to fully extend, one to the left, the other to right. When ascended to shoulder level, loosely clench palms into fists, and rotate fists to face the front (due east), the fore part of each fist facing the other, with a distance of approximately 10 cm. The fist eye formed by root of thumb and forefinger of each hasd faces down. Your weight remains on right foot; your sight unchanged; your attention focused on right fist. (Fig. 151)

Self-feeling: Right leg distended and warm; either side of rib cage at ease.

Practical application: Continuing, when the opponent is leaning forward to you, clench your hands into fists and move them from back of your body to the front for the fore parts of two fists to face each other till they strike at the opponent's two ears. (Fig. 21/7, 21/8)

Fig. 21/5

Fig. 21/6

Fig. 151 Fig. 152

Posture XXII. Dodge and Kick (4 movements)

Explanation of posture name: In this posture one turns body to dodge and then delivers a kick.

1st movement: Fists turn rightward

Relax right heel to turn left (toes pointing south), and following the turn transfer your sight along direction of your fists to front right (southeast corner). Your weight still rests on right foot; your left heel is still raised; look out from between two fists; your attention is on your two fists. (Fig. 152)

Fig. 21/7

Fig. 21/8

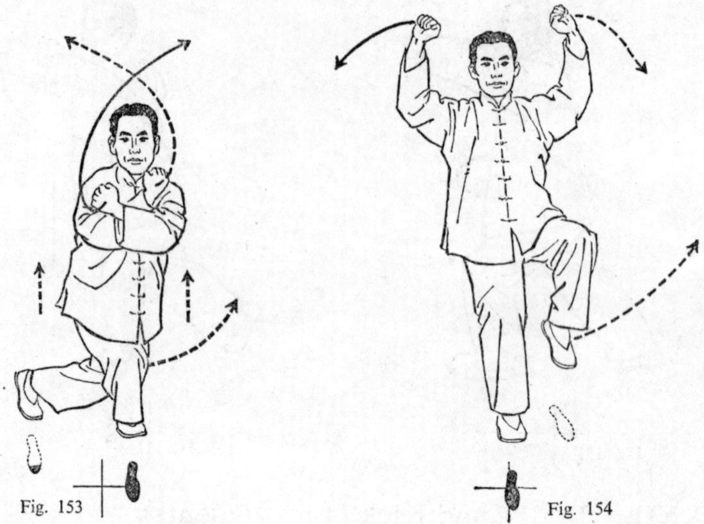

Fig. 153

Fig. 154

Self-feeling: Right leg distended and warm; two fists and left sole wriggling.

Practical application: If an opponent has grabbed your two wrists to pull you toward him, while attempting a kick with his right foot at your groin, you may allow your wrists to follow on his pull, his upper torso will lean backward. Then you may rotate your torso slightly to right, so when he has kicked in vain and must drop down his foot, he will find his body in an awkward position. (Fig. 22/1, 22/2)

Fig. 22/1

Fig. 22/2

2nd movement: Cross fists

Turn torso and arms to due south. Loosen waist and lower torso, left leg will be devoid of weight, left heel raised. At same time, move left fist to right, left wrist adhering to the back of right wrist to form an X, palms of fists facing in. Your weight is still on right foot; look out toward front left; your attention on right fist. (Fig. 153)

Self-feeling: Right leg distended, warm and sore; back warm.

Practical application: Continuing, go on with the rotation of your torso till it has turned 90 degrees to right. At same time, by relaxing shoulder and sinking elbows rotate arms inward for two forearms to form an X; moreover, bend left leg under right leg to form a resting stance, thus you are dodging, and the opponent's body is unsteady. (Fig. 22/3)

3rd movement: Fists uprise

Raise crossed fists, torso rises in correlation. When crossed fists have ascended overhead, separate fists to left and right, perpendicular to two elbows, palms of fists facing out. Lift left knee, left foreleg hanging, leaving right leg only to support the whole body. Look straight ahead. Focus your attention on two fists. (Fig. 154)

Self-feeling: Right foot planted into the ground; back warm.

Practical application: Continuing, in case the opponent did not topple but released both hands and dropped his right foot forward, you can raise overhead your fists, while getting your left foot ready for a kick. (Fig. 22/4)

4th movement: Separate hands to kick with heel

Unclench fists, with little fingers leading, separate two hands, one to

Fig. 22/3 Fig. 22/4

front left, the other to rear right to form an angle of about 135 degrees. Let left heel kick to left, left leg parallel with left arm. Now left palm faces right, fingers pointing forward; right palm faces front, finger extended. Your weight ramains on right foot; your sight rests on left thumb; your attention on right palm. (Fig. 155)

Self-feeling: Right toes grabbed onto the ground; strength of left foot transferred to its heel; two palms warm.

Practical application: Continuing, when the opponent is staggering, kick with your left heel aiming at his right hipjoint. He will be kicked well off. (Fig. 22/5)

Posture XXIII. Turn Around and Kick (4 movements)

Explanation of posture name: Here the body rotates 180 degrees before delivering a kick with heel, hence the name.

lst movement: Left foot right turn

Loosen left ankle, shift your sight to right thumb, and drop left foot down along an outward arc for its heel to set down at front right of right foot. Your weight is still on right foot; look ahead over right thumb; focus your attention on right palm. (Fig. 156)

Self-feeling: Two sides of rib cage extended at ease; right palm and left sole warm.

Practical application: Continuing, when the opponent has evaded your kick with your left foot and now attempts to kick your substantial right foot

Fig. 22/5

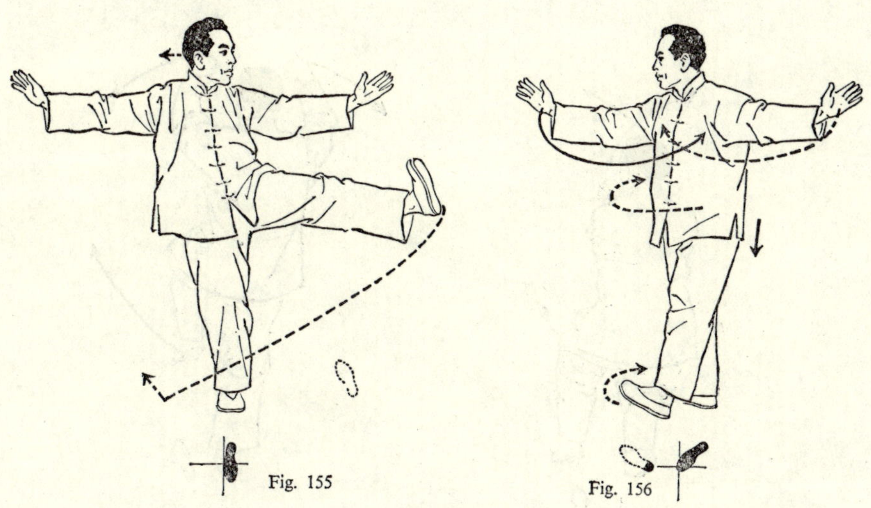

Fig. 155

Fig. 156

with his right foot, you can drop your left foot (following rotation of your body) in front of your right toe, your left heel touching, left toes slanting up. Thus your upper torso has rotated 90 degrees in evasion. (Fig. 23/1, 23/2)

2nd movement: Cross fists

Turn in left toes as far as possible and set whole foot on ground, while rotating body rightward. Lower body to a cross-legged sitting position, but lifting slightly right knee and right heel, with its toes barely touching. At same time loosely clench both hands into fists, their wrists forming an X, right

Fig. 23/1

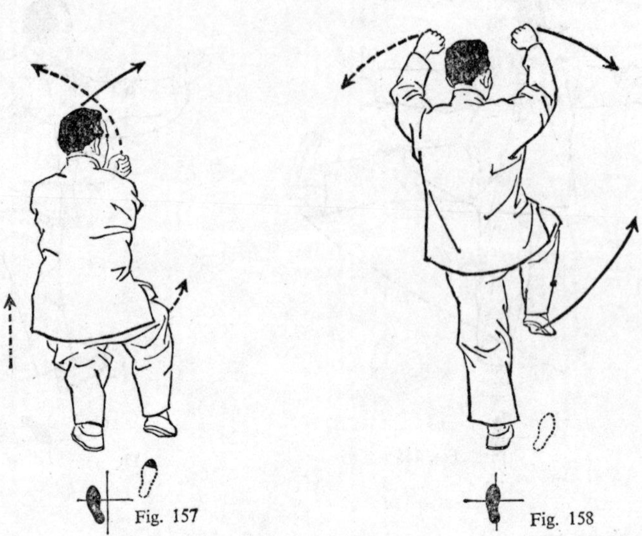

Fig. 157 Fig. 158

fist at the outer side, both palms of fists facing in. Your weight has shifted onto left foot; look out to front right; focus your attention on left fist. (Fig. 157)

Self-feeling: Left leg distended, warm and sore.

Practical application: Continuing, having dropped down your left foot, continue to turn your torso 90 degrees to right. Cross your forearms, squat with your weight on left foot with right toes lightly touching ground. You have thus dodged an attack by the opponent's right leg. (Fig. 23/3)

3rd movement: Fists uprise

Fig. 23/2

Fig. 159

Raise crossed fists, torso rises in correlation. When crossed fists have ascended overhead, separate fists to both sides, palms of fists facing out. Lift right knee, right foreleg hanging, with only left leg supporting the whole body. Look toward front right. Your attention is on left fist. (Fig. 158)

Self-feeling: Left foot planted into the ground; back warm.

Practical application: Continuing, when the opponent dropped the foot which has kicked at nothing, and now aims at your right temple with his right fist, you can block his approaching fist with your crossed fists. At same time lift your right leg ready for a kick. (Fig. 23/4)

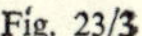

Fig. 23/3

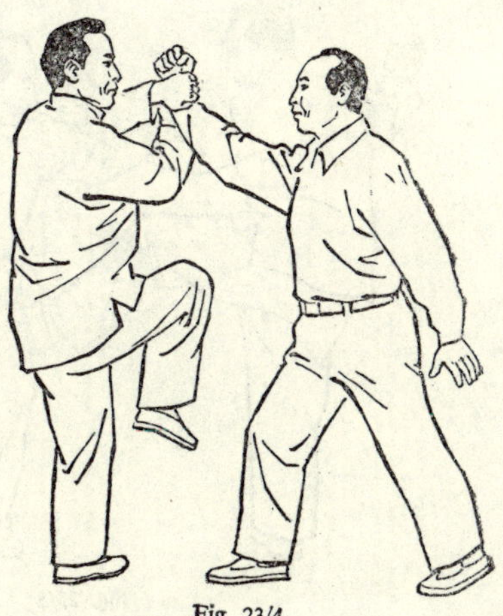

Fig. 23/4

4th movement: Separate hands to kick

Unclench fists, with little fingers leading, and separate two hands, one to front right, the other to rear left to form an angle of about 135 degrees. Let right foot kick with heel to right, right leg parallel to right arm, right palm facing left, fingers pointing forward; left palm faces front, fingers extended. Your weight remains on left foot; your sight rests on right thumb; your attention on left palm. (Fig. 159)

Self-feeling: Left toes grabbed onto ground; strength of right foot transmitted to its heel; both palms warm.

Practical application: Continuing, extend your left hand to rear left in order to strike the opponent's face with your right hand. At same time hit the opponent's right hipjoint with your right heel. (Fig. 23/5)

Posture XXIV. Press Face with Palm (4 movements)

Explanation of posture name: The palm is thrusted forward with a forward step on the same side of body. With two hands rotating, thrust of one hand is promptly succeeded by the thrust of another hand, constituting the effect of pressing and covering of the opponent's face.

1st movement: Left hand down push

Relax left knee and waist to lower upper torso. Drop right foot, heel touching ground to assume left sitting stance. In coordination with the dropping of right foot, push down left hand to right side of body at a level between brest and abdomen, palm down, fingers pointing to right; meanwhile bend right arm at 90 degree angle near your right flank, palm up. Your weight

Fig. 23/5

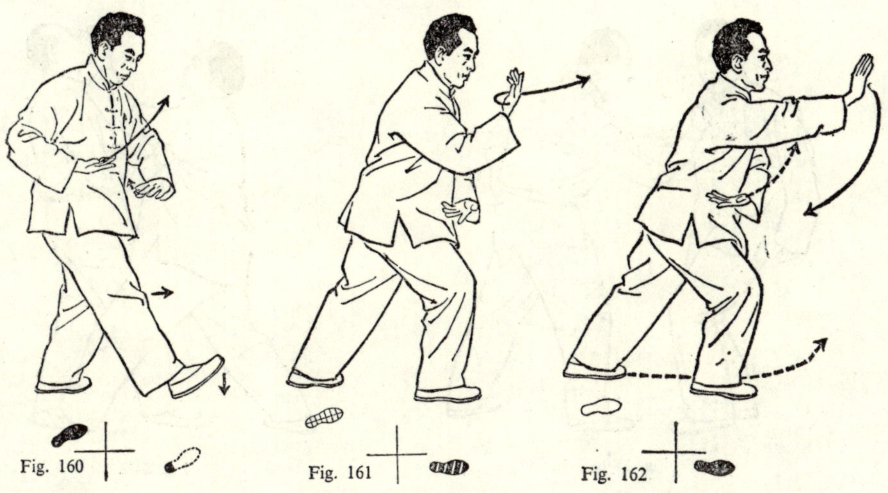

Fig. 160　Fig. 161　Fig. 162

is on left foot; your sight passing left hand to rest at lower front; your attention on left palm. (Fig. 160)

Self-feeling: Left leg distended, warm and sore; left palm and right foot wriggling.

Parctical application: Should an opponent strike at your chest with his right hand, adhere with your left hand to his forearm and pull it down. His upper torso would topple forward. (Fig. 24/1)

2nd movement: Right hand forward push

Raise head to look gradually forward while setting toes gradually down and bend right knee forward to assume right archer stance. At same time rotate left hand to rest beside right ribs, palm up; ascend right hand to the level of right eye and to push forward, palm facing front, thumb aligned with tip of nose (right knee and right palm reach their destination at same moment). Your weight is now on right foot; look ahead over your right thumb; your attention on right palm. (Fig. 161, 162)

Self-feeling: Right leg distended, warm and sore; right palm and left sole wriggling.

Practical application: Continuing, you have pulled down the opponent's right arm with your left hand and he is toppling forward, you may quickly follow up with your right palm lightly pushing on his face. At the same instant bend your right knee, stretch rearward your left leg to assume a right archer stance. The opponent will be pushed away. (Fig. 24/2, 24/3)

3rd movement: Right hand down push

Repeat 1st movement "Left hand down push" of this Posture, except to

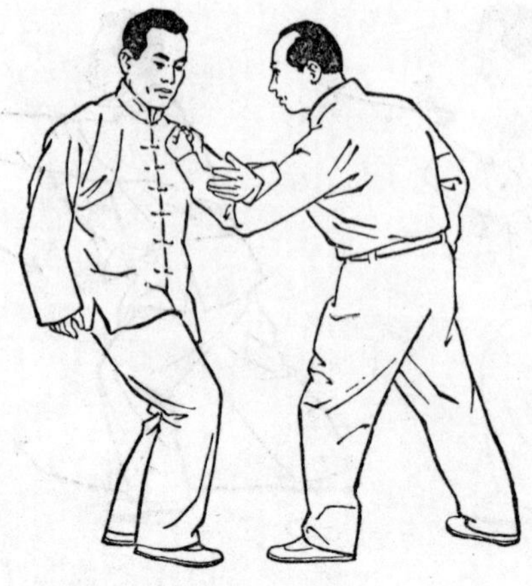
Fig. 24/1

Fig. 24/2

reverse left and right. (Fig. 163)

4th movement: Left hand forward push

Repeat 2nd movement "Right hand forward push" of this Posture, except to reverse left and right. (Fig. 164, 165)

Posture XXV. **Cross-form Kick** (Sweep Lotus with Single Hand) (4 movements)

Explanation of posture name: The coordinated movement of left arm

Fig. 24/3

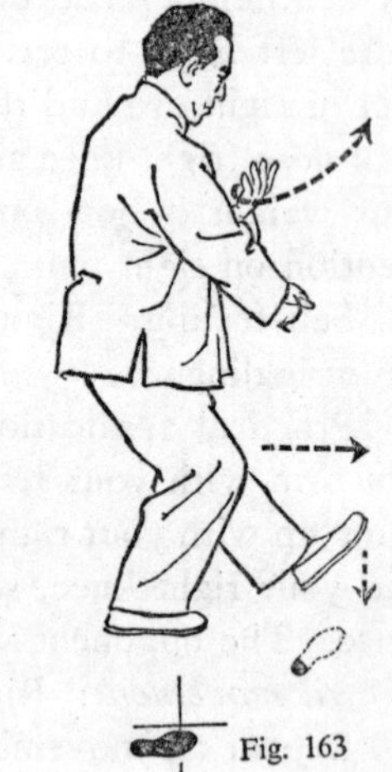
Fig. 163

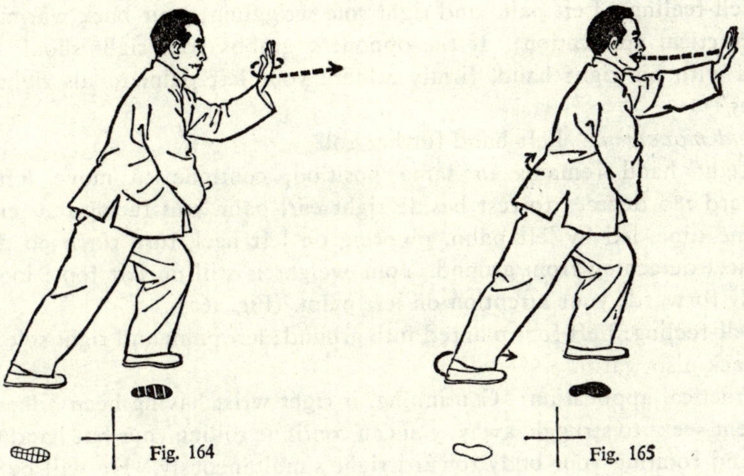

Fig. 164 Fig. 165

and right leg in passing and touching each other is in the form of X, and is likened to the wind sweeping the lotus.

1st movement: Left hand rightward roll

Right hand remains in same position, move left hand rightward with its forefinger leading, and your sight following the forefinger. At same time pivoting on right toes and lightly lifting right heel, turn right foot to point to south, left foot still pointing east. Your weight is still on left foot; your sight on left forefinger; your attention still on left palm. (Fig. 166)

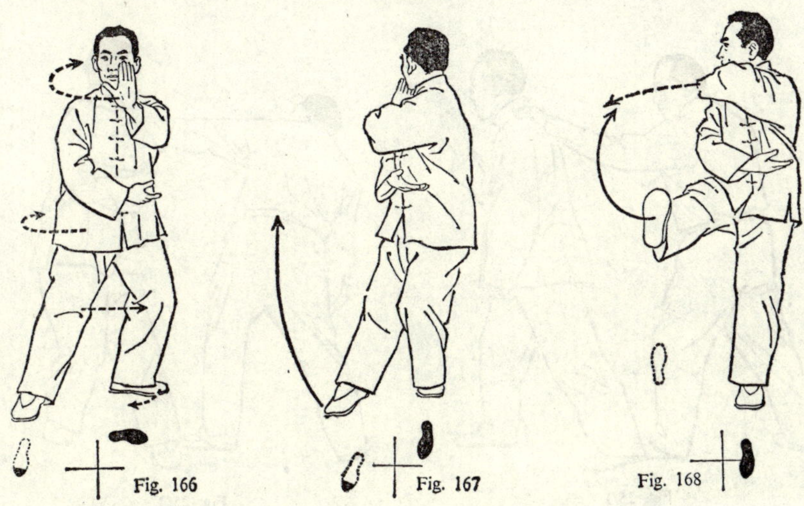

Fig. 166 Fig. 167 Fig. 168

Self-feeling: Left palm and right sole wriggling; your back warm.

Practical application: If the opponent grabbs your right shoulder from behind with his right hand, firmly adhere your left palm to his right wrist. (Fig. 25/1)

2nd movement: Left hand further roll

Right hand remains in same position, continue to move left hand rightward 180 degrees to rest beside right ear, palm still facing out, ends up. At same time, led by left palm, pivoting on left heel, turn torso 90 degrees, right heel detaching from ground. Your weight is still on left foot; look horizontally forward; your attention on left palm. (Fig. 167)

Self-feeling: Left foot planted into ground; left palm and right sole warm; your back also warm.

Practical application: Continuing, if right wrist having been adhered the opponent seeks to struggle away, you can continue rolling your left hand toward right and rotating your body toward right simultaneously. He will be off his balance. (Fig. 25/2)

3rd movement: Right foot uplift

Lift right foot, its toe leading, toward front left; simultaneously stretch forward left hand, forefinger leading, to shoulder level, palm down. Your weight and sight not shifted; your attention still on left palm. (Fig. 168)

Self-feeling: Both legs warm; left palm warm, its fingertips distended.

Practical application: Continuing, having taken hold of the opponent's right arm, now you may lift your right foot ready to kick. (Fig. 25/3)

Fig. 25/1 Fig. 25/2

4th movement: Right foot rightward sweep

Sweep right foot in the curve toward upper right till its toe aligned with tip of nose at a natural distance. At same time sweep left hand leftward to get in touch with right foot at your front. Let right foot drop at front right, heel touching, toes slanting up to assume left sitting stance. Let your left hand continue sweeping to rear left till arm is fully stretched. Your weight is still on left foot; your sight follows left forefinger; your torso rotates naturally after left hand; your attention on left palm. (Fig. 169, 170)

Self-feeling: Left leg planted into ground; left palm and right sole wriggling.

Practical application: Continuing, after you have lifted your right leg, see if there is any change on part of the opponent. Should there be no change, allow the instep of your right foot to strike at his Mingmen point, while your palm strikes (palm leftward) at his chin or the Yifeng point behind his ear lobe. (Fig. 25/4)

Posture XXVI. Brush Knee and Punch at Underbelly (4 movements)

Explanation of posture name: This Posture is same as the 3rd Posture "Brush Knee and Twist Step" except that the last movement here uses fist instead of hand to attack the opponent's underbelly.

1st movement: Right hand down push

Loosen left wrist for the curve between thumb and forefinger to get close

Fig. 25/3

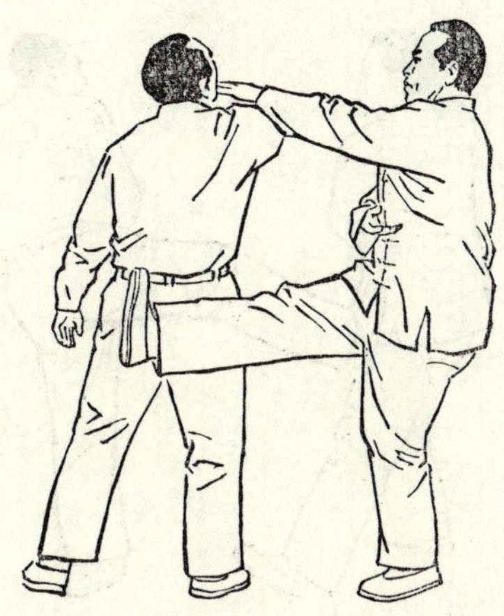

Fig. 25/4

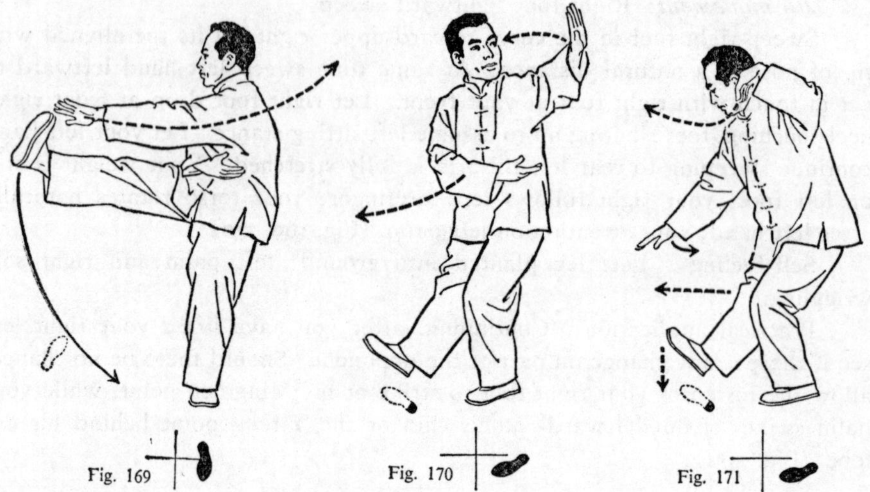
Fig. 169 Fig. 170 Fig. 171

to left ear, then loosen left shoulder and sink left elbow. Meantime, right hand will naturally push down toward lower front till its palm is in vertical line with right toe. Your sight follows right forefinger; your attention on left palm; your weight still on left leg. (Fig. 171)

Self-feeling: Left leg distended, warm and sore; both palms warm.

Practical application: Continuing, should the opponent withdraw to evade your kick and turn to kick at your right waist with his left leg, you can brush his left knee with your right hand and lift left wrist to left ear ready to attack. (Fig. 26/1, 26/2)

Fig. 26/1

Fig. 26/2

Fig. 172

Fig. 173

2nd movement: Left hand forward push

Set down right foot, bend forward right knee to assume right archer stance, while pushing forward left hand, its ring finger leading, palm forward, ends up. At same time bring right hand naturally to side of right hipjoint. Your weight is now on right foot. Look out over left thumb. Focus your attention on right palm. (Fig. 172)

Self-feeling: Right leg distended and warm; right palm and left sole warm.

Fig. 26/3

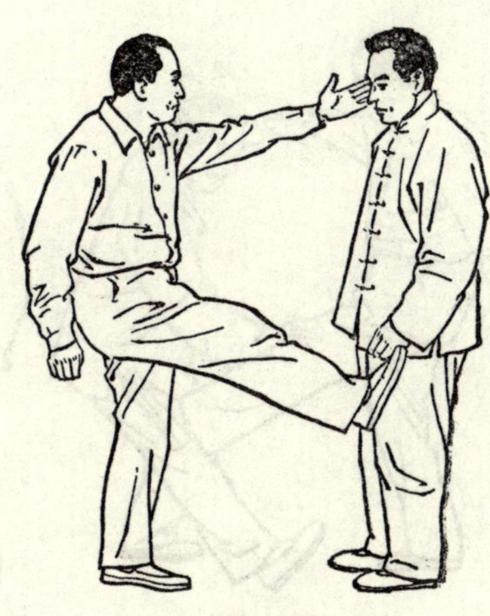

Fig. 26/4

Practical application: Continuing, after the opponent's left foot has dropped on ground, thrust your right knee to the inner side of his left knee, and simultaneously deliver your left hand at his face or the sensitive point near his armpit. (Fig. 26/3)

3rd movement: Left hand down push

Push left hand, its forefinger leading, forward and downward to the front of right knee, while loosening right wrist to lift it to right ear. At same time, draw back left foot to set down a step forward, heel touching, toes slanting up. Your weight is still on right foot; your sight on tip of left forefinger; your attention on right palm. (Fig. 173)

Self-feeling: Right leg distended, warm and sore; both palms warm.

Practical application: Suppose an opponent strikes your face with his left palm and your underbelly with his right foot, you may lift up his left wrist by attaching your uplifting right hand to it, simultaneously allow your left hand to push down his right knee to set him off balance. Your taking a step forward with your left foot to thrust your knee against the inner side of his right knee will prevent him from evading your next attack. (Fig. 26/4, 26/5)

4th movement: Right fist punches at underbelly

Swing right hand up toward rear, let your eyes follow right forefinger, and left hand will rise naturally. When right hand has stretched out to the rear, gradually clench it into a fist, and while sinking right elbow bring the fist along a screw path to rest beside right ribs, eye of fist upward, your sight transferred to left forefinger. Gradually set down left foot, bend forward left knee to assume left archer stance. At same time punch forward right fist over the front of left knee, eye of fist upward, and left hand will naturally attach

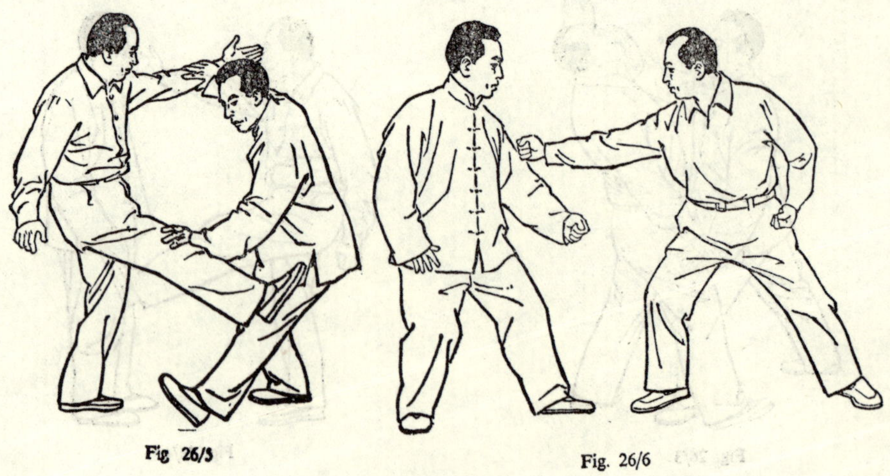

Fig 26/5 Fig. 26/6

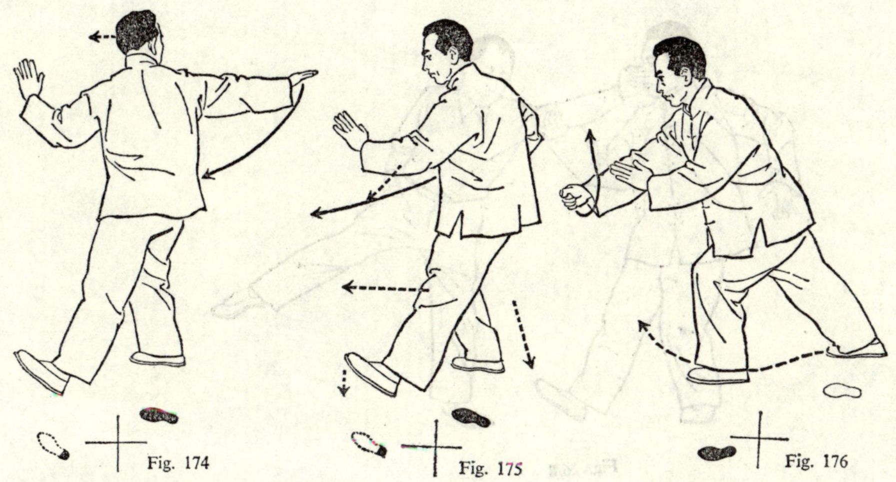
Fig. 174 Fig. 175 Fig. 176

to right forearm at its middle point. Your weight is now on left foot; your sight rests on eye of right fist; your attention is on left palm. (Fig. 174, 175, 176)

Self-feeling: Left leg distended and warm; both sides of your rib cage feel loosened and comfortable; your back warm.

Practical application: In case an opponent punches at your chest with his right fist, attach your left hand to his right elbow. At same moment swing up right hand toward rear right, then bring it to your right ribs. Clench it into a fist and punch it toward the opponent's underbelly. (Fig. 26/6, 26/7, 26/8, 26/9)

Fig. 26/7

Fig. 26/8

Posture XXVII. Front Single Whip (6 movements)

Explanation of posture name: When one's waist is straightened, top of head lifted up and legs squatting, the body is likened to the handle of a whip; whereas the spreading arms are likened to the leather lash of the whip. The downward motion of the handle transmits the force to the lash. Hence the posture name is given.

1st movement: Turn over fist and step forward

Fig. 26/9

Turn over right fist and stretch it upward to front left, palm of fist facing up, left hand still attached to right forearm; at same time sink right elbow and straighten waist and let right foot move a step forward, heel touching, to assume left sitting stance. Your weight is now on left foot; your eyes looking at right fist; your attention on left palm. (Fig. 177)

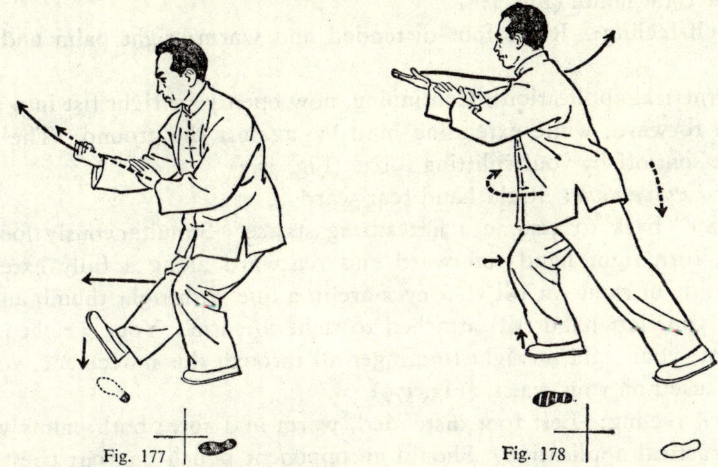

Fig. 177   Fig. 178

Self-feeling: Left leg distended, warm and sore; back warm.

Practical application: Continuing, if the opponent has grabbed your right wrist, sink your right elbow to turn palm of fist upward; simultaneously step forward right foot to lock his hind leg. Your left hand should adhere to his right hand to prevent him from retreating. (Fig. 27/1, 27/2)

Fig. 27/1   Fig. 27/2

2nd movement: Step down and unclench fist into palm

Set down right foot on ground and bend forward right knee to assume right archer stance. At same time open right fist to resume palm to ward up to front right, palm up. Your weight is on right foot; your sight follows right forefinger; your attention focused on Wai Laogong point at centre of the back of your right hand. (Fig. 178)

Self-feeling: Right foot distended and warm; right palm and left sole warm.

Practical application: Continuing, now open your right fist into palm and stretch forward, while extending hind leg against the ground. The opponent will be sent off by your splitting force. (Fig. 27/3)

3rd movement: Right hand rear ward

"Sit" back to assume a left sitting stance. Simultaneously loosen right elbow, turn right hand rightward and rearward along a fully extended arc to the side of right ear till your eyes are in a line with right thumb and middle finger, your left hand still attached to right forearm. Your weight is now on left foot; your sight on right forefinger all through this movement; your attention focused on your waist. (Fig. 179)

Self-feeling: Left foot distended, warm and sore; both palms wriggling.

Practical application: Should an opponent punch on your chest with his right fist, thrust your right arm below his right arm, then with your right forefinger leading ward up toward your rear right, while relaxing your left knee to "sit" back to form a left sitting stance. Your opponent will be warded off a good distance. (Fig. 27/4, 27/5, 27/6)

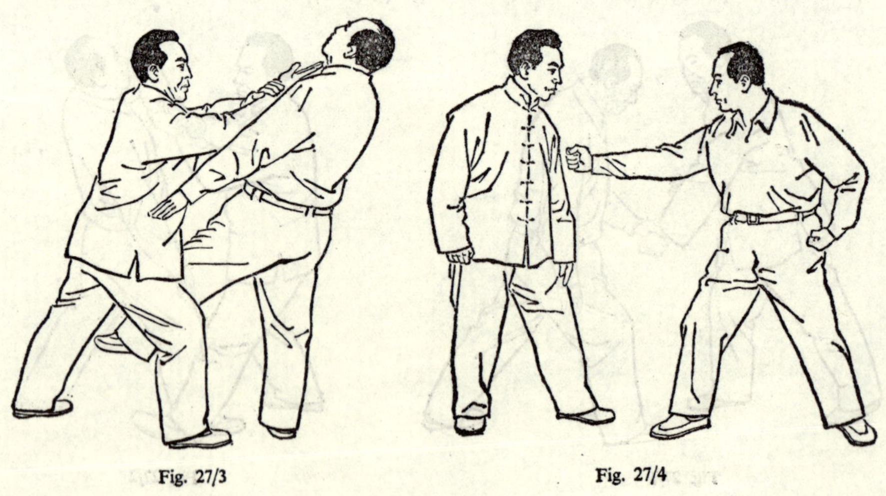

Fig. 27/3 Fig. 27/4

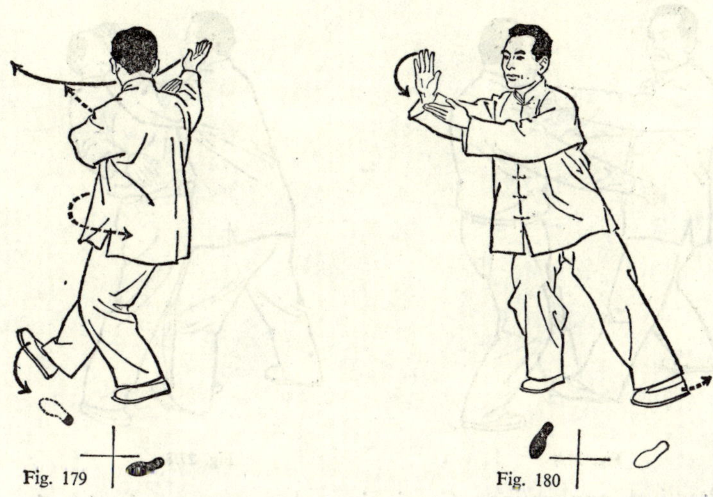

Fig. 179　　Fig. 180

4th movement: Right hand forward push

Loosen waist slightly, sink right elbow slightly forward, and turn in right toe 45 degrees. At same time push right hand to the direction of the turned-in right toe, palm facing out, ends up. The middle finger and ring finger of left hand attached to right wrist at the point where one's pulse is taken. Bend forward right knee when right toes settled down on ground. Your weight is now on right foot; your sight rests on right forefinger; your attention on Shanzhong point (between brests). (Fig. 180)

Self-feeling: Right leg distended and warm; back warm.

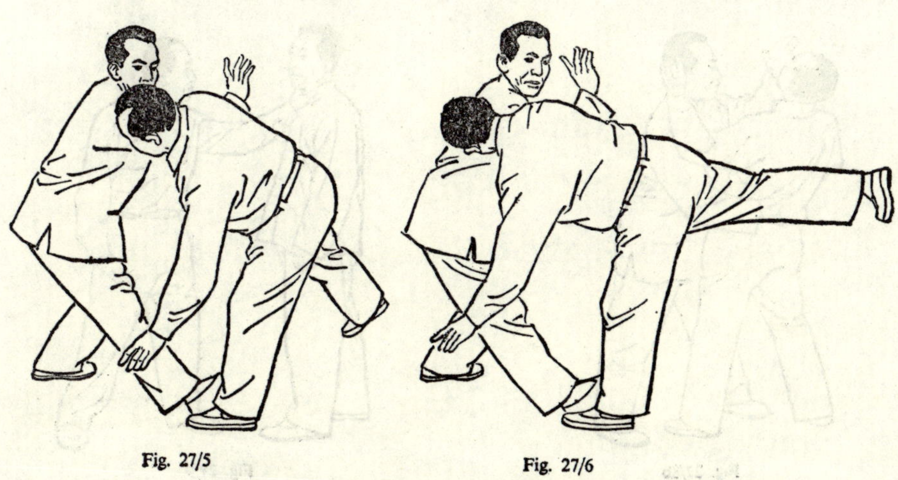

Fig. 27/5　　Fig. 27/6

Fig. 27/7

Fig. 27/8a

Practical application: Continuing, the opponent having been warded up he would seek to retreat. Move your left hand down along his spine down to the Mingmen point at his lower back. (Here this movement is different from that in solo practice.) At same time turn in right toe and push your right hand at the opponent's face or shoulder. He will be pushed down. (Fig. 27/7, 27/8a, 27/8b)

5th movement: Turn hand into hook and step laterally

Loosen right wrist, gather fingers of right hand into a hook, protruding its wrist. When point of the hook hangs down, extend right wrist to upper

Fig. 27/8b

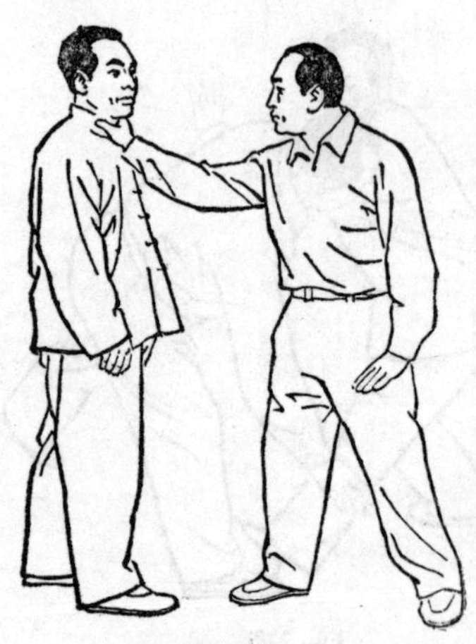

Fig. 27/9

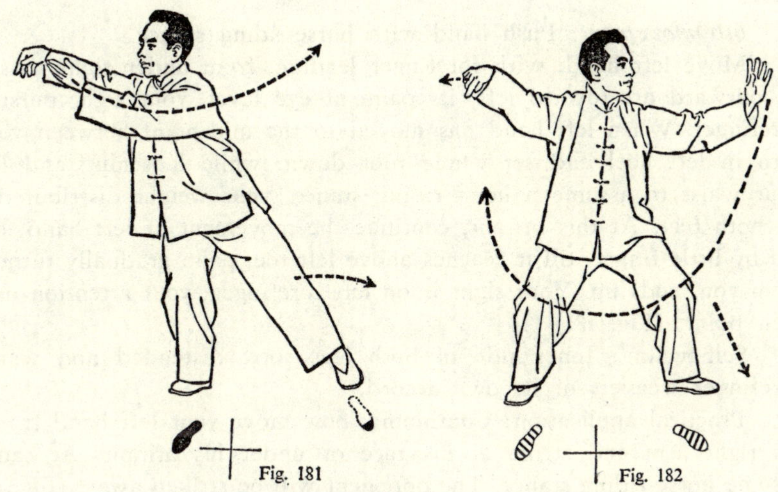

right, simultaneously draw left foot laterally to left, its toe barely touching ground. Your weight is still on right foot; your sight on right wrist; your attention focused on left foot. (Fig. 181)

Self-feeling: Right leg distended, warm and sore; right palm and left sole wriggling.

Practical application: If an opponent grabs at your neck with his right hand, grasp his right wrist with your right hand. At same time turn torso slightly to right to step laterally to left in order to block his hind leg to prevent him from escaping. (Fig. 27/9, 27/10, 27/11)

6th movement: Push hand with horse-riding stance

Move left hand, with forefinger leading, from under right wrist, along an outward arc toward left, its palm at eye level, your sight pursuing left forefinger. When left hand has moved to the mid-point between your legs, turn in left heel and set whole foot down, while loosening and lowering your waist to assume a horse-riding stance, your weight distributed evenly on both feet. At this instant, continue the movement of left hand, but now led by little finger, till it reaches above left toe, palm gradually turned away from you, ends up. Your sight is on left forefinger; your attention on Mingmen point. (Fig. 182)

Self-feeling: Inner side of both legs sore, distended and warm; left forefinger weavers of its own accord.

Practical application: Continuing, now move your left hand from under his right arm and strike at his face or under his armpit. At same time assume horse-riding stance. The opponent will be striken away. (Fig. 27/12)

Posture XXVIII. Wave Hands Like Clouds (6 movements)

Explanation of posture name: The continual and intersected circling of the two arms in even tempo is likened to the sailing of clouds in sky.

1st movement: Left hand down roll

Loosen left wrist to swing left hand, forefinger leading, downward toward right to pass left knee and then right knee to finally reach near right ribs. Concurrently shift your weight in coordination to right foot and bend

Fig. 27/12

Fig. 183

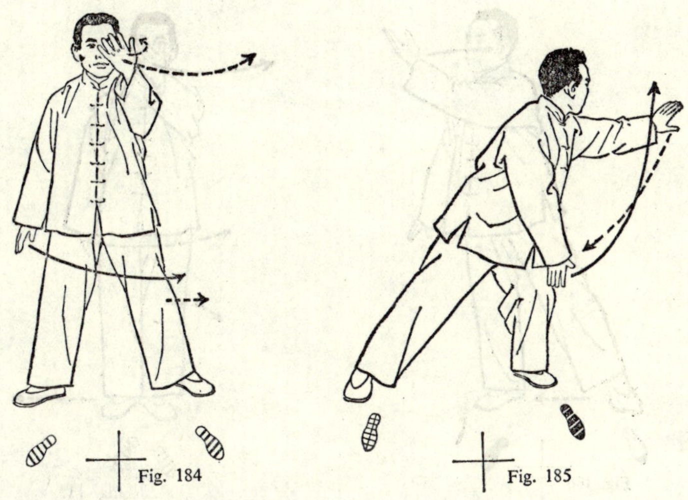

Fig. 184 Fig. 185

right knee. When left hand has reached right ribs, open right hook into palm and extend fully to right, its forefinger leading, palm down. Your weight transferred onto right foot; your sight rests on right forefinger; your attention on right palm. (Fig. 183)

Self-feeling: Right foot planted in the ground like a tree; right palm and left sole wriggling.

Practical application: If the opponent attempts to slap your face with his left hand, adhere your right hand to his left wrist and roll your left hand toward the rear right of your right heel. The opponent will lose his balance. (Fig. 28/1, 28/2)

2nd movement: Left hand lateral push

Move left hand upward, led by forefinger, toward bend of right arm, and then upward to front right, palm turning in. Continue moving up this hand, but now toward left, torso straightened up following the ascending of this hand. When this hand has reached your front, your weight naturally transfers towards your left foot, so your weight is evenly distributed between two feet. Gradually turn out left palm, little finger leading. When left hand has moved to front left, shift your weight to your left foot and bend slightly left knee. When left hand finally reached due east push it down to shoulder level. Simultaneously at the beginning of this movement, move right hand along a downward arc to pass right knee and stop in front of left knee. Your weight is now on left foot; your sight on tip of left forefinger; your attention focused on left palm. (Fig. 184, 185)

Self-feeling: Left leg warm and sore; left palm warm.

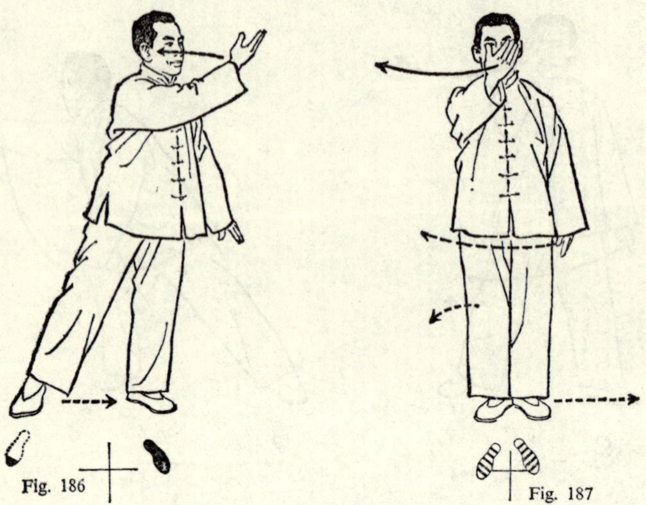

Fig. 186

Fig. 187

Practical application: Continuing, at the instant when the opponent has lost his balance, lift your left hand toward left along the inner side of his left arm to strike at his face. He will fall down. (Fig. 28/3)

3rd movement: Right hand lateral push

Move right hand upward, led by its forefinger, toward bend of left arm, and then to front left as far as possible, your torso straightened up following the ascending of your hand, simultaneously withdrawing right foot next to left foot. Continue moving right hand toward right. When it reaches your front, your weight is on both feet, but as it proceeds to front right,

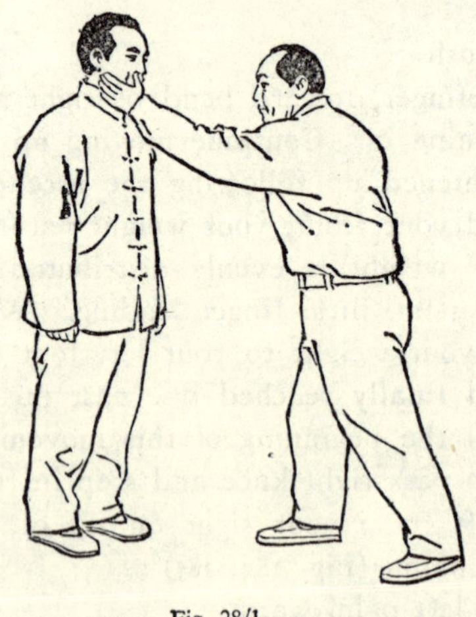

Fig. 28/2

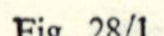

Fig. 28/1

Fig. 188

transfer your weight onto right foot, and bend slightly your right knee. When right hand reaches right (due west), push hand down to shoulder level. Simultaneously at the beginning of this movement, move left hand along a downward arc to pass left knee and stop at right knee. At this instant draw left foot a lateral step to left, its toes barely touching ground. Your weight is now on right foot; your sight on tip of right forefinger; your attenion on right palm. (Fig. 186, 187, 188)

Self-feeling: Right leg warm and sore; right palm warm.

Practical application: If the opponent attempts to hug your neck, turn

Fig. 28/3

Fig. 28/4

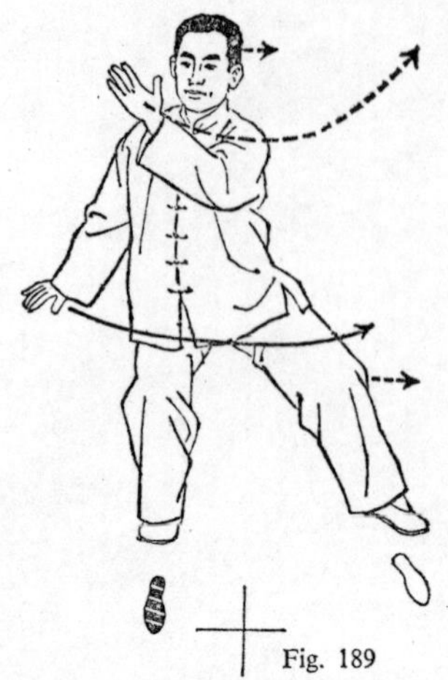

Fig. 189

Fig. 190

torso and adhere your left hand to his right wrist, then thrust up your right hand along outer side of his right arm, while withdrawing your right foot to left foot and turning out right hand to "pat" his shoulder. Simultaneously let your left foot move a lateral step. The opponent will fall on ground. (Fig. 28/4, 28/5, 28/6, 28/7, 28/8)

4th movement: Left hand lateral push

Repeat 2nd movement "Left hand lateral push" of this Posture. (Fig. 189, 190)

Fig 28/5

Fig. 28/6

For Practical application, repeat that of 3rd movement "Right hand lateral push" of this Posture, except to reverse left and right.

5th movement: Turn hand into hook and step latearlly

Move right hand upward, led by its forefinger, toward bend of left arm, and then to front left as far as possible, your torso straightened up following the ascending of your hand, simultaneously withdrawing right foot next to left foot. Continue moving right hand toward right. When it reaches your front, your weight is on both feet, but as it proceeds to front right, transfer your weight onto right foot, and bend slightly your right knee. When right hand reaches right (due west), push it down to shoulder level. Simultaneously at the beginning of this movement, move left hand along a downward arc to pass left knee and right knee. When left hand has ascended to bend of right arm, loosen right elbow for right hand to shift slightly to left and for the point where one's pulse is taken to contact tip of left middle finger and ring finger. Now loosen right wrist to gather five fingers to form a hook, and left foot naturally takes a lateral step to left, toes touching ground. Your weight is now on right foot; your sight on the wrist of right hook; your attention at the point of right hook. (Fig. 191. 192, 193)

Self-feeling: Right leg warm and sore; right palm and left sole warm and wriggling.

Practical application: If the opponent punches with his right fist on the left side of your rib cage, turn torso slightly to left to evade the punch. At same time adhere to his right elbow with the bend of your left elbow, and let your left hand move to your right elbow via your right knee. The

Fig. 28/7

Fig. 28/8

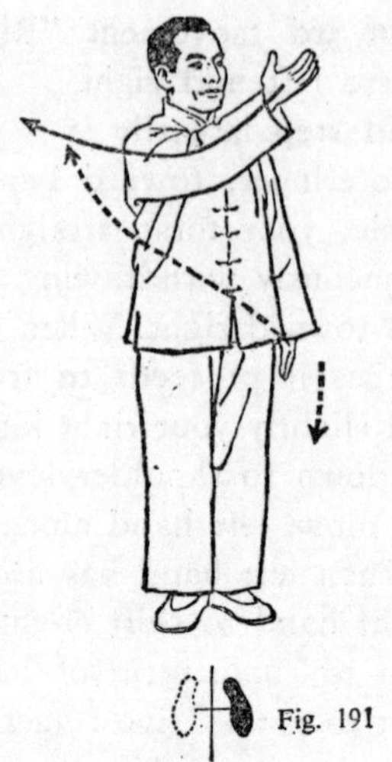
Fig. 191

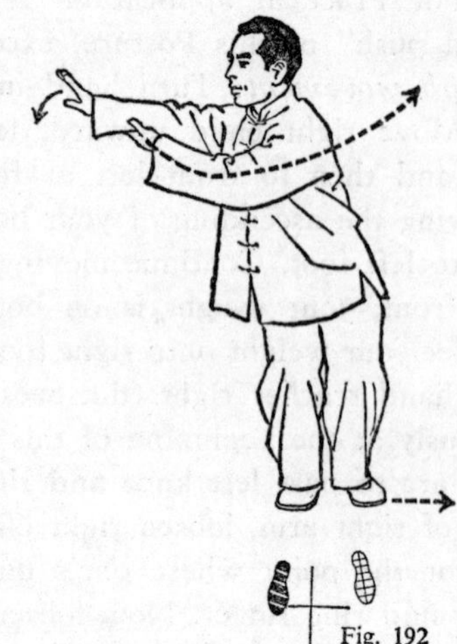
Fig. 192

opponent will be off balance and incline forward. Now gather your right fingers to form a loose hook and allow your right wrist to strike the opponent's chin, while your left foot makes a lateral step with toes lightly touching ground. (Fig. 28/9, 28/10)

6th movement: Push hand with horse-riding stance

Move left hand, with forefinger leading, from under right wrist, along an outward arc toward left, its palm at eye level, your sight pursuing left forefinger. When left hand has moved to the mid-point between your legs, turn in left heel and set whole foot down, while loosening and lowering

Fig. 28/9

Fig. 28/10

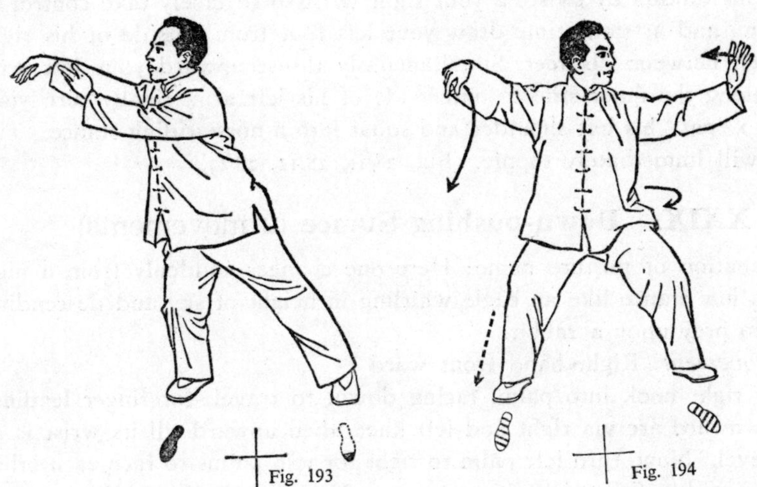
Fig. 193 Fig. 194

your waist to assume a horse-riding stance, your weight distributed evenly on both feet. At this instant, continue the movement of left hand, but now led by little finger, till it reached above left toe, palm gradually turned away from you, ends up. Your sight is on left forefinger; your attention on Mingmen point. (Fig. 194)

Self-feeling: Inner side of both legs sore, distened and warm; left forefinger will weaver of its own accord.

Practical application: Continuing, if the opponent leans back to evade your attack and pushed aside your right wrist with his left hand, you can

Fig. 28/11

follow up his motion by twisting your right wrist to reversely take control of his left arm, and at same time draw your left foot from outside of his right foot to step between his feet. Simultaneously thrust upward your left arm, palm in, along the inner side to outer side of his left arm, finally turn your palm out to "pat" his left shoulder and squat into a horse-riding stance. The opponent will immediately topple. (Fig. 28/11, 28/12, 28/13)

Posture XXIX. Down-pushing Stance (2 movements)

Explanation of posture name: Here one changes suddenly from a high stance to a low stance like an eagle whirling in height of sky and descending suddenly to prey upon a rabbit.

1st movement: Right hand front ward

Open right hook into palm, facing down, to travel, forefinger leading, with a downward arc via right and left knee, then upward till its wrist is at shoulder level. Now, turn left palm to right for two palms to face each other by shoulder width, fingertips pointing east. Your weight has shifted to left foot following the travelling of right hand to left. Your sight is directed toward east; your attention focused on left palm. (Fig. 195, 196)

Self-feeling: Left leg and hipjoint warm and sore; palms have wriggling feeling.

Practical application: If the opponent pushes against your chest with two hands, lift up your right hand to adhere to his right wrist, your left hand

Fig. 28/12

Fig. 28/13

Fig. 195

Fig. 196

holding his right elbow. At same time draw your right leg to rear. The opponent is now off balance. (Fig. 29/1, 29/2)

2nd movement: Palms back roll

Loosen and lift wrists, fingers half bent, while straightening torso up to evenly distribute your weight on two feet. Let your right elbow lead torso to turn to front, then squat toward right to shift your weight to right foot till right hand is above right knee. Meanwhile let your left wrist lead left hand to rest above left knee, both palms facing down. Your left leg is now

Fig. 29/1

Fig. 29/2

Fig. 197

Fig. 198

naturally straightened to assume a right down-pushing stance, both feet pointing south. Your upper torso should be kept erect; your sight directed to front left; your attention focused on right palm. (Fig. 197, 198, 199, 200)

Self-feeling: Right leg distended and warm; both palms feel wriggling.

Practical application: Continuing, you have had control of the opponent's right arm and were drawing your right leg to the rear, now pull down his right elbow and wrist toward your rear right. The opponent wil lose balance and fall forward. (Fig. 29/3, 29/4, 29/5)

Fig. 29/3

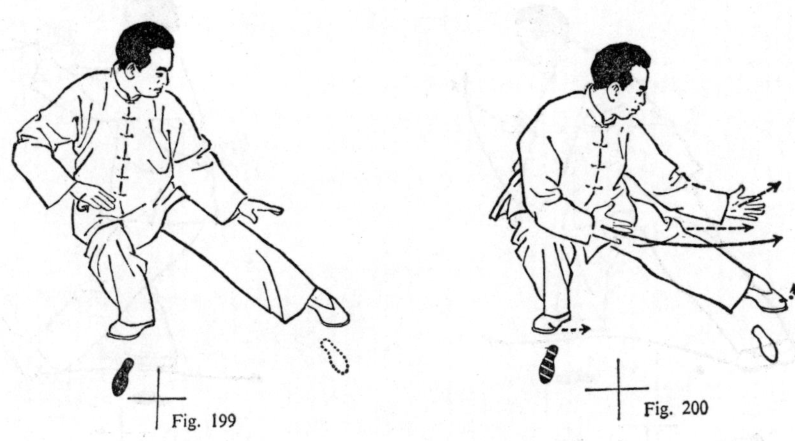

Fig. 199

Fig. 200

Posture XXX. Step Forward to Form Seven Stars (2 movements)

Explanation of posture name: In this posture the following seven parts of the body, the head, two shoulders, two elbows, two hands, two hipjoints, two knees and one foot constitute the shape of the constellation of the Big Dipper.

1st movement: Right hand down thrust

Thrust fingertips of left hand forward while turning left toes toward

Fig. 29/4

Fig. 201

Fig. 202

left to face east. At same time, thrust right hand, with its forefinger leading, downward over left knee, palm facing up. At this instant bend left knee to assume left archer stance, your left palm naturally gets close to bend of right elbow. Your weight is now on left foot; your sight directed to lower front; your attention focused on left palm. (Fig. 201)

Self-feeling: Left leg and right palm warm.

Practical application: Continuing, in case the opponent has not been rolled out by you, and is watching for a chance to chop at your head, you can adhere your left hand to his left elbow and push it aside, while straightening up your body, led by the left hand, to assume left archer stance; simultaneously hit his underbelly with your right hand. (Fig 30/1, 30/2)

Fig. 29/5

Fig. 30/1

2nd movement: Hands up ward

Raise right hand, forefinger leading, along the under side of left arm to stretch forward to cross left wrist from its outside, right palm facing left, left palm facing right. Straighten up your upper torso and loosen your right knee to draw forward right foot to assume left sitting stance. At the beginning of this movement look at right forefinger, after two hands have crossed each other, look out from the cross. Your attention is on left palm. (Fig. 202)

Self-feeling: Left leg warm and distended; the outer edge of right hand extended with energy; left palm and right sole warm.

Practical application: Continuing, now thrust your right hand from under his right arm to slant up to hit his right shoulder or the sensitive point near

Fig. 30/2

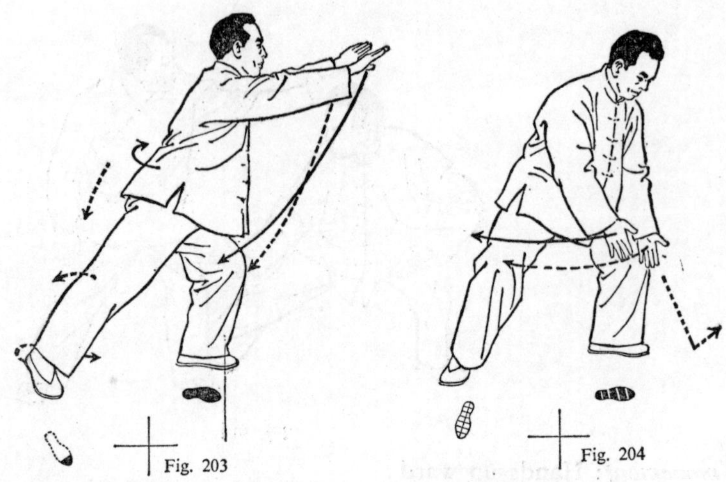
Fig. 203
Fig. 204

his armpit. At same time thrust forward your right foot to pass round the opponent's foreleg to kick at his hind leg with an uplifting force. The opponent will fall on his back. (Fig. 30/3, 30/4)

Posture XXXI. Step Back and Ride Tiger (2 movements)

Explanation of posture name: The posture whereby one sits on one foot, with the other foot barely touching ground, and separates one's hands,

Fig. 30/3
Fig. 30/4

the rear hand in hook, is called in Chinese pugilism a Tiger-riding Posture.

1st movement: Hands forward ward

Relax both wrists to separate hands to extend forward, palm facing down. Simultaneously draw right foot as far as possible to rear, toes touching ground. Keep your weight on left foot; look out from between two hands; focus your attention on left palm. (Fig. 203)

Self-feeling: Left leg warm and distended; chest and ribs at ease; palms warm.

Practical application: If an opponent punches at your face, ward up your hands to block his approaching hand with one of your hands, and to take advantage of this chance to hit the opponent's face with your other hand. (Fig. 31/1, 31/2)

2nd movement: Front palm rear hook

Roll down two hands to the front of left knee and set down right heel, its toe pointing south. Swing two hands to right knee, your weight automatically transfers to right foot, left toes slanting up. Now keep your weight on right foot, but roll two hands again to outer side of left knee. Lift right wrist to right ear and ward forward to south, palm facing left, thumb upward. Concurrently gather left fingers into a hook and swing backward, point of hook upward. At same time withdraw left foot to the side of right foot, toes barely touching ground. Your weight is on right foot; your sight directed to front left (southeast); your attention on right palm. (Fig. 204, 205, 206, 207a, 207b)

Self-feeling: Right foot rooted onto ground like a tree; rib cage relaxed; right palm and left sole wriggling.

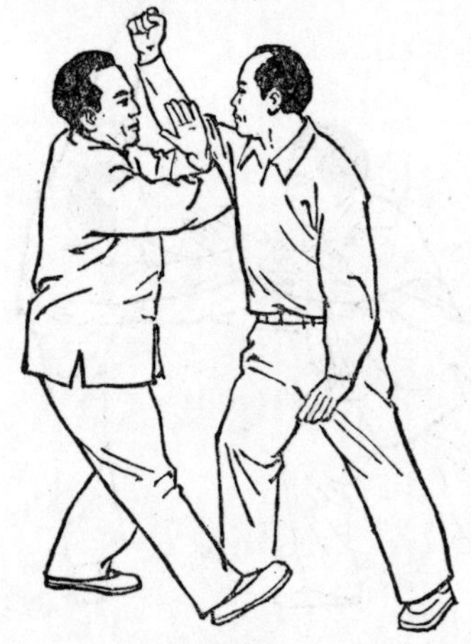

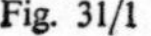

Fig. 31/1

Fig. 31/2

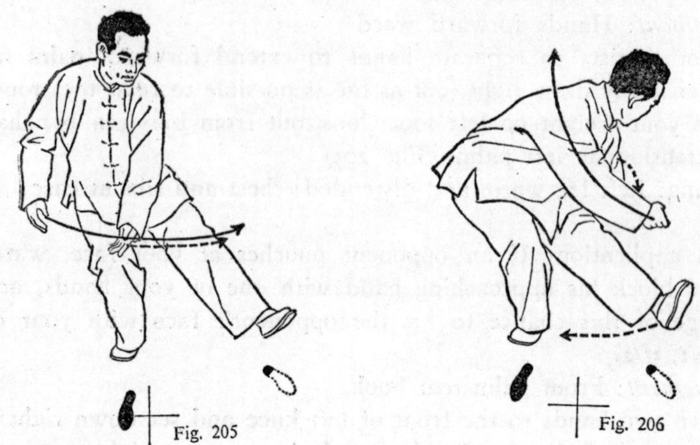

Fig. 205

Fig. 206

Practical application: Continuing, if the opponent now attempts to tread on your left knee with his right foot, and to hit your face with his left hand, you may hook his approaching right foot with your left hookhand; simultaneously let your right hand adhere to and block his approaching left hand. Now separate your hands, one to the front, the other to the rear, with a sudden rotation of your body withdraw your front leg, thus to dodge and beat his attempt. He will fall down sideways. (Fig. 31/3, 31/4, 31/5)

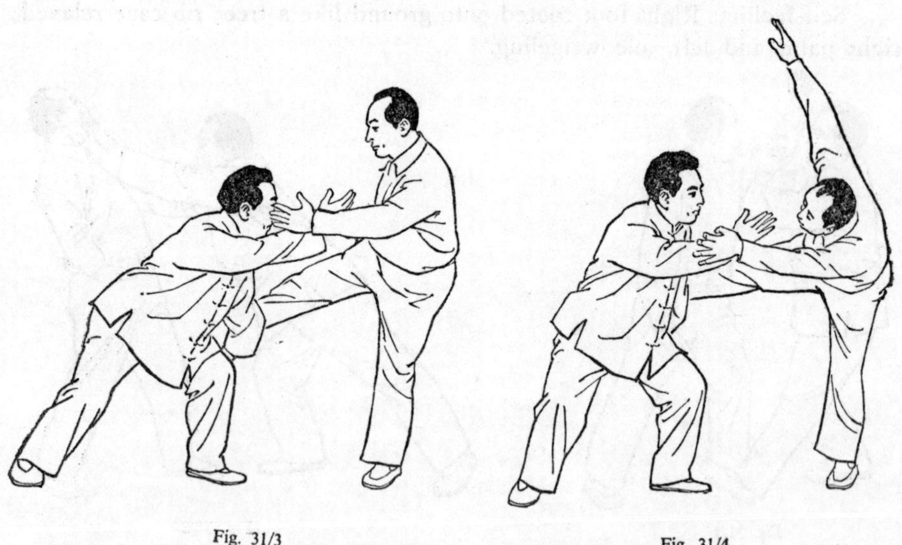

Fig. 31/3

Fig. 31/4

Fig. 207a

Fig. 207b

Posture XXXII. Turn Around and Press Face with Palm (2 movements)

Explanation of posture name: The torso turns 180 degrees to press the opponent's face with your palm, hence the name.

1st movement: Right hand rightward move

Move right hand, led by its forefinger, to right (pointing west), palm down; turn torso with the turning of right hand. Left hook naturally resumes palm, facing up, and rests near your left rib cage. Your weight is still on right foot; your sight follows right forefinger; your attention focused on right palm. (Fig. 208)

Fig. 31/5

Fig. 208

Fig. 32/1

Self-feeling: Right leg warm and distended; tips of right fingers distended.

Practical application: If an opponent punches your rib cage from your right side, turn your torso to right and fake a thrust to his eyes with your right fingertips. The opponent's offensive will be tardy due to this sudden attack and he has to draw back his torso. (Fig. 32/1, 32/2)

2nd movement: Left hand forward push

Raise left hand, with forefinger leading, passing left side of rib cage to the bend of right arm, while right hand turning its palm up. Left hand continues its move by extending forward to west as far as possible. When left

Fig. 32/2

Fig. 209 Fig. 210

hand meets with right hand, left foot passes over right toes to land on ground. When left foot has just landed, push forward your left palm to west, palm facing out, ends up. At same time bend forward left knee, turn out right heel to asume left archer stance. Withdraw right hand to left side of rib cage, palm up. Your weight is on left foot; look over tip of your left forefinger; focus your attention on left palm. (Fig. 209, 210)

Self-feeling: Left leg distended and warm; back rounded and full of energy; both palms warm.

Practical application: Continuing, when your right hand has made a fake thrust at the opponent's eyes, you can now withdraw your right hand, palm up, to pull down his right arm with back of your hand; meanwhile deliver your left palm from your chest to press on his face. At same time, in close coordination with your hand, thrust your left foot to block his hind leg, and to promptly assume left archer stance. The opponent will be pushed away. (Fig. 32/3, 32/4)

Posture XXXIII. Turn and Kick Horizontally (Sweep Lotus with Both Hands, 4 movements)

Explanation of posture name: The horizontal circling of right foot, touching in turn the left hand and the right hand which are also circling horizontally, but in reverse direction, is likened to lotus sweeping in the wind.

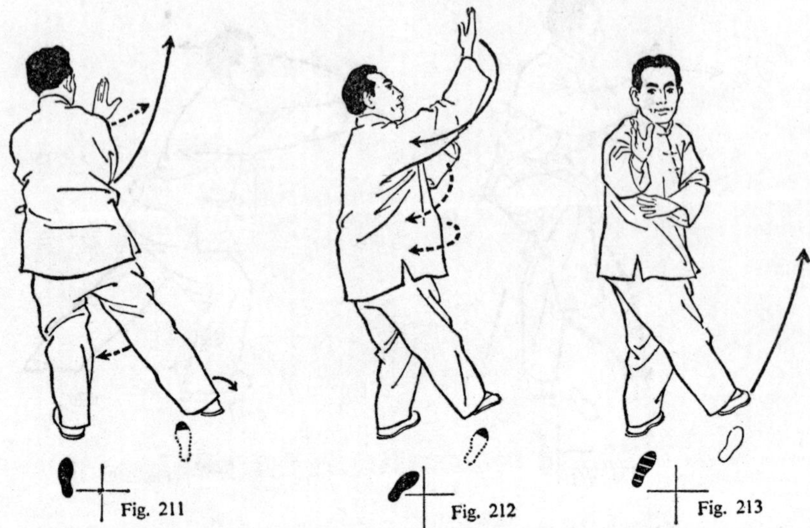

Fig. 211 Fig. 212 Fig. 213

1st movement: Left hand right roll

Without moving right hand, turn left hand to right, forefinger leading and your sight following the forefinger. Simultaneously turn left toes to right to point to north. Your weight is still on left foot; your sight on left forefinger; your attention focused on left palm. (Fig. 211)

Self-feeling: Palms wriggling; back warm.

Practical application: Should the opponent grabbed your right shoulder

Fig. 32/3 Fig. 32/4

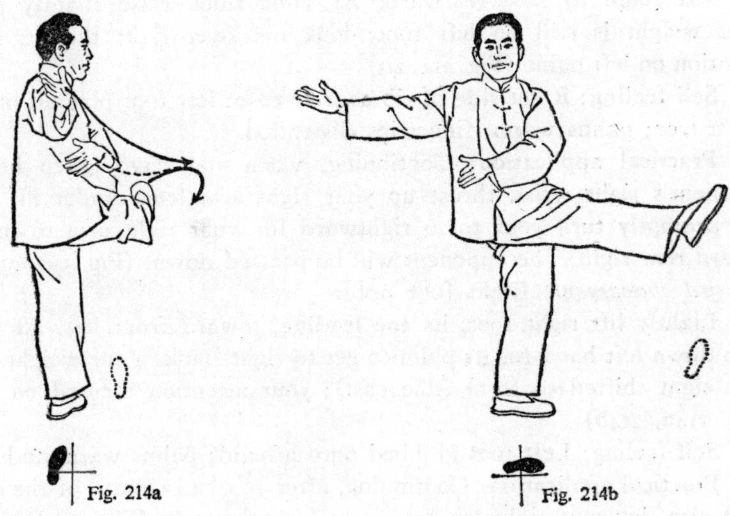

Fig. 214a   Fig. 214b

with his right hand from your rear, you can turn rightward and adhere to his right hand with your left hand. (Fig. 33/1, 33/2)

2nd movement: Right hand back roll

Move right hand, forefinger leading, to right from under left arm, along an outward arc. When the bend of right arm reaches left hand, and right palm facing in, turn torso to right and lower both hands down to rear right to shoulder level, wrists turn as they descend, for right palm to face forward

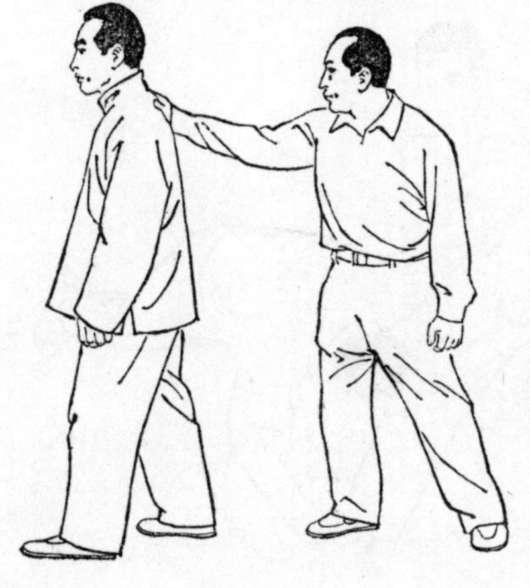

Fig. 33/1

Fig. 33/2

and left palm to face rearward. At same time, raise slightly right heel. Your weight is still on left foot; look out over right thumb; focus your attention on left palm. (Fig. 212, 213)

Self-feeling: Right side of rib cage at ease; left foot planted onto ground like a tree; palms warm; fingertips distended.

Practical application: Continuing, when you have taken hold of the opponent's right wrist, thrust up your right arm from under his right arm and promptly turn your torso rightward for your right arm to press down toward rear right. The opponent will be pressed down. (Fig. 33/3, 33/4)

3rd movement: Right foot uplift

Lightly lift right foot, its toe leading, toward front left. At same time push down left hand for its palm to get to right flank. Your weight unshifted; your sight shifted to front (due east); your attention focused on left palm. (Fig. 214a, 214b)

Self-feeling: Left toes grabbed onto ground; palms warm and wriggling.

Practical application: Continuing, after you had control of the opponent's right arm, let your right leg get ready for an attack. (Fig. 33/5)

4th movement: Right foot right swing

Swing right foot gradually upward for its toe to be aligned with tip of nose. And at this instant let right foot get in touch, in your front, with tip of each hand one after the other, which are swinging leftward. Then without ceasing, swing right foot gradually to front right to descend, heel touching ground, to assume left sitting stance. The two hands continue their swing to

Fig. 33/3

Fig. 33/4

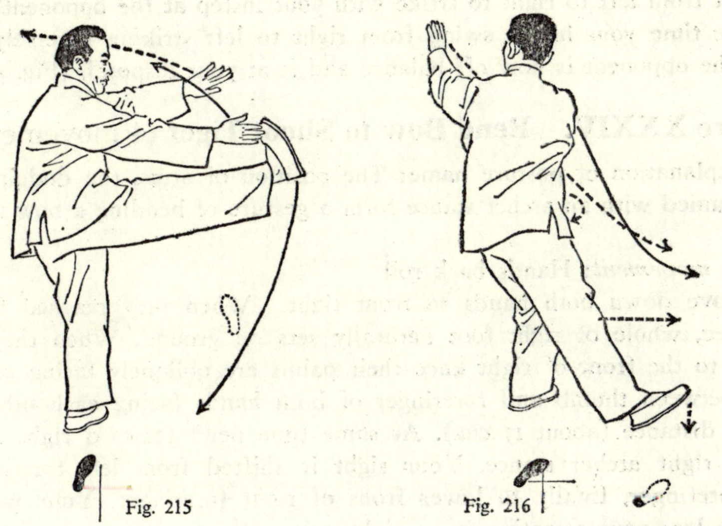

Fig. 215 Fig. 216

extend to upper rearleft, both palms obliquely downward, right palm at the bend of left arm. Your weight is still on left foot. After both palms and right foot got in touch, your sight follows tip of left forefinger; your attention focused on left palm. (Fig. 215, 216)

Self-feeling: Five toes of left foot grabbed onto ground; chest and back warm; tendons of two arms stretched.

Practical application: Continuing, after having raised your right foot,

Fig. 33/5 Fig. 33/6

swing it from left to right to strike with your instep at the opponent's waist. at same time your hands swing from right to left striking reversely at his face. The opponent is now off balance and is at your disposal. (Fig. 33/6)

Posture XXXIV. Bend Bow to Shoot Tiger (4 movements)

Explanation of posture name: The position of arms, the dodging body accompanied with an archer stance form a gesture of bending a bow to shoot tiger.

1st movement: Hands back roll

Move down both hands to front right. When they reached front of left knee, whole of right foot naturally sets on ground. When they move further to the front of right knee their palms are obliquely facing rear, the curve between thumb and forefinger of both hands facing each other at a natural distance (about 15 cm.). At same time bend forward right knee to assume right archer stance. Your sight is shifted from left forefinger to right forefinger, finally to lower front of right forefinger. Your weight is on right leg; your attention is on right palm. (Fig. 217)

Self-feeling: Inner side of right thigh warm and sore; waist and back warm; right palm and left sole wriggling.

Practical application: If the opponent punches on your chest with his right fist, turn torso slightly to left, and put your right hand on the bend of his right arm, your left hand on his right wrist. Following up his attack, roll with both your hands his right arm slightly up to left, then forward to lower right. The opponent will be off balance. (Fig. 34/1, 34/2)

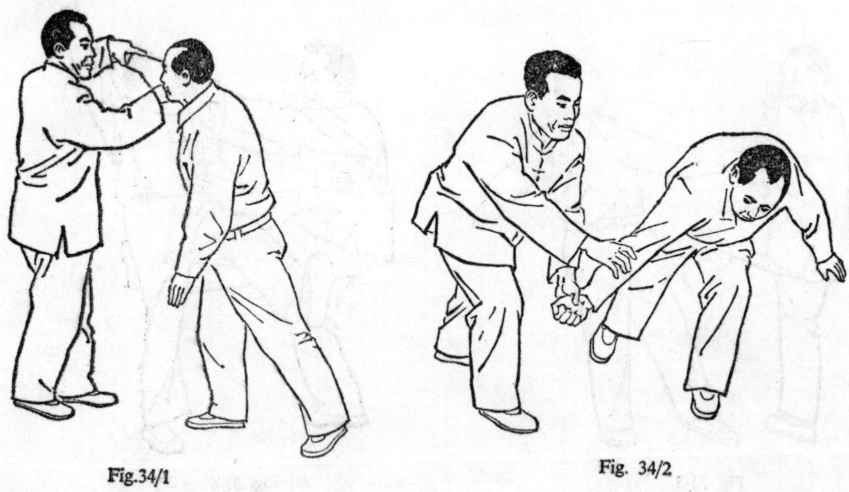

Fig.34/1 Fig. 34/2

Fig. 217 Fig. 218 Fig. 219

2nd movement: Punch with both fists

Relax elbows for two hands to clench gradually into light fists to ascend to outer side of right ear. Look at the fist kunckle of right forefinger, the eyes of two fists facing each other. At same time turn torso slightly to right and then to left. Deliver a punch with right fist from right ear toward front left, the left fist accompanying underneath, eyes of two fists still facing, right fist above left fist, left elbow aligned with right knee. Your weight is still on right foot; your sight directed along first knuckle of right forefinger to front left, your attention on rgiht fist. (Fig. 218, 219)

Fig. 34/3 Fig. 34/4

Self-feeling: Right foot planted firmly onto the ground like a tree; foreleg warm; right fist and left sole warm.

Practical application: Continuing, the opponent having evaded, again attempts to punch your head with two fists, you can follow up his attack to roll his hands upward. Quickly raise your fists to right ear to deliver one fist at his head, the other fist at his flank. He will be sent off. (Fig. 34/3, 34/4, 34/5)

3rd movement: Hands back roll

Gradually unclench both fists and move up both hands toward rear right. When they have extended as far as possible relax left knee for left foot to take a step forward, heel touching ground, then roll and push down hands towards front left. When they pass the right knee, set down whole left foot; when they pass the left knee, bend left knee to assume left archer stance. Now both palms are obliquely facing rear, the curve between thumb and forefinger of both hands facing each other at a natural distance (about 15 cm.). Your sight is shifted from right forefinger to left forefinger, and finally along left forefinger to lower front. Your atention is focused on left palm; your weight is on left leg. (Fig. 220, 221)

Self-feeling: Inner side of left thigh warm and sore; waist and back warm; left palm and right sole wriggling.

Practical application: Continuing, if the opponent withdraws to evade your two fists and chops your neck with his right palm, you can grab his right wrist with your right hand, adhere to his right elbow with your left hand, and bring them up toward rear right. At same time, draw forward

Fig. 34/5 Fig. 34/6

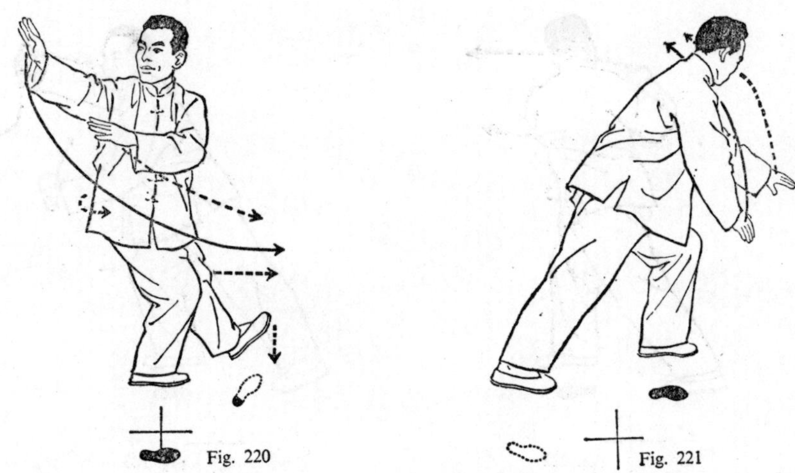

Fig. 220

Fig. 221

your left foot to assume left archer stance, while with both your hands roll down his right arm toward front left to topple him. (Fig. 34/6, 34/7, 34/8)

4th movement: Punch with both fists

Relax elbows for two hands to clench gradually into light fists to ascend to outer side of left ear, the eyes of two fists facing each other. At same time turn torso slightly to left and then to right. Deliver a punch with left fist from left ear toward front right (southeast), the right fist accompanying underneath, eyes of two fists still facing, left fist above right fist, right elbow aligned with left knee. Your weight is still on left foot; your sight

Fig. 34/7

Fig. 34/8

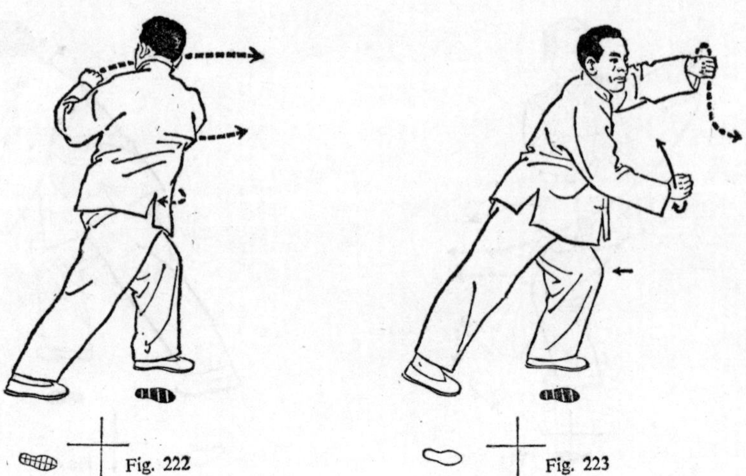

Fig. 222

Fig. 223

directed along left fist knuckle to front right; your attention on left fist. (Fig. 222, 223)

Self-feeling: Left foot firmly planted onto the ground like a tree; foreleg warm; left fist and right sole warm.

Practical application: Continuing, if the opponent attempts to embrace your waist, turn your upper torso first to left and then quickly turn to right. At same time turn hands into fists and lift them to left ear and then to punch at the opponent below his right armpit or on right ribs. (Fig 34/9, 34/10, 34/11, 34/12)

Fig. 34/9

Fig. 34/10

Posture XXXV. Step Back, Deflect, Parry and Punch (4 movements)

Explanation of posture name: The opponent's offensive force is being deflected to left and right by your two hands accompanied with a backward stepping. The opponent's approaching hand is then parried by your upright left palm and the opponent's chest is punched by your right fist.

1st movement: Step back and deflect rightward

Lower left elbow to rotate left fist counterclockwise to the front of chest, palm of fist upward; simultaneously bend right elbow to rotate right fist clockwise, and to move to right side of your chest. Now carry two fists in opposite directions to intersect each other, and at the end of intersection unclench both fists to move to front right (deflect), until right arm is stretched out, palm down, left palm facing up at the middle of right foream. At same time relax right knee to sit back, transferring your weight to right foot. Then withdraw left foot and stretch it as far as you can to the rear, toes slightly touching ground. Your sight follows left fist first, but shifted to right forefinger after fists have unclenched. Your attention is focused on right palm. (Fig. 224, 225)

Self-feeling: Tendons of limbs stretched to give a feeling of comfortable extension. Right leg feels distended and warm; both sides of rib cage comfortable.

Practical application: Continuing, if the opponent has grabbed your left wrist with both his hands, you can lower your left elbow to turn up palm of left fist and sit back to thrust upward your right fist along the bend of

Fig. 34/11 Fig. 34/12

Fig. 224 Fig. 225

your own left arm. Unclench right fist to "pat" on the opponent's right shoulder. At same time stretch your left foot backward. He will topple and fall. (Fig. 35/1, 35/2, 35/3)

2nd movement: Step back and deflect leftward

Bend right elbow to rotate right hand counterclockwise to the front of right chest, palm up; simultaneously rotate left hand, clockwise, for its palm to turn down and to face right palm at a distance of about 10cm. Then thrust both hands to front left till left arm is stretched out, palm still downward, right palm facing up, at the middle of left forearm. At same time

Fig. 35/1

Fig. 226 Fig. 227

relax left knee to sit back, thus transfer your weight to left foot. Now withdraw right foot and stretch as far as you can to the rear, toes lightly touching ground. Fix your sight on left forefinger, and focus your attention on left palm. (Fig. 226, 227)

Self-feeling: Tendons of limbs stretched to give a feeling of comfortable extension. Left leg distended and warm; both sides of rib cage comfortable.

Practical application: If the opponent pushes at your chest with both his hands, allow your right hand to adhere to his left elbow and to push his left shoulder laterally with your left hand, simultaneously allow your

Fig. 35/2

Fig. 35/3

right foot to thrust backward to assume a left archer stance. He will be toppled. (Fig. 35/4, 35/5)

3rd movement: Left hand backward parry

Loosen waist and gradually shift body weight to right leg. Move left hand, its forefinger leading, along a slightly outward curve toward rear left, right hand follows underneath. When all body weight has been shifted onto right leg, forming right sitting stance, thrust up left hand toward your front until its forefinger is aligned with tip of your nose, palm rightward; meanwhile clench right hand gradually into a loose fist and lower it toward

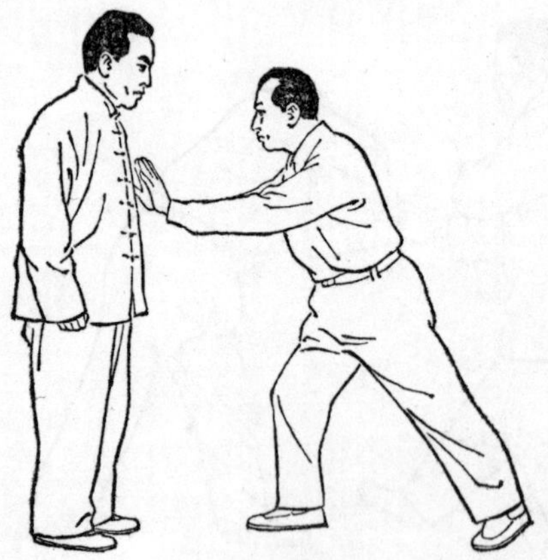

Fig. 35/4

Fig. 35/5

rear right to rest beside right flank. Your weight is now on right foot; look ahead over tip of left forefinger; focus your attention on the palm of right fist. (Fig. 228)

Self-feeling: Right leg distended and sore; palm of right fist and left sole warm.

Practical application: If the opponent attempts to punch at your chest with his right fist, draw a step backward and parry with your left forearm any forward movement of his arm. Meanwhile clench your right hand into a fist at your right flank ready to turn into offensive. (Fig. 35/6)

Fig. 35/6

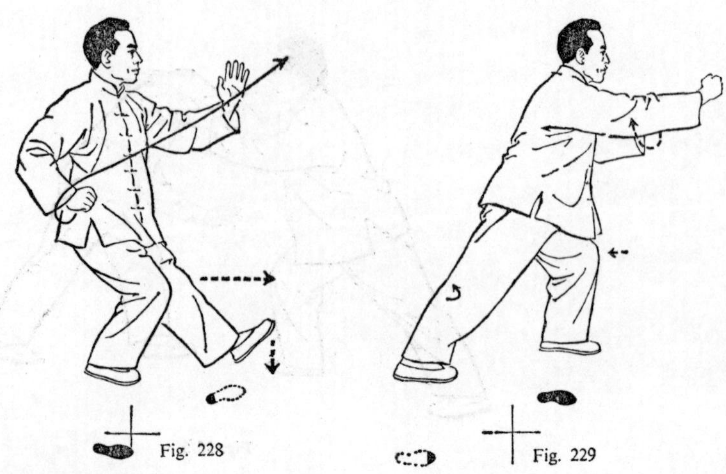

Fig. 228

Fig. 229

4th movement: Right fist forward thrust

Thrust right fist gradually to front to pass the right side of left palm. When whole left foot has set down to a left archer stance, continue the thrust forward of right fist till right arm and left leg are straight, the second knuckle of forefinger of right fist is aligned with tip of your nose. Your weight is now on left foot; your attention on fore part of your fist; your sight is directed ahead over right fist. (Fig. 229)

Self-feeling: Right leg distended and warm; right arm fully stretched.

Practical application: Continuing, when you have parried with your left forearm the opponent's offensive right arm, instantly send your right fist to pass from under his right arm to attack his chest or the sensitive point near his right armpit. (Fig. 35/7)

Posture XXXVI. Seeming Close Up (2 movements)

Explanation of posture name: When the two arms cross each other in shape of X, they are similar to two strips of paper pasted in X shape for sealing a door. Again when the two hands push forward they are similar to the closeing-door movement. The technical terms in Chinese pugilism for the above are respectively "Sealing & blocking" and "Intersecting & closing."

1st movement: Hands back roll

Move left hand to outer side of right elbow, palm facing left. Shift your weight gradually to right leg, right fist carried backward by your body. Unclench right fist when it is aligned with left palm. Spread two hands naturally at shoulder width, palms facing you, ends up; simultaneously loosen

Fig. 230 Fig. 231

shoulder and lower elbows till wrists are at shoulder level, while loosening waist to "sit" back to assume right sitting stance. Your weight is now on right foot; your sight directed to far front; your attention focused on right palms. (Fig. 230, 231)

Self-feeling: Right leg distended, warm and sore; centres of both palms and tips of ten fingers warm and distended.

Practical application: If the opponent pushes with both hands at your chest, let your left hand scoop up and adhere its radius to ulna of his left arm.

Fig. 35/7

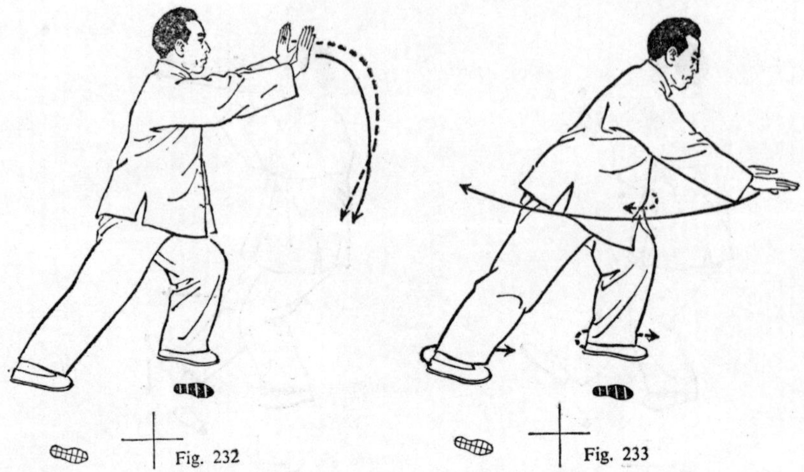

Fig. 232 Fig. 233

At same time, draw your right foot to the rear to assume a right sitting stance to shift his centre of gravity to the right. (Fig. 36/1, 36/2)

2nd movement: Hands forward push

Let two little fingers take the lead, turn both palms outward and push them to the front as far as you can, but keep elbows slightly bent, while shifting your weight to left foot to assume the left archer stance. Your weight is now on left foot; your sight directed from between your hands to far front; your attention on left palm. (Fig. 232)

Self-feeling: Left leg distended and warm; palms wriggling.

Fig. 36/1 Fig. 36/2

Practical application: Continuing, when you have spread your hands to cause the opponent to incline forward, now push with both your hands at his left forearm or left shoulder. He will be pushed away. (Fig. 36/3)

Posture XXXVII. Embrace Tiger and Return to Mountain (Cross Hands Closing From, 6 movements)

Explanation of posture name: Two arms are here separated to turn and to embrace. Then two hands are crossed in front of chest to gradually resume the beginning potsure, as is usually done after practising a whole series of postures.

1st movement: Hands forward thrust

Loosen both elbows but extend forward all fingertips to push hands downward till weight of body has transferred to left foot. Now look forward from between hands, your attention on left palm. (Fig 233)

Self-feeling: Left thigh very warm; arms feel fully stretched; fingertips distended.

Practical application: Should the opponent again try to push you with both his hands, you may imitate his action and push forward likewise. When both parties get into contact, the opponent will be bumped away. (Fig. 37/1)

2nd movement: Spread hands

Move right hand rightward, with its forefinger leading. When it has reached due south, draw in right heel, pivoting on its toes, till right foot points

Fig. 36/3

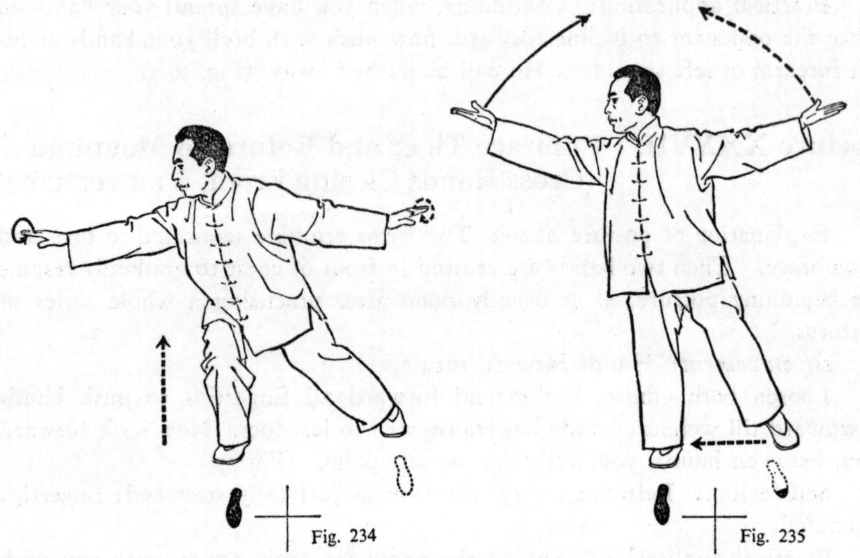
Fig. 234
Fig. 235

to south. Then when right hand, continuing its move, has reached due west, draw out left heel, pivoting on its toes, till left foot also points to south. While right hand begins to move rightward at the start of this movement, left hand also begins its move toward left. Both hands are spread to shoulder level, palms downward without change. Your weight is now shifted to right foot; your sight rests on tip of right forefinger; your attention focused on right palm. (Fig. 234)

Fig. 37/1
Fig. 37/2

Self-feeling: Arms fully extended; chest and back comfortable.

Practical application: If the opponent, left foot forward, pushes with his hands at your abdomen, turn your torso slightly toward left while thrusting your right foot from behind toward the mid-point between his feet to assume a half-perpendicular half-splay stance, and extend forward your right hand to adhere firmly to his right ribs. The opponent will be out of balance and to fall backward. (Fig. 37/2, 37/3, 37/4)

3rd movement: Hands up ward

Rotate right hand, its thumb leading, to turn its palm gradually upward. When this palm is up and arm fully extended, let your body rise with the hand. Simultaneously and likewise allow your left hand to execute the same movement. Your weight remains on right foot; your sight is on right forefinger; your attention on right palm. (Fig. 235)

Fig. 37/3

Fig. 37/4

Fig. 37/5

Fig. 236

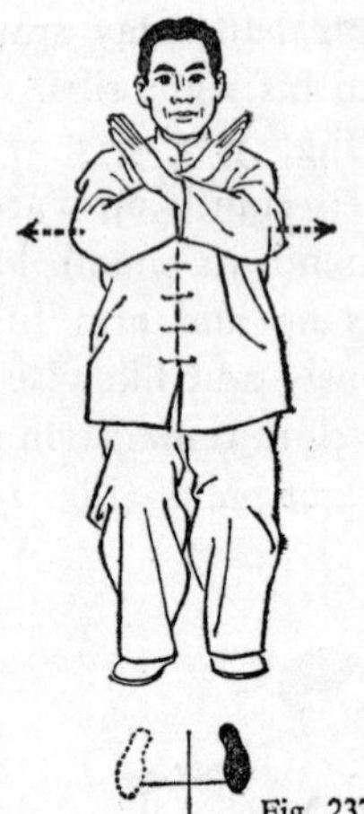

Fig. 237

Self-feeling: Both sides of rib cage light and comfortable; palms warm; tips of all fingers distended.

Practical application: Continuing, after you have locked the opponent's legs and spread your hands near his middle section, now turn your palms up and rise up. The opponent will be uprooted, unless your right palm is turned downward to hold him from falling on back. (Fig. 37/5, 37/6)

Fig. 36/6

4th movement: Lower elbows

Raise both arms overhead and withdraw left foot next to right foot. Then relax knees to gradually lower upper torso to a half squat. At same time relax shoulders to loosen and lower elbows. Your wrists will naturally cross one another at shoulder level in front of your chest. Your weight is on both feet; your sight directed forward over the crossed hands; your attention focused on tips of all fingers. (Fig. 236, 237)

Self-feeling: Whole body light and comfortable.

Practical application: Should the opponent chop at your head with both hands, just raise his arms overhead with both your hands, he will be warded up. At this instant lower your elbow and cross your wrists so his wrists will be crossed and he will be in an awkward position to be easily thrown away. (Fig. 37/7, 37/8)

5th movement: Spread elbows

Loosen both elbows to spread to both sides, thus the crossed hands will gradually separate and descend to the chest. Let tips of two middle fingers get into slight touch, then let tips of forefingers and that of thumbs also get into slight touch. Your sight rests on tips of forefingers; your weight is still on both feet; your attention focused on back of both hands (the Wai Laogong points). (Fig. 238)

Self-feeling: Your waist (Mingmen point) hot; both palms and soles warm; both thighs and shanks distended and warm.

Fig. 37/7

Fig. 37/8

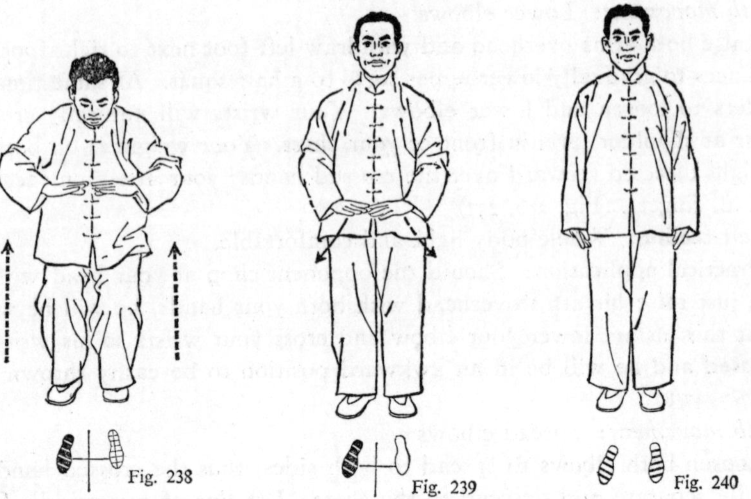

Fig. 238 Fig. 239 Fig. 240

Practical application: If the opponent attempts to embrace you, rotate your body and strike his rib cage with your elbow. (Fig. 37/9, 37/10)

6th movement: Return to Taiji position

Relax both ankles, knees, and hipjoints, your body will stand up of its own accord. Detach your sight from tips of forefingers to look horizontally afar. Then relax your shoulders, elbows and wrists. While doing the above, think consciously of loosening these parts as if they were falling from your body like the decomposed skin of old wall, which falls off at a

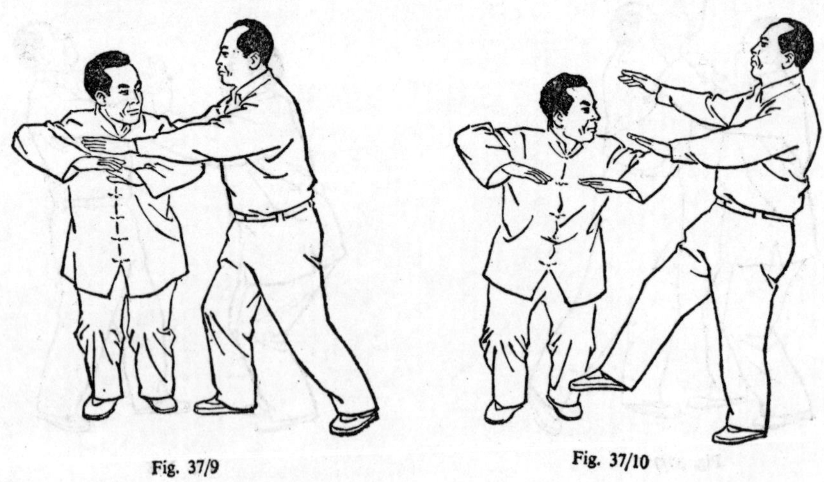

Fig. 37/9 Fig. 37/10

mere touch. Finally, think in turn from thumbs to little fingers for all the nails to drop from your fingers. (Fig. 239, 240)

Self-feeling: Perspiring lightly all over the body which is now light and comfortable. All joints are loosened and give you a light and agile feeling. Blood circulates right to the fingertips. You feel spirited and energetic.

Practical application: Should the opponent attempt to push you off balance with both his hands, just think of your Mingmen and Dantian points, you will be able to stand firmly like a rock. (Fig. 37/11, 37/12)

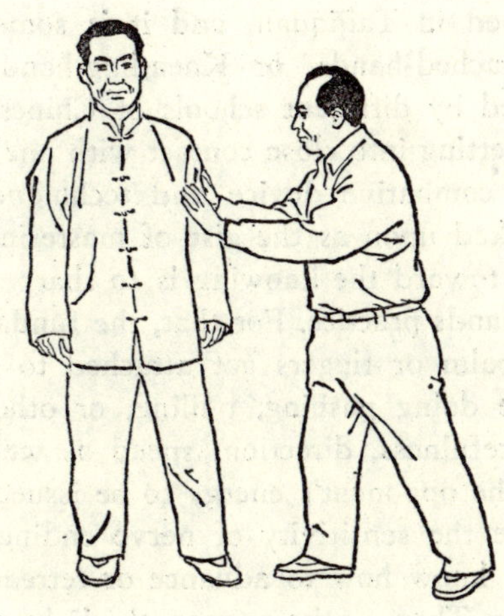

Fig. 37/11

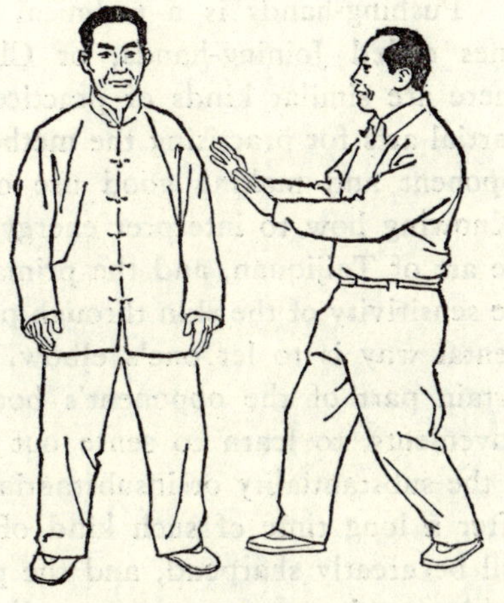

Fig. 37/12

TAIJI PUSHING-HANDS EXERCISES

What is Taiji pushing-hands? What should one pay attention to when learning and practising pushing-hands?

The solo form sequence practice and duet form pushing-hands exercise are the two component parts of the art of Taijiquan. Doing sequence practice enables one to learn the substance of Taijiquan, while doing pushing-hands exercise trains one to apply the art to actual self-defence. Therefore, after having learned how to do well a complete sequence of Taijiquan, one should proceed to learn pushing-hands. Only when one has become proficient in both, can he be counted as being possessed of the substance as well as the application of the art of Taijiquan.

Pushing-hands is a form of exercise to sharpen the sensitivity of one's nerve endings to the degree as sensitive as that of the feelers of a cricket. The feelers are not only very quick in sensing out what the cricket is facing against, but are also very quick in directing the insect to dodge nimbly an attack with the slightest necessary shifting movement, or to be fully attentive in locating and taking advantage of any of the opponent's weak points. Such kind of exercise will enhance one's interest and arouse the spirit of enquiry and analysis in the process of learning Taijiquan.

Pushing-hands is a technical term used in Taijiquan, and it is sometimes called Joining-hands, or Closely-attached-hands, or Kneading-hands. There are similar kinds of practice adopted by different schools of Chinese martial arts for practising the methods of getting into close contact with one's opponent and making good use of some combative device and technique. "Knowing how to interpret energy" is looked upon as the gist of mastering the art of Taijiquan, and the primary step toward the knowing is to sharpen the sensitivity of the skin through pushing-hands practice. For that, the fundamental way is to let one's elbow, wrist, palm or fingers get attached to a certain part of the opponent's body while doing pushing, pulling, or other movements, to learn to sense out the forcefulness, direction, speed as well as the substantiality or insubstantiality of the opponent's energy to be issued. After a long time of such kind of practice the sensitivity of nerve endings will be greatly sharpend, and the pair will know how to advance or retreat, and how to issue energy or neutralize it aptly. Then, at the opponent's slightest stir, one will know instantly the direction, the forcefulness, the speed as well as the substantiality or insubstantiality of the energy he is to issue. Such ability is known as "knowing how to interpret energy."

After one is capable of "knowing how to interpret energy", one's art will become more and more refined through further practice. In an encounter with an opponent, taking an accurate measure of him is of utmost importance, and the basis of an accurate measure is knowing oneself and one's opponent. There is an old Chinese saying: "Knowing oneself and also one's opponent will make one a hundred times victorious in a hundred battles." Sensitive feeling is the meduim for knowing the self and the opponent. So the fundamental theory of pushing-hands is actually not very complicated. Of course, from the point of keeping one's body centered and in equilibrium, it is harder to be so with the duet form pushing-hands than with the solo form sequence practice, for the latter calls for keeping balanced in doing different sorts of movements by oneself only, while the former demands keeping balanced under an opponent's every measure to set him off balance, and losing no opportunity to set the opponent off balance. The often cited saying "Seeking to know one's own energy through the sequence practice, and the other's energy through pushing-hands exercise" shows that the two actually serve the same purpose of knowing oneself and knowing one's opponent.

Only through constant practice can one obtain true knowledge. Whether in doing pushing-hands exercise or sequence practice, one must observe the prescribed way of doing them, and must try one's best to do every posture and to apply any method as correctly as possible. In pushing-hands, the insubstantiality and the substantiality of the two legs must be clearly differentiated. For instance, the foreleg must bend to the required degree when taking the "archer stance", and one must sit back firmly on the rear leg when assuming the "sitting stance." Also, one's trunk must be kept centered and in equilibrium as in doing the sequence practice. The eight forms of hand-methods: warding, rolling, pushing, pressing, pulling, splitting, elbow-striking and shoulder-striking should be practised one by one again and again, to obtain accuracy. Therefore, a beginner is asked to devote his full time and attention to "rotation-practice" which is a system of exercise done cooperatively by two persons. When A does warding, B counters it with rolling aside, then A changes to pressing, B overcomes it with pushing, or vice versa. Going on this way in rotation round after round till tired, it is not unusual to do up to a few hundred rounds at a practice session. In the older days, some had done up to a few thousand rounds, and even to ten thousand rounds! When the above four forms of hand-methods are mastered, the pair should proceed to four more forms: pulling, splitting, elbow-striking and shoulder-striking in the training system called Da Lu. Only after one has become proficient in the use of these eight hand-methods, should one start to make enquiry (to test) the opposite party's energy. In pushing-hands, the movement of eyesight generally follows that of the hands.

Form a habit of doing all these in a correct way. When a good foundation is laid, it will be easier to reach the advanced stage of development. It is necessary to observe the rule of gradual progression. Avoid any hasty desire for success. Kungfu (skill developed through a long time of hard training) is an accumulation of improvement day by day and bit by bit.

There are quite a number of diferent forms of pushing-hands exercise. The basic four hand-methods practice on fixed stance, the same practice with moving steps, and Da Lu are the chief ones; while the so-called "Rib-reaching", "Folding up" and "Old Cattle Energy" are more advanced auxiliary exercises designed to develop a certain skill or power; and finally there is "Free-flower-picking" as a form of free sparring. However, pushing-hands on fixed steps is fundamental to all. Therefore, it is necessary to start with it in learning the art of pushing-hands.

When starting to do rotation practice, all the movements should be done to the required degree and it is advisable to gradually enlarge the movements and make them more and more rounded, avoiding any appearance of bumps and holes in one's posture, any severance and discontinuity in one's movement, and any defectiveness in the methods employed. Pushing-hands on fixed stance allows no moving of the rear foot, and any such moving is usually counted a loss of one point in a contest. Therefore, in the practice one should increase his reach only by extending the movements of his arms and trunk and his counterpart should evade the closing in by sitting back on his rear foot as far as needed, and then neutralize the on-coming force at the apt moment. It is not allowed to resist or to ward off it with force. Only when one is so closely pressed by the on-coming force that any neutralizing movement is no more possible, will he be allowed in praetice to move a step backward, and if only half a step is needed, then just retreat half a step, not any more. Whether advancing or retreating, the two should maintain attachment to each other. Practising in such a manner, a kind of adhering and sticking energy will be gradually developed as time goes by.

The next step is to take up folding up practice and Da Lu to develop further the flexibility and tenacity of the waist and legs, and for the training of advanced skills. One important thing to remember is not to let yourself go into inquiring (testing) your opponent's energy too early. The common saying "Practice makes perfect" is most suitably applied to pushing-hands. Just concentrate your effort and attention on doing your daily practice, by and by, there will develop in you the sense of knowing how to "interpret energy." When you really knows this you will be able to make use of the technique of overcoming hardness with pliability, and to "use four ounces to deflect a thousand pounds."

The sentence "Use four ounces to deflect a thousand pounds" in the "Song of Pushing-hands" denotes a method with the highest efficiency employed in pushing-hands. To achieve this, the primary demand after getting into contact with the opponent is "no letting go and no resistance". Though the phrase "no letting go" surely denotes not getting separated from each other, but in fact it is not that simple. One should let some part of his arm, by his keen sense of touch, get adhered to the opponent's. And in this state of adherance, one should follow the opponent's movement, at the same time, issue a very slight amount of energy to try to drive the opponent into a disadvantageous or unstable position. At this juncture, if no counter-acting energy is felt (that is, at the moment when a sense of lightness appears from a sense of heaviness), one could use any hand-method that deemed fit to send the opponent off his feet. And if a sense of heaviness is felt at the attached point, one should slightly loosen the attachment to let the opponent have a sudden feeling of emptiness, and follow with an attack immediately. That will send the opponent away much farther. Such is the effect of first making use of the principle of "no resistance", to leave one's opponent in a state of being suddenly lifted from his root, and then immediately followed with the technique of "no letting go" to set him off balance. The phrase "no resistance" may be understood from the wording as not to use any strength and let oneself be handled in any way by the opponent, however, it is not entirely so. To be handled in any way by the opponent will place oneself in a passive position, while "no resistance" embodies an active spirit in making one's movement suited to any of the opponent's. Therefore, in pushing-hands, while it is necessary to be able to receive whatever comes from the opponent, it is also imperative to use one's keen sense of touch to find out the substantial and the insubstantial parts on the opponent's body, and to discriminate the real and the fake of his offensive or defensive movements so as to be able to adapt one's own movements to that of the opponent's.

To counter an opponent's forceful attack with forceful resistance is a commitment of the most serious fault in Taijiquan, the "double-weighting" (this term will be explained in detail later). To hit back at any on-coming stroke right away is but a kind of natural reaction and not the way of Taijiquan. The way adopted by Taiji pushing-hands is "to neutralize the on-coming force first, then to follow with a counter attack". And it is also necessary to get oneself into a superior position, and one's opponent, an awkward position before making the counter attack. Thus, one will be able to gain victory without spending much effort. This is in accordance with what is said in the Taijiquan treaties: "To meet hardness with softness is termed getting away"; "to get oneself into a superior position, and one's opponent, an awkward position, is called adhering to." One should take any on-coming force, big or small, as a hard one, and not to resist it with force, but to meet it softly while evading from the attack. This is what is meant by "getting away." To creat a superior position before making the counter attack, one must catch the right opportunity and make use of the advantageous situation, or try to get out from an awkward and disadvantageous position in time.

It is naturally uncomfortable in an awkward position, and to transfer from being uncomfortable to comfortable, one must also do as pointed out in a Taijiquan classic: "If you fail to catch a good opportunity or to gain an advantageous position, your body will be in a state of disorder and the cause of such a fault must be sought from the waist or legs." That is: in pushing-hands, if the waist senses some discomfort, adjust the legs and the trouble will be gone; and when the legs are not properly placed, hard to bare one's weight and feeling uncomfortable, adjust the waist, and the problem will be solved. We must also see that when one's own body is in a comfortable state, there is no question that the other party is in a state of discomfort, and vice versa. And when one is in a superior position, this is the time to issue energy to upset the opponent. And remember: not a split-second's delay; any delay, the opportunity is lost and the situation is changed. Thus the aim of pushing-hands training is not to improve our natural reaction, to make it quicker and more forceful, but to inhibit and remould it. And it does not mean "not to use any force", but to use a necessary amount of force at the right moment and with much greater effects.

The principle "no letting go and no resistance" is one of prime importance in pushing-hands practice. The relationship between advance and retreat could be made more interrelated. The two persons engaged in this practice should neither stick together too closely, nor get separated, but to be linked into one in the continuous rotation practice. The procedure of practice is to let one party take up the role of an attacker, the other the defender, and then have the two changed around later. If the attacker advances one inch, the defender yeilds one inch, if one foot, also one foot, not a bit more or less. Yeilding less will result in resisting, while yeilding more will result in letting go. And one must remember that all advancing or retreating must take a curved path, not a straight one. Another important point is that to practise "no resisting", it is necessary not only to yeild with the hands, but to turn the waist and sit back at the same time. Otherwise, because of lack of coordination between one's own hands and the trunk, should the trunk stay unmoved while the hands are already retreated, it will offer the opponent an opportunity of discarding the hands and reach directly for the trunk. That is why in pushing-hands, it relies chiefly on one's waist and leg-work. To train the waist and legs, aside from laying emphasis on fundamental training, such as the practice of the various forms of foot stance: the archer stance, the riding stance, the insubstantial stance, the resting stance and the sitting stance, etc., as well as the various forms of turning and twisting the trunk, one must take note of the training procedure of "seeking first for extending and opening; seeking later for closing and compacting."

Formerly, speaking of pushing-hands, there is one way called "getting the gate tightly closed", and another, "leaving the gate wide open". The idea of "getting the gate tightly closed" is that as a defensive measure against any offensive move, one should block the entrance leading toward one's own body. It is generally correct but not always so. If one has in his command good waist and leg-work, it is all right for him to leave the gate wide open, enticing the opponent to come in. On the contrary, if one only pays attention to closing the gate in his daily practice, and has no experience in leaving the gate wide open, then, at the instance of actual encounter, should the gate be opened by his opponent, he will find himself in great alarm and not knowing what to do. Therefore, in daily practice, one should first seek to make one's postures more and more open and extended, and later on, more and more close and compacted. It is quite the same as in learning calligraphy.

To be good at writing small size characters, one generally starts with writing big size charcters to build up a strong foundation of penmanship. When one is already good at writing big size characters, one can achieve success in writing small size characters after a comparatively short time of practice. As it is harder to extend one's movement when one is already accustomed to compacting, the training of Taijiquan demands extending one's movements first to increase the reach in applying the techniques of "adhering, connencting, sticking and following, without letting go and with no resistance", so as to make possible "With the upper and lower parts acting in unison, it will be difficult for the opponent to come in", no matter how far-reaching is the opponent's movement. It is required that one's movements be more and more compacted later, so one can be quicker and nimbler in making any change of movements which will be harder to be sensed by the opponent. This is the training method designed for reaching a higher level of accomplishment: to make one's sense of touch more sensitive, one's "hearing" (sensing) of the on-coming energy more precise, one's "answer" (response) to an "inquiry" (the opponent's testing move) more adequate and to discriminate the insubstantial and substantial more clearly.

Finally, a detailed exeplanation of "double-weighting" and the way to avoid it is given below.

Generally speaking, double-weighting means that substantiality and insubstantiality are not clearly differentiated. It is said in the Taijiquan classics, "The insubstantial and the substantial should be clearly discriminated. Each single part of the body has both an insubstantial and a substantial aspect at any given time, as does the body in its entirety." Therefore, in every posture taken, and in the way of issuing energy, there should be differentiated aspects of the substantial and the insubstantial. In pushing-hands, one must first seek to find out the insubstantial and the substantial aspects of the opponent's postures and movements, as well as in his way of applying a defensive or offensive technique and in issuing energy. Then one should make good use of the opponent's insubstantiality and substantiality found by attacking the insubstantial and evading from the substantial, and at the same time, one should make subtle and varified changes of the insubstantial and substantial aspects of his own, so as not to let them be found out by his opponent, or to puzzle and mislead the opponent by feinting. If one could not have the insubstantiality and the substantiality either of his own or of his opponent clearly discriminated, or to meet substantiality with substantiality, he is bound to be defeated in the pushing-hands. Therefore, double-weighting is the most serious fault that must be avoided in pushing-hands.

It is said in the Taijiquan treaties: "Many people have spent years in practising Taijiquan, yet are often seen unable to apply it for practical use, but to be generally subdued by others as the result of not having perceived the serious fault of double-weighting." This shows that double-weighting is not only like an unnoticeable pitfall that one is liable to fall into at any time, but is also like a sickness that could not be easily diagnosed and got rid of.

Letting both feet exert force against the ground to bear the weight of the body equally is certainly double-weighting. If both feet are exerting force but letting a greater part or the whole of one's body weight be borne by one foot, with the other foot bearing a lesser part of body weight or just for the sake of balancing the body, that is not double-weighting. This is the generally accepted view. However, in actual practice, many Taijiquan learners are not quite clear about how to be in the state of non-double-weighting.

More often than not, they will think that it is not necessary for the insubstantial foot (leg) to exert any force. They fail to see that only when it is also exerting some force, can the body be kept in equilibrium and the centre of gravity stabilized. However, the force of the insubstantial foot should not be exerted against the ground, but in the emptiness just for balancing. If the insubstantial foot exerts force against the ground, one's centre of gravity will tend to move out of the base; or if the insubstantial foot does not exert any force, he will be easily set off balance by the opponent's slight push or pull. This is why we find such a statement in the Taijiquan classics "To be insubstantial is not a state of totally devoid of effort." And we must also study and make good use of its counterpart, "To be substantial is not a state of being totally fixed onto the ground", the gist of being in such a state is rather simple: think of your head as if being lifted upward by a string suspended from above.

If one has no understanding of both sides of the same issue, he may have no more trouble with double-weighting, but he may be again involved with a new fault of letting all the weight dropped down and all the force exerted at one side.

In all, double-weighting denotes the stereo-form of not having the insubstantial and the substantial differentiated. To avoid double-weighting, one must be capable of making rapid and subtle changes from being insubstantial to being substantial, or vice versa, related to any part of his body or to what is on his mind. At the moment when any of the substantial part on his body is about to be shaken, one should think of letting it become insubstantial immediately and vice versa. The training procedure is to make such changes going along from a bigger part to a smaller and smaller part of one's body, up to the size of one square inch or a single finger. Of course, such kind of refined training and high level of achievement is beyond the reach of beginners. The beginners should only follow a course of gradual progression. They should, in their rotation exercise, try to make their movements more and more open, extended and rounded at first, and more and more closed and compact, but still rounded later on. The circular form is the ideal form for smoothly neutralizing any on-coming force at any point of contact and for quick change of movements at any time. And having one's movements well rounded is a prerequisite for attaining a high degree of harmony and continuity. There could be in one's outer movements, many different forms of circles: the regular, the semi, the vertical, the horizontal and the oblique circles, as well as the ovals for one assortment; and the hand, elbow, shoulder, chest, abdomen, hip, knee and foot circles for another assortment. As to one's inner activities, there should also be some sort of circular movements, one should think of his internal organs making some slight turning and inter-massage with the assistance of deep abdominal breathing. This will aid the sending out of inner spiraling energy from Dantian (a point about two inches below navel). This will also help making one's circulation system, one's main and collateral channels (a network of passages, through which vital energy circulates and along which the acupuncture points are distributed) unimpeded. With proper guidance and ceaseless endeavour, the beginners will eventually become masters of the art of pushing-hands.

A DETAILED COURSE OF TAIJI PUSHING-HANDS EXERCISE

This illustrated course is arranged in the order of learning:

I. Solo exercise
- A. Warding
- B. Pressing
- C. Rolling
- D. Pushing

II. Duet exercise
- A. Single-hand pushing
  Preparatory posture — single hand contacting
  1. Single-hand pushing and kneading in horizontal circles
  2. Single-hand pushing in vertical circles
- B. Two-hands pushing
  Preparatory posture — two hands contacting
  1. Pushing-hands using the four basic methods
  2. Pushing-hands using the eight methods; or Da Lu

I. Solo exercise

When doing the solo exercise, stress is to be laid on the four methods of warding, pressing, rolling and pushing. It is required to focus one's attention on moving according to instructions instead of on the exerting of energy. Until well versed in the aforementioned four methods, can one then proceed into duet exercise. The succeeding four illustrations, figures P1, P2, P3, and P4 are basic postures of these four methods.

A. Warding

Stand facing due south, move right hand from your right ribs toward your upper front, thumb in line with tip of nose, palm facing in. Loosen knees to lower torso, draw right foot forward, heel touching, toes slanting. Meantime, raise left hand forward until its thumb gets to the bend of

Fig. P1 Fig. P2 Fig. P3

right elbow, palm facing forward. Now set down right foot and bend right knee to lower torso slightly and straighten hind leg naturally to assume a right archer stance. Simultaneously turn forward right palm, set sight on tip of right forefinger and focus your attention on left palm. This is "warding." (Fig. P1)

B. Pressing

Continue with the preceeding movement without moving steps. Gradually drop right hand, little finger leading, to the level of tip of its elbow, palm facing in, fingertips pointing left. Right arm is now bent to a 90 degree angle, horizontally in front of chest. At same time, slide forward left hand till its wrist touches upper side of right arm bend, palm facing out, fingers pointing up. Direct your sight far ahead over left forefinger. Your weight is on right foot, and your attention focused on your back. This is "pressing." (Fig. P2)

C. Rolling

Succeeding the previous movement, let your right hand descend toward front right, little finger leading, for the whole arm to stretch out naturally. Turn up right palm (imagining supporting the opponent's left elbow). Move up left hand toward rear left, its forefinger leading, till left palm is at a natural distance from left side of your forehead. Now the two palms have 10 cm. between them, both palms facing out, all fingers slanting up, the left hand slightly higher than the right one. At same time relax left knee, "sit" backward to shift your weight to left leg. Right leg is stretched in your front, with heel touching the floor, toes slanting up, assuming the left sitting stance. Look at tip of left forefinger, your attention focused on the centre of left palm. This is "rolling." (Fig. P3)

D. Pushing

Succeeding the previous movement without moving steps, shift your sight from left forefinger to right forefinger, your weight remaining on left leg. At same time, without any change of the distance between the two palms, relax shoulder and sink elbows, the two hands will of their own accord descend and turn toward right, wtih your torso naturally turned toward right too. When torso turned to front (due south), bend slightly two arms, for both palms to settle horizontally in your front, facing down. The left hand should be in level with your brests, while right hand be in level with your navel. Your sight is still on right forefinger, your attention on Shanzhong point (a point between your brests). This is "pushing." (Fig. P4)

II. Duet exercise

A. Single-hand pushing

Preparatory posture — single hand contacting

Two partners stand facing each other. Each takes a step forward with right foot and draws forward right hand from own right ribs with an upward arc. Each assumes a sitting stance, with back of wrist attached to that of the other's in a cross form. (Fig. P5)

Fig. P4

Fig. P5

1. Single-hand pushing and kneading in horizontal circles

Two partners stand facing each other, both assume preparatory posture of single hand contacting. Then,

(1) A (in Chinese dress) lowers right palm against B's right wrist to push it toward B's chest. B (in shirt sleeves), to neutralize A's attack, sits back on left leg, bends right arm, and draws right hand horizontally back toward own left shoulder, palm in ward, along half a horizontal circle.

(2) B continues moving of right hand to own right shoulder and turns wrist for palm to face out, waist follows naturally the turning.

(3) B now pushes toward A's chest. The movements are same as those of A in (1).

(4) A draws hand back with kneading movements. The movements are same as those of B in (1) and (2). Here also, a horizontal half circle is being formed. Repeat the back and forth pushing and kneadiny along the half circles, until both are familiar with these basic movements. Movements by the right or left limbs are the same. (Fig. P6: a.b.c.d.)

2. Single-hand pushing in vertical circles

Two partners stand facing each other, both assume preparatory posture of single hand-contacting, Then,

(1) A rotates and presses down on B's wrist with outer edge of own right hand.

(2) A follows up by pushing toward B's face with own palm.

Fig. P6a

Fig. P6b

Fig. P6c

Fig. P6d

(3) B bends arm to adhere to A's forward push, then withdraws own hand downward along the lower half of a vertical circle.

(4) B lets hand pass own right ribs to push forward toward A's abdomen. (Fig. P 7: a, b, c, d)

A slightly turns waist and wrist to press downward B's hand, then go on with movements (2), (3), (4) . . . . After repeating many rounds, then A and B change around. Also practise with left hands in contact.

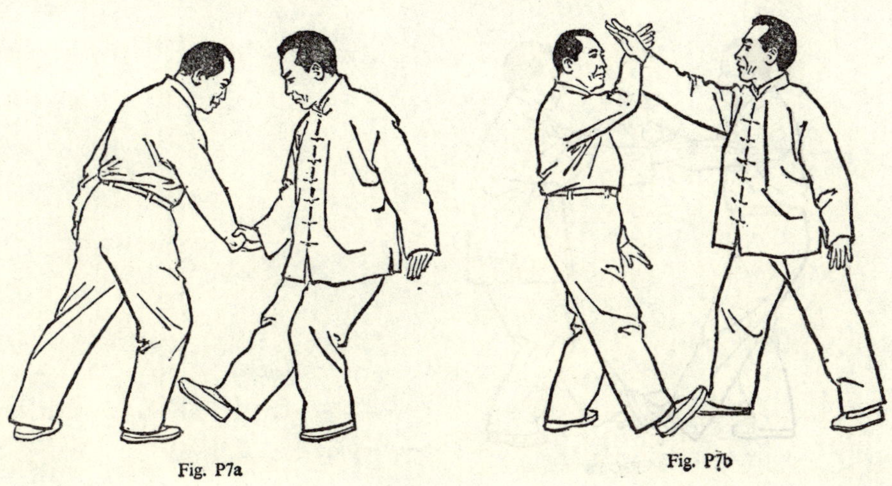

Fig. P7a

Fig. P7b

Fig. P7c Fig. P7d

B. Two-hands pushing

Preparatory posture — two hands contacting

This posture is same as that of the single-hand pushing, except the rear left hand is moved to the front, attached to the opponent's right elbow. Imagine the point of contact of the two wrists to be the centre of a big circle, and each side occupies half of the circle. That means each holds a fish-like half of the circle like the sign of Taiji. (Fig. P 8)

1. Pushing-hands using the four basic methods

The four basic methods are: warding, pressing, rolling and pushing. When two partners are doing pushing-hands, the movement of warding

Fig. P8

Fig. P9a

Fig. P9b

represents (not actually towards) the direction of north, rolling the south, pressing the east and pushing the west. Repeated circling movement is kept on by the back and forth pushing and kneading between the two partners. The circling begins with the preparatory posture. Then,

(1) A (in shirt sleeves) and B (in Chinese dress) both employ the movement of warding at the start. If A's force is stronger than that of B's, B should bend his knee to "sit" backward, and also bend his arms with elbows sinking. Next, he should with one hand lighted on A's elbow, the other on A's wrist, roll back toward own right side of chest and then slant upward. This is called "A warding, B rolling." (Fig. P 9: a, b)

(2) Taking advantage of this situation, A bends right arm horizontally to a 90 degree angle to press toward B's chest in order to block B's wrists, and to attach own left palm to B's left wrist to enhance the force of press. As A presses at B's elbow, B can turn waist slightly to left, and losing no time to push down at A's left elbow and wrist, till the opponent can no longer carry on the offensive. This is called "A pressing, B pushing." (Fig. P 10: a, b)

(3) When A's left elbow is being controlled by B's pushing, and A is sensing the pushing through an awkwardness at his waist, A instantly detach his right hand and attach it under B's left elbow to force B's left elbow to slant diagonally. This is called "dodge hand, uphold elbow." (Fig. P 11)

(4) B's left elbow having been raised by A, he seeks to turn waist slightly

Fig. P10a

Fig. P10b

toward left and move both hands toward front left, each hand along an arc to ward off and to neutralize A's raising force. This is called "turn waist, ward off with arcs." (Fig. P 12)

(5) Following B's warding force A tries to neutralize it with rolling. (Fig. P 13)

(6) Following A's rolling force, B becomes attacker with the pressing. A follows B's pressing force, and tries to nullify it with pushing. (Fig. P 14)

Fig. P11

Fig. P12

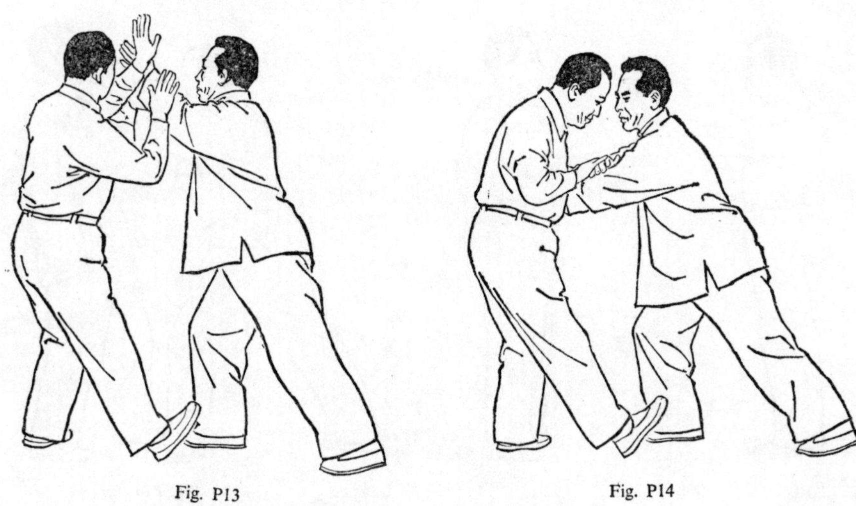

Fig. P13　　Fig. P14

The recurring of the circling in this way is called "pushing-hands using the four basic methods" or "doing the rotation."

2. Pushing-hands using the eight methods or Da Lu

Footwork plays an important part in Da Lu Pushing-hands. It is a combined training of all the eight basic methods. Besides the four methods just given above, the methods of pulling, splitting, elbow-striking and shoulder-striking (representing the four corners) are added. It takes constant practice of the above methods to form correct movement by habit. Only thus can one gradually achieve body coordination on a new level and attain such advanced skills as dodging, extending, springing up, position-shifting, getting-close-to, exerting force with a snap, pressing against, leaning against, self-shrinking, self-softening, making ingenious moves, etc. Below is the exercise.

(1) A warding B rolling

1) A and B stand to attention facing each other, their right wrists in contact in cross form, right palms facing in, with thumbs aligned with own noses. Both direct eyesights over own thumbs at the opposite partner. (Fig P 15 Single hand contacting)

2) A draws forward right foot to block B's left heel, and turns right palm forward with thumb aligned with tip of B's nose, and with tip of forefinger brushing (from a natural distance, not touching) B's left eyebrow, from its thick end to its thin tip. At same time A supports lightly B's right elbow with own left palm and thinks for own Mingmen point to settle upon own Huantiao point, and A's right knee will naturally bend forward, and the muscles at

Fig. P15

Fig. P16

the back of his left knee will fully extend. So A's body weight is now shifted to right leg forming the right archer stance. A's sight is directed forward, passing the left side of the nail of his right forefinger. (Fig. P 16 A warding)

3) B draws left foot a big step toward rear left, sets this foot on floor and stretches out this hind leg, while he bends forward right knee to sustain his body weight. At same time, with right palm still adhered to A's right wrist, B adds left palm in support of A's right elbow, and rolls A's right arm upward toward rear right. B's sight rests on tip of own right forefinger. (Fig. P 17 B rolling)

(2) A pressing B pushing

1) A moves forward left foot to block B's right heel, and bends right arm to a 90 degree angle for it to stay horizontally before own chest, palm in, fingers pointing to left, while he moves left wrist forward to the bend of own right arm, left palm away from self, fingers pointing up. In mind, A thinks for own back to fall on front foot, while bending his left knee, stretching out right leg to shift body weigth to left leg and assuming the left archer stance. (Fig. P 18 A pressing)

2) B draws right foot diagonally backward toward rear right, sets this foot on floor and stretches out this hind leg, while he bends forward left knee to sustain his body weight. At same time, B lets his left palm adhere to A's left wrist, his right palm adhere to A's left elbow, and with his two hands he pushes downward

Fig. P17

Fig. P18

toward the front of his left foot. Now, his attention is focused on his Shanzhong point (between two brests), and his sight rests on tip of his left forefinger. (Fig. P 19 B pushing)

(3) A elbow-striking B pulling

1) A inserts right foot between B's two feet. Then A bends forward right knee and stretches out left leg to shift weight to right leg, assuming a right archer stance. At same time he sets tips of left fingers at the bend of own right arm, and then bends right arm for its palm to get close to own right shoulder. He directs eyesight forward along where the point of his right elbow is pointing at. His attention is focused on his right Jianjin point. (Fig. P 20 A

Fig. P19

Fig. P20

Fig. P21a

Fig. P21b

elbow-striking)

2) B, without any moving of feet, keeps left thumb in line with tip of own nose while setting right palm above A's right wrist or elbow to pull it downward. At this moment focusing attention on own Xuanguan point (between two eyebrows), B looks at own right Jianjin point, and keeps his right kneecap perpendicular to his right toe, right leg sustaining 70% of his weight, and his left kneecap perpendicular to left ankle, sustaining 30% of his weight. And his torso will of its own accord lower a little. (Fig. P 21a, P 21b B pulling, front and back views)

(4) A shoulder-striking B splitting

1) Without any shift of feet A moves right hand toward upper front, with forefinger leading. Then with right hand taking hold of B's right wrist and left hand rolling backward B's right elbow, A turns upper torso to right for own left shoulder to get close to B's chest, and quickly turns head toward right to direct own eyesight backward to be in a straight line with own left shoulder. His palms are facing down, the arcs formed between thumb and forefinger of two palms facing each other. His attention is focused on Yuzhen point (the indented point where the back of head connects with neck). (Fig. P 22 A shoulder-striking)

2) The moment A issues the shoulder-stroke B takes hold of A's left wrist with own left hand and adheres to A's left elbow with own right hand. Then B turns upper torso slightly toward left, and lifts left foot from the outer side to inner side of A's right knee,

but keeping it uplifted. B's weight is sustained on his right leg, his eyesight on his left forefinger, and his attention focused on the centre of his right palm. (Fig. P 23 B splitting)

The above 8 forms of exercises of Da Lu pushing-hands have A taking the offensive with the four methods of warding, pressing, elbow-striking and shoulder-striking, while B neutralizes with the four methods of rolling, pushing, pulling and splitting. To go on with the Da Lu exercise by reversing the offensive and defensive sides, B can set down his uplifting left foot in-between A's two feet, and then bend forward left knee and stretch out right leg to shift own weight to left leg, assuming a left archer stance. In the meantime, B allows own left thumb to be aligned with tip of A's nose, and left forefinger to brush (with a natural distance) from the thick end of A's right brow to its thin tip, while with own right palm adhered to A's left elbow warding off to the front.

In quick response, A withdraws right foot and thrusts it toward rear right. With body weight on left foot he assumes a left archer stance. Simultaneously A adheres to B's left hand with own left palm and supports B's left elbow with own right palm, to roll up toward rear left. Thus the movement is shifted to "B warding A rolling." This will naturally be followed with a full set of "B pressing A pushing", "B elbow-striking A pulling", "B shoulder-striking A splitting." The last movement will bring the partners to the beginning "A warding B rolling", etc. Such repeated rounds in pushing-hands form the most important exercise for pushing-hands with movable steps. Only through constant practice of these movements to be fully familiar with them can one attain pliability and nimbleness. Only thus one will be able to apply it either as a martial art or as a means of maintaining good health.

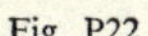

Fig. P22

Fig. P23

[illegible] has [illegible] A's [illegible]. B's weight is concentrated on his [illegible] his left [illegible], and his [illegible] forward [illegible] his [illegible] (Fig. [illegible]) following [illegible].

The above movements [illegible]. The pushing-hands [illegible] with the four [illegible] of warding, pressing, elbow-striking and shoulder-striking, [illegible] with the four [illegible] pulling and splitting. [illegible] the [illegible] and [illegible] sides [illegible] down his [illegible] A's [illegible] left, [illegible] and [illegible] left forward [illegible] right leg [illegible] weight to his left leg, assuming a left [illegible] stance. [illegible] B [illegible] his own left thumb to be aligned with [illegible] A's [illegible] and [illegible] finger to [illegible] (with a natural distance) from the [illegible] of [illegible] right [illegible] his right palm [illegible] A's [illegible] elbow [illegible] off [illegible] front.

In quick response, A withdraws his right foot and [illegible] body weight on his left foot, he assumes a left [illegible] stance. Simultaneously A [illegible] B's left hand with own left palm and supports B's right elbow with own right palm, [illegible] pull up toward rear left. [illegible] movement [illegible] A rolling. This will naturally be followed with a [illegible] B pressing A [illegible], B elbow-striking A [illegible], B shoulder-striking A [illegible]. The last movement will bring the partners to the beginning, A warding B rolling. [illegible] repeated [illegible] the most important exercise for pushing hands with movable steps. Only through constant practice of these movements can the [illegible] with [illegible] plasticity and [illegible]. Only [illegible] will be able to [illegible] as a martial art or as a means of maintaining good health.

The Famous Teacher Yang Yuting

PRACTICAL GUIDANCE TO LEAD YOU THROUGH THE GATE OF TAIJIQUAN

— *Teachings of the Famous Teacher Yang Yuting*

"Verbal instructions are necessary to lead one through the right gate and onto the right path, while mastery of the art comes from one's incessant self-cultivation."

— *"Chant of the Thirteen Postures"*

Brief Introduction to the Famous Teacher Yang Yuting

Born in 1887, died in 1982, Yang Yuting was a famous Taijiquan master with a rich teaching experience of about sixty years in Beijing. He was a direct disciple of Master Wang Muzhai who was a direct disciple of the illustrious founder of the Wu School Taijiquan, Master Quan Yu (also known as Wu Quanyu). Master Yang's students came from different walks of life, including the well known General Fu Zhuoyi, the outstanding Beijing Opera Kungfu actor Chang Yunxi, the chief Taijiquan instructor of the famous Beidaihe Sanatorium, Master Li Jingwu, the dean of the Chinese Martial Arts Teaching Centre of the Eastern District of Beijing, Master Li Bingci and the authors of this book, etc. Master Yang had always been much respected for his strict and detailed instruction and the no-flowery-talk teaching manner. In the course of his teaching, he laid great emphasis on the standardization of form and the clear understanding of the characteristics of the art, and then proceeded to render individual treatment according to different personal conditions. He had been holding the vice-chairmanship of Beijing Wushu (Chinese martial arts) Association for many years up to his death at 95. Master Yang had stopped teaching Taijiquan since 1966. In 1961, he prepared a series of lecture notes for his students. Not long before his death, I obtained permission from the master to condense and revise a part of the valuable material to be offered to the public, so the readers of this book may have the opportunity of receiving the famous teacher's guidance to lead them through the gate of Taijiquan and onto the way to the mastery of the art.

Master Yang's Scheme of Graded Teaching and Learning

As Taijiquan is quite complicated in its movement formation and demands a high degree of technical exactness and adaptability, and as the art emphasizes a gradual and natural development of subtle mind control, keen sensation and alert reaction, there is no short cut to the mastery of the art, and it is not advisable to design a quick learning course. The right path to success is one of ceaseless endeavour following a scheme of gradual progression leading to a deeper and deeper understanding of the principles and techniques of the art and a finer and finer degree of controlling the body by the mind. Based on his long years of teaching experience Master Yang divided the teaching and learning period into three stages, each with its particular aspects to be emphasized as follows:

1st stage

1) Learn the postures one by one, and each posture movement by movement, as closely as possible as taught by the instructor or as laid down in a teaching manual. Proceed to teach/learn a new posture only after the former one could be quite accurately executed. Repeated practice of a single posture dozens of times in continuation is usually needed for the students to remember the proper movement sequence and to form a correct movement pattern. Holding a certain stance in its correct form from a few seconds to a few minutes or more without any motion, called taking a pile-stance, is a common practice and a very effective means of building up stronger leg strength, greater sinking power and stamina, so as to gradually build up the solidity of the lower part of one's body as if rooted into the ground.

2) Form a habit of keeping the different parts of one's body in the manner deemed natural and fundamental by the Taijiquan classics, with special regard to the following six points:
   (1) The head should always be kept straight with its top pointing upward without exerting any force as if it were suspended by a string from above;
   (2) The lowest vertebra should be kept plumb erect;
   (3) The chest should be held in slightly and naturally;
   (4) The back muscles should be loosened while its top part lifted slightly upward;
   (5) The shoulder should be kept sunk;
   (6) The elbows should be kept lowered.

3) Form a clear perception of the characteristics of Taijiquan movements: relaxed, pliable, slow, rounded and even. Try to direct your movements more and more in such a manner. Though it takes a long time

to get rid of the clumsiness and tenseness generally exhibited by the beginners, one should try hard to obtain a little bit of improvement day by day. Easiness and naturalness will surely come up after a year or so.

2nd stage

1) Polish up the more difficult postures, such as those requiring standing on a single foot or turning the body 180 degrees or more.
2) Improve the ability of keeping yourself centered without the slightest loss of balance at all times.
3) Improve gradually the coordination of the hands, eyes, trunk and feet, paying special attention to the waist. See to it that there is always some waist movement, big or small, or even very slight, in connection with any movement of the other parts of the body. Observe well the principle that whenever you make a move, all the related parts of the body should all move in unison; and once any movement turns into stillness, a state of tranquility should prevail in your whole self.
4) Differentiate the insubstantial from the substantial more and more distinctly.
5) Improve the smooth linkage of a number of postures at a time, and then proceed to practise the whole sequence of movements in one continuity.

3rd stage

1) Pay special attention to performing the whole set of Taijiquan in a light, agile and flowing manner without any abruptness or discontinuity.
2) Learn the combative functions of every movement of every posture, and practise them with a picture in your mind as if facing an opponent.
3) Vary the speed of practice from time to time: the normal; the slower than normal; the faster than normal; as slow as you can without showing any discontinuity of movement and wavering of attention; and as fast as you can without exhibiting any rash and incorrect movement or a hasty and careless attitude. However, most of your practice should be done with normal speed or slower than normal speed.
4) Try to couple the different movements with diaphragm breathing as naturally as possible.
5) Learn and practise the "Pushing-hands" exercise: proceed from the one arm to the two arms; from the fixed steps to the active steps; from applying the four basic Pushing-hands postures (warding, pressing, rolling and pushing) to eight postures (warding, pressing, rolling, pushing, pulling, splitting, elbow-striking and shoulder-striking).

Master Yang's Practical Instructions on Some Important How-to

(1) What is meant by "Yi" and how to let "Yi" conduct the body?

The word "Yi" denotes intent or thought, or thinking, or idea.

In practising Taijiquan, "to let 'Yi' conduct the body" means that you must first have a clear idea and a definite intent of what you are going to do in your mind and to let the body do it accordingly. Sometimes, it just indicates which part of the body the mind should be thinking of, or your attention should be focused on. Though it is nothing unusual to have first in one's mind of what one is going to do just before doing it, nevertheless, it is not a common practice in one's daily doings to think of or to be aware of how he is doing a thing all the way through, from the beginning to the end, and, at the same time, to make modifications if the body is not doing precisely as the mind wills it, especially when one's attention or thinking is not to be put only on his outer movements but on his inner activities as well. Thus it needs a period of training to get used to doing it this way and months and years to make the conducting more and more subtle and the response more and more refined.

As Taijiquan is quite complicated in its movement formation and demands a high degree of inner and outer coordination, it is unlikely that one can form a clear integrated picture of what and how a posture, not to mention a whole set, should be done in one's mind in a short time. The training procedure devised by Master Yang is: to set one's "Yi" first on the starting point and the ending point of each movement only; when one has become proficient in doing so, then shift one's "Yi" to make clear the line or the path each movement goes through; and then to do every movement, with the "Yi" leading, the body following, from the starting point all the way through the process a movement takes, up to the ending point; and then try to do every posture and finally the entire set of Taijiquan this way; then, when one has again become proficient in doing so, discard the concept of line or path and substitute it with a moving point in the mind, and let the movement of one's body follow closely the movement of this moving point — when it moves, one moves; and when it retreats, one advances. After doing one's daily practice in such a way for some time, he will be able to perform the complete solo set of Taijiquan flowingly and lively as does the running water or the drifting cloud.

As Taijiquan is basically an art of conducting the body with "Yi", the finer the body part to be conducted, the easier for the conducted part to relax; and the more sensitive the feeling and the quicker the response of the body, the deeper the interest in practising and studying could be developed in the doer and the greater the charm of the art would appeal to him.

Usually, when the instructor says to place the "Yi" on a certain part of the body, it simply means to think of that part. But the body part one's "Yi" is to be placed on and the shifting of "Yi" from one part to another should be smaller and smaller, finer and finer. For instance, one's "Yi" could be placed on one hand and then it could be shifted to another, but when one is thinking of one of his hands, a finer way is to think of the palm first and then to let his thinking be shifted onto the fingers or from one finger to another, or even from the root of a finger to its nail. There could be an infinite degree of fineness to be reached, hence, there is no limit to the development and achievement of the art. The more advanced one is, the finer and more subtle his using of "Yi" should be.

2) What is the "Song" demanded of the doer of Taijiquan, and how to be "Song"?

To be "Song" means that the entire body should be kept naturally relaxed but not slackened. The limbs should neither be straightened forcefully nor bent sharply and with stiffness, but be kept naturally relaxed at their joints. So even when one is delivering a straight forward blow towards one's opponent, he could still be doing what is termed in Taijiquan "Seeking the straight thro the curved". Excepting those involved in performing a certain movement or to maintain the body in a certain posture that needs to be duly tensed, all tne rest of muscles, tendons and joints should be kept naturally relaxed. The purpose of being "Song" is: firstly, to facilitate the outer body movements be done slowly, smoothly, roundedly, evenly, nimblely, co-ordinately and flowingly; secondly, to keep the abdomen and the waist loosened, so the diaphragm could be expanded downward to its lowest position to let one's breath fully fill the lungs and one's "Qi" abide by the "Dantian", thus making the whole body vitalized and keeping one's centre of gravity lowered and stabilized.

How to be "Song"? Checking your postures and movements constantly, see if there is any stiffness in any part of your body, and then loosen that part is generally helpful; while the fundamentally preventive way is to observe that your are carrying yourself in the manner deemed natural by the Taijiquan classics with special regard to the six points afore-mentioned in the "Graded Teaching and Learning Scheme."

Beginners will often find: while it is not too difficult to be "Song" in stillness, it is generally rather hard to keep "Song" in motion. Why? Master Yang's observation and analysis is that most of them are not doing the movements in keeping with the standard form taught by their instructors, and therefore are not in harmony with the natural physical constructions of the human body and the rational set up of the Taijiquan movements. Thus, moving a step little too far forward or backward, or making a turn too sharp or insufficient, etc., will impart an awkwardness to the movement and some discomfort to the doer that makes it impossible to be "Song". Therefore it is wise and better to teach and learn every movement, every posture slowly and accurately with repeated demonstrations and a lot of concentrated practice, so what is learned could conform as closely and naturally as possible to that taught by a competent instructor or laid down in a good teaching manual right from the very beginning.

One's Taijiquan will not look like and will not be Taijiquan if devoid of the "Song" required of the doer. A "Song" body, as well as a tranquil mind is an essential element that renders Taijiquan a superior system of physical/mental culture and a unique form of martial art.

3) How to stabilize one's centre of gravity and what to pay special attention to in shifting it?

Keeping one's centre of gravity stable in whatever position he takes and also in the process of transferring from one position to another is a fundamental Kungfu (the cultivated ability or skill to do something difficult through a long period of training) a student of Taijiquan should seek to build up through his daily practice. To be able to maintain one's own balance at all times and to detect his opponent's centre of gravity as soon as one comes into contact with an opponent and to sense and make use of the opponent's slightest loss of balance instantly is what distinguishes the outstanding from the ordinary.

Taking the body as a whole, whether one's contre of gravity is stable or not depends largely on whether his torso is straight and centered or otherwise. When standing straight, one's centre of gravity is generally at the point about 7 cm. in front of the third coccygeal vertebra, and that point would be at a different place for a person of different height, build and age. Of the same person, the centre of gravity changes along with the changes in his blood circulation, breathing, and especially with the postures taken.

In practising Taijiquan one very seldom stands erect but takes various forms of postures, most frequently the "archer stance" and the "sitting stance." A stabilized centre of gravity could be maintained in these two stances if the following requirements are met:

(1) viewed from the front or the sides:
the tip of nose in vertical line with the inner side of the knee cap, and the big toe of the fore foot (archer stance), or the rear foot (sitting stance).

(2) viewed from the side:
the top of head in vertical line with the arch of fore foot (archer

stance), or with the arch of the rear foot (sitting stance).

(3) viewed from the back:
the sacrum in vertical line with the heel of the fore foot (archer stance), or with the heel of the rear foot (sitting stance).

In the process of changing one's movement or posture from one to another, one should be all the more careful in the shifting of one's centre of gravity. The saying in the Taijiquan classics: "one must heed to the transformation of the insubstantial and the substantial" stresses just this point. The shifting of the centre of gravity is closely related with the stableness of the whole body, if not properly done, your body will be in a state of disorder. There is also a saying: "Rising from the root and lowering from the root." And there is another: "Of tens of thousands of changes, none is unrelated with the root." Here, the word "root" denotes the "foot" as well as the centre of gravity. In other words: See to it that every change of movement in any posture, whether rising or lowering, advancing or retreating, or turning, etc. is in unison with the smooth and stable shifting of one's centre of gravity.

Any change of movement and posture, concomitant with the shifting of centre of gravity, should not be done abruptly but gradually.

The following is an illustration of how to shift one's centre of gravity in advancing, retreating and stepping to the sides:

(1) When shifting the centre of gravity forwards (changing from a sitting stance to an archer stance):
Let the centre of gravity of the substantial leg (the rear leg in the sitting stance) drop downward loosely first; at this juncture, the toes of the tipped-up foot of the front leg gradually drop down, and when the sole is set lightly flat on the ground, continue to advance lightly the front knee; at this moment the centre of gravity of the rear leg moves gradually and lightly forward; when the front knee reaches the point in vertical line with the toes of the front foot, continue to move the hip joints lightly forward; finally, loosen the waist. Now the centre of gravity has gradually shifted to the front leg and the sitting stance is changed into the archer stance.

(2) When shifting the centre of gravity backward (changing from the archer stance into the sitting stance):
Again the centre of gravity of the substantial leg (the fore leg of the archer stance) should first be dropped loosely downward. At this juncture, let the hollow of the back knee bend lightly, with the centre of gravity feeling as if it were dropped down onto the toes of the rear foot, and finally onto the rear foot as the bending of knee continues. Meanwhile, the center of gravity of the fore leg is moving gradually

downward and backward; when the knee cap of the rear leg comes in vertical line with the toes of the rear foot, continue to draw backward the hip bones lightly; finally loosen the waist; now the centre of gravity has been shifted backward to the rear leg and the archer stance is changed into the sitting stance.

(3) When shifting the centre of gravity to the side (changing from the movement of "Grasp Bird's Tail" to the horse-riding stance of "Single Whip"):
Move the left foot sideways to its left side with the toes touching the ground lightly first when commencing the "Single Whip", then the left hand should move in an arc from the right upward to the front left and then turn downward and sideways to the left; at this juncture, first the toes and then the entire sole of the left foot should gradually step down flat on the ground, then continue to loosen the left knee downward; when the right hip joint is influenced by the leftward moving hand to rise a little and turn a little toward the left, loosen the left hip joint downward. At this time, the centre of gravity, following the turn of the waist, has been shifted to the middle point between the two feet. Then loosen the waist again, and let the two knees, and finally the two feet bear the weight of the body evenly.

From the three examples given above, aside from learning the ways of shifting the centre of gravity, one should also take heed of the following four points:

(1) When shifting the centre of gravity, the parts of the body below the waist should make their changes one by one, and in continuity: first the foot, then the knee, then the hip joint, and finally the waist. Such an order must be observed, whether advancing, retreating or stepping to the sides.

(2) When shifting the centre of gravity, that of the waist should not be shifted right straight forward, backward, or sideways, but in a slightly downward curve first, when advancing or retreating; and let that of the waist be raised a little bit till all the joints of the insubstantial leg are well adjusted, and then let it be shifted sideways and downward as the insubstantial leg steps aside. Using the downward curve and the slight raising and lowering as a buffering element during the shifiting, it will be easier to keep the centre of gravity stable.

(3) One must take heed to transform the substantial leg into an insubstantial one gradually and smoothly. Using a simple analogue: taking the gravity of the substantial leg as 10, and that of the insubstantial leg as 0, in the process of shifting, the gravity of the insubstantial leg

increases from 0, 1, 2 . . . 8,9, and finally to 10, while the gravity of the substantial decreases from 10, 9, 8, . . . 2, 1, and finally to 0. The transformation is not done abruptly but smoothly and gradually, and they are in correspondence with each other at all times.

(4) Whatever one does in his Taijiquan practice, it should be in accordance with the principle: "Conduct the body with Yi", and in the process of shifting one's centre of gravity, one's Yi should still be concentrated on the prescribed body parts, so the transformation could be done naturally, smoothly, lightly and lively.

4) How to couple the Taijiquan movements with proper breathing?

All the different postures of Taijiquan are basically composed of two opposite yet co-existant types of motion or state in continuous alternation: the "opening" and the "closing" motions, or the "insubstantial" and the "substantial" states. Our breathing is also composed of two opposite yet co-existant types of motion or state in continuous alternation: the inhaling and the exhaling. The traditional ideal way of coupling the Taijiquan movements with breathing is: inhaling while doing an "opening" motion or coming into an "insubstantial" state; exhaling while doing a "closing" motion or going into a "substantial" state. Bending, retreating, facing upward, raising, energy-accumulating, and neutralizing are classed as "opening" motions and being "insubstantial"; stretching, advancing, facing downward, dropping, energy-issuing and attacking are classed as "closing" motions and being "substantial". From the point of "Yi", any part of the body where "Yi" is concentrated on, that part is "substantial", then its counterpart is "insubstantial". For instance, if your "Yi" is on your right hand, then that is the "substantial" hand, and your left hand is the "insubstantial" one.

However, owing to the differences in the formation of Taijiquan movements and postures, the speed of doing the movements, the depth of one's breath and other physiological capacities as well as the degrees of proficiency of the doer, it is usually not quite possible to couple the entire set of Taijiquan movements with one's breathing in the traditional ideal way. As long as one is not holding his breath to cause any discomfort, but breathing naturally, it is quite all right for the beginners.

The next step is to try to couple the two types of motion with inhaling or exhaling as stated above at the end of a movement. And if a certain movement is too long or too complicated and if you are practising with a speed too slow that before coming to the end of that movement you are unable to continue the inhaling or exhaling as deemed fit, you can intersect the inhaling with a short exhale, or intersect the exhaling with a short inhale, then you will be able to accomplish the proper coupling at the end of the movement.

Then, when your breathing capacity has notably increased, and the way of your breathing has become longer, deeper, finer and more even as a natural result of your constant practice with a gradually increasing training load, you should try to adopt an optimal speed with your practice to meet the aforementioned requirements in coupling the movements with proper breathing. And when that way of coupling gradually and finally becomes natural to you, you can forget all about it, and let your "Yi", "Qi", and "Shen" (the vital spirit) be merged into one, and let your body be truly vitalized after each session of practice.

The Famous Master Wu Tunan

HOW TO PRACTISE TAIJIQUAN TO ATTAIN SUPER HEALTH AND LONGEVITY

— *Teachings of the 98 Year Old Famous Master Wu Tunan*

CHINA DAILY carried a report in its Nov. 11, 1981 issue, entitled "A Long Life of Taijiquan." The opening three paragraphs read as follows: "At 96, Wu Tunan still has good eyesight and hearing, is alert and clear in speech. His tall figure with its straight back and steady walk is that of a much younger man."; "Doctors find that Wu's heart functions like that of an athlete, his blood pressure is normal, he can walk several dozen miles, and once a week he climbs the hills at Badachu, a scenic spot on the outskirts of Beijing. His wife Liu Guizhen, 10 years his junior, is almost as healthy."; "Wu and his wife attribute their health to the practice of Taijiquan, traditional Chinese shadow boxing. Wu, who is vice chairman of the Beijing Wushu Association, has been practising Taijiquan for nearly 90 years."

Aside from the above, the writer has often listened with admiration to the Master's quoting from memory famous passages found in traditional Chinese literary, medical, historical and philosophical works; and watched with keen interest how the old man could still toss a student, 50, 60 or 70 years his junior several feet away in the pushing-hands exercise.

Longevity plus such super health and clarity of mind is surely something to be envied at and worth striving for. The way of attainment sounds rather simple - the practice of Taijiquan. But why and how?

There are now in operation 161 Taijiquan teaching posts with about 750 coaches in Beijing. The yearly enrolment in 1981 amounted to nearly 50,000, reaching a total of over 250,000 since 1974. Statistics have shown that of those participants with chronic diseases, over 90 percent have obtained marked improvement, and many have returned to their jobs. However, men as old and healthy as Master Wu are still rare, even among Taijiquan practicians. Is it because Master Wu is an exception to nature's rule? Or is it because the majority of Taijiquan practicians, enthusiastic and benefited as they are, have not practised Taijiquan in the way as Master Wu has? If so, how should it be done to attain such super health and longevity?

One fine morning, the writer had a long chat with the Master, seeking an answer. Through our discussion, the Master's teachings emerged. My questions, and Master Wu's replies, are as follows:

Zeng:

Factors contributing to health and longevity are many. Why do you attribute your super health to the practice of Taijiquan and not to anything else? Tens of thousands of people practise Taijiquan every morning in Beijing, and as a result of its very good health promoting effects, the number is still growing. However, compared with what you have attained, it seems the majority are not getting the full benefits promised by the art. Is it chiefly because the other factors influencing their health and longevity are possibly not as favourable as yours? Or is it because they have not practised Taijiquan as you have or as you deem it should be?

Wu:

Factors influencing health and longevity, favourable or unfavourable, are indeed numerous. Some important ones, like heredity, geographical environment, living and working conditions, affect us more basically than Taijiquan. Obviously, these factors are either beyond our control, or not easily altered by us. However, their ill effects may be lessened, and good effects enhanced by the practice of Taijiquan. In my own case: I was not born strong but very weak. I suffered lung, liver and spleen troubles as a child, until taking up Taijiquan at the age of nine. I gradually overcame my weakness after eight years of vigorous training under the tutorship of Wu Jianquan, plus another four years under the strict coaching of Master Yang Shaohou.

My health originally was less favourable than the average person's. As to living conditions, I have been through very stressing times. But I persisted in correct practice of Taijiquan under all circumstances.

Zeng:

In other words, it is not just the practice of Taijiquan, but the persistent and correct practice which leads to super health and longevity. Right?

Wu:

Precisely so. But I must add: by persistence, I mean life-long persistence. By correctness, I mean full accordance with the fundamental principles set in the Taijiquan classics.

Zeng:

Such a high standard is very hard to attain.

Wu:

Yes, and no.

It is certainly hard for the sceptics and the half-hearted. These often quit after having missed a few lessons, or upon finding their movements still awkward after a mere few months of practice. But those who are serious in their pursuit of super health and longevity, and who realize they are indeed attainable are therefore determined to spend the necessary time and effort required. They are usually attentive to their instructors and sensitively aware of the subtle differences in their own movements and feelings, depending on whether they follow the instructions faithfully or not. Generally, after learning and practising in such a manner for a year or so, the movements of these students become much more coordinated and flowing, their health noticeably improves. The hour or so of daily practice becomes a time of joy, relaxation and self-achievement. Persistence then is no longer a problem. The only issues are how to make the best possible progress in keeping with age, constitution, time available for learning and practising, and the finding of a good teacher and good practice companions.

Zeng:

That I can well see from my own experience. I started learning Taijiquan at 46 when I found my old favourite sport, weightlifting, a bit beyond my age. As Taijiquan is in many ways very different from weightlifting, I found the movements quite complicated and I did them awkwardly at first. However, with some knowledge of Taijiquan's health promoting effects, I determined to learn this traditional system of health promoting exercise and martial art. It was new to me, and not only suitable to my age but an art I could practise to the end of my days. After a year of intensive learning and practice I was doing the movements more easily. A feeling of relaxation and well-being arose with every practice session.

Even when conditions would not allow me to do Taijiquan I tried to practise it in my mind, coupled with diaphragm breathing. In this way, I had not only managed to have avoided forgetting the sets I had learned, but also could relax under conditions of stress. At the end of 1974, though then already 59, I started to learn new sets of Taijiquan. I found improvement possible even with two knees suffering from bone arthritis, in fact I was the runner-up in the 1978 Beijing Taijiquan Contest for the Aged. What a great joy and satisfaction!

Today, Taijiquan is as much a daily necessity to me as eating and sleeping. What I am most eagerly seeking now is a deeper understanding of the art. As you are one of the oldest Taijiquan masters of our time, you have studied both traditional Chinese medicine and western medicine and are one of the earliest advocates of scientific Taijiquan, I admire you sincerely.

Now what is your interpretation and evaluation of the cardinal principles of the Taijiquan classics from a scientific point of view? What are the most important points to observe in Taijiquan in order to get the best possible results?

Wu:

I am pleased with what you have experienced and that you are eager to hear from me. Let me say first that the basic principles and methods of Taijiquan and the healthful benefits ensurd by this age-old system are in harmony with recent findings in physiology, medicine, sports science and other related fields.

Zeng:

This is very interesting and important. Please elaborate.

Wu:

Of course, I am not prepared to give you a comprehensive presentation, but I will try to cover the most salient points.

The first thing to note is the tenet in physiology that a proper functioning of the nervous system, with the cerebral cortex as its core, is a prerequsite to the proper functioning of the different systems of the human body. Compare this with the cardinal principle of Taijiquan that the art depends primarily on the mind, not on the muscles, and that one must cultivate the subtle directing power of the mind and maintain an ever tranquil state, free from all outside disturbances and vexations. This cultivation is realized through an ever higher coordination not only of such body parts as the hands, eyes, feet and the torso, but also a harmony of the external body movements with the inner changes of the mind-intent, the respiration and the movement of the "qi." Such a state is termed in Taijiquan: "The upper and lower in correspondence; the internal and the external in unison."

To practise or seek such a high coordination for 30-60 minutes everyday is very beneficial to the nervous system and therefore to the whole body, in two ways. Firstly, it will greatly improve the efficiency of the directing power of the mind through exciting, by concentration, a certain part of the cerebral cortex. Secondly, according to the phenomenon of negative inducement in physiology, increasing the excitation of one part of the cerebral cortex will necessarily lessen the excitation in the others, thus suppressing excitation focuses due to chronic illness or prolonged stress and vexation, and so encouraging recovery.

Zeng:

That certainly is an important basic concept to be kept in mind. Are there any recent findings relevant to the directing power of our mind?

Wu:

Recent findings in physiology, brain science and other related fields have further revealed that not only voluntary muscles are under the control of our mind; by focusing attention on certain parts of one's body and thinking in a certain way, after a short period of training with the help of the technique and instrumentation called "bio-feedback", certain inner activities can be controlled or aroused by one's mind as well (the same kind of phenomenon had long been noticed and made use of by Taijiquan masters hundreds of years ago in China.) One successful experiment made in recent years in the West is the raising or lowering of fingertip temperature by the will of mind, which actually is the result of the opening or closing of the capillaries brought about by one's focused thinking. This offers a scientific interpretation of the slight distension and wriggling often sensed by many Taijiquan practicians in their fingertips or palm centres together with a visible reddening of these parts when their minds are focused on them. Sometimes one can also feel a stream of warmth running through a certain part of his body when performing a certain movement, that could well be the widening of some bigger blood vessels, allowing more blood to circulate through.

According to the Taijiquan classics, that something running inside is "qi". And according to the traditional Chinese medical theory, "qi" is something innate in man from birth, something invisible but vital to life. The free moving of "qi" clears the way for the blood to circulate freely, though "qi" circulates through its own network of main and collateral channels, along which the acupuncture points are distributed. The existence of "qi" had never been scientifically identified until a few years ago, when some Chinese scientists with the help of modern instruments, succeeded in finding out first in 1978 that the "qi" emitted from the palm centre of a "qigong" master is a kind of far infra-red radiation adjustable by the rise and fall of low frequency electrical waves. Then in 1979, it was again demonstrated that the "qi" emitted from the fingertips of another "qigong" master was a current of fine particles with electrical charge. Although a comprehensive understanding of "qi" is still a subject for further research, and whether the sense of warmth and wriggling is the result of a freer movement of blood, or of "qi" or of both remains to be ascertained scientifically, practising Taijiquan in the way of "letting the mind direct the qi; and letting the "qi" circulate through the body" will greatly improve your health and lead to longevity. If not practised in this manner, you will still receive some benefits, but not much more than spending the same amount of time walking or doing calisthenics.

Zeng:

Your talk on the relationship between the most salubrious effect and the most characteristic feature of Taijiquan is a point of great interest to me. Now, what would you rate as next in importance and ingenuity?

Wu:

There are a few more points that I would like to mention, but not necessarily in the order of their relative importance and ingenuity. One special feature that almost everyone can see when watching a good Taijiquan performance or practice is the slow, pliable, even, rounded and continuously flowing movements done smoothly without apparent effort from the beginning to te end of a complete set which generally lasts about 5-8 minutes for the shortest simplified version and 20-40 minutes for the longer ones. When it comes to an end, one usually finds light perspiration on the performer's skin even in cold weather, but without finding him out of breath.

Zeng:

This is quite a unique feature. How does it come about, and what particular benefits and advantages does it offer?

Wu:

Aside from what are noticeable to the casual observer as described above, there is, or should be, in these continuously flowing movements, an alternative change from "insubstantiality" to "substantiality" or from "to open" to "to close" as they are termed in the Taijiquan classics. Or simply as the actions themselves show: there is a constant shift of body weight, letting the greater part of it be borne on one of the legs (bent to a certain angle) alternatively, as well as an alternative change of stretching-out and drawing-in movements, keeping the whole body alternatively in a stretched or relaxed state both internally and externally. Practising Taijiquan with a greater part of bodyweight borne on a single and bent leg alternatively for 20-40 minutes in continuity is certainly demanding both to the mind and the body, thus comes the perspiration. Keeping a part of or the entire body in a stretched or relaxed state alternatively is a good means of conserving energy and a way of letting the workload be shared evenly by the different body parts. That, together with coupling deep respiration naturally with body movements in rhythmic harmony as far as possible, makes a good supply of oxygen available right from the beginning to the end of the workout. Thus no oxygen debt is formed, and the performer will not be out of breath.

The benefits and advantages concomitant to this unique feature are many: as the exercise is actually quite demanding, so it enhances cardiovascular efficiency, increases the elasticity of the lung tissue and improves digestion and assimilation. As it is generally done slowly and gently, it is not too hard a task even for the aged or the weak. And as a good supply of oxygen is available at all times and no oxygen debt is being built up throughout the whole practice, it is entirely suitable for those with chronic illness such as high blood pressure, or pulmonary tuberculosis.

Zeng:

That explains the popularity of Taijiquan with people of different ages and health problems. Are there any new findings regarding the health promoting effects in relation to this aspect of its uniqueness?

Wu:

There certainly are. I'll just cite one of the latest. As reported in the newspaper Tiyubao (The Sports Gazette) a researcher at the Henan Medical College made an observation of the changes in the immune functions of nineteen 50-68 years old Taijiquan practicians and twenty-five 18-32 years old middle and long distance runners after their workouts. The procedure is to let the two groups walk slowly to a designated place after rising from bed in the morning, then with the Taijiquan group doing a set of simplified Taijiquan and the runners group running in full speed a distance of 1,600 metres. Both before and after their workouts, samples of their saliva were collected and tests were made of the contents of the immune substance, the secretive type globulin (SlgA) contained in their saliva. The result was that an increase of SlgA was found in about two thirds of the Taijiquan group, while a decrease was found in about two thirds of the runners group right after the workout. It shows that exercises of different intensity will bring about good or bad influence, at least right after the workout, to the immune functions of the human body and an exercise of moderate intensity like Taijiquan will bring about a good influence. This is another proof offered by modern scientific analysis of the multivalent effects of this unique and popular traditional Chinese form of mental and physical culture.

Zeng:

All that I have learned from you today is most interesting and enlightening. Now is there anything else that you would consider of particular importance for me to observe?

Wu:

Well, yes. Though you are much younger than I, you are now already sixty-six, and as enthusiastic as you are, it is all the more necessary to be aware of over training. Anything done in harmony with the law of nature is liable to bring you good results, and aging is a natural law. Don't take yourself as still young when you are already old, or are becoming older. In my own case, I used to train not less than three hours a day when a youth. The whole program was very strenuous, including "keeping pile-stance" (holding a fixed position for a number of minutes, a sort of isometric training) in several different stances; kicking a foot high up forward, touching the forehead with the toe and kicking a foot high up backward, touching the back of head with the heel; doing a set of Taijiquan under a kind of long rectangular table only a few inches higher than a dining table, so as to make sure that I was taking a very tiring low stance, etc. Then about 2 hours during my middle age. After sixty, about one hour and a half. Over seventy, about an hour. Over eighty, less than an hour. Over ninety, about 30 minutes. Now I do only about 15 minutes early every morning and sometimes another 15 minutes before going to bed, and I have kept myself all the time fit and healthy.

The second thing I want you to keep in mind is that the healthy and strong body one has built up through long years of Taijiquan practice or any other sports activity is not one that can stand limitless abuses. Over-eating, over-smoking, over-drinking, over-indulgence in sex, and working beyond a certain limit will surely ruin the mind and the body.

Finally, I hope you will not limit the application of the basic principles of the art to your daily Taijiquan only. For instance if, while walking, you remember to stick up the top of your head lightly, loosen up your hip joints and raise the knees, you will instantly feel spirited and nimble. If something vexes you, you can throw it off by a few minutes of deep breathing, slowly and evenly, and, by shutting off all disturbing thoughts, as you do in the "Preparation Form". Then follow with an actual round of Taijiquan, or just picturing it in your mind. When you are at a scenic spot or in a place full of sunshine, fresh air and fresh food, don't hesitate to take these good things into your body and form a deep impression of them in your mind, to be recalled with joy afterwards, by doing a set of Taijiquan on the spot. That will certainly help you attain super health and longevity.

Zeng:

Thank you ever so much for your valuable and detailed advice. As the old saying goes: "I profit more from one consultation with you than from ten years of reading." I wish you a long, long life and I hope that more and more Taijiquan enthusiasts will learn of your teachings and be benefitted by them.

Appendix I

PROGRESSION DIAGRAM OF 37-POSTURES WU STYLE TAIJIQUAN

NOTES:

1. One of the fundamental requirements in designing a Taijiquan solo sequence is that the Closing Form should be taken place at where the Beginning Form started. One should also try to meet this requirement in practice or exhibition.
   The progression of the different postures of the entire set, though making several turns facing opposite directions, actually takes place more or less on one straight line. Since it is impossible to give a progression diagram on one straight line, so we have spread apart the otherwise superimposed images in the diagram.

2. The acute angle of a triangle denotes the direction a practitioner is facing. The number inside a triangle represents a given posture, or one of several steps of a single posture, e.g.:
   no. 1 represents the Beginning Form
   no. 15 (1) represents Left and Right Instep Kick (lst step).

3. Generally a practitioner is facing south at the Beginning Form, and therefore he has his back toward north, to his left is east, to his right is west.

4. The proper space required is usually 2 metres in width and 5 metres in length for practising the whole sequence.

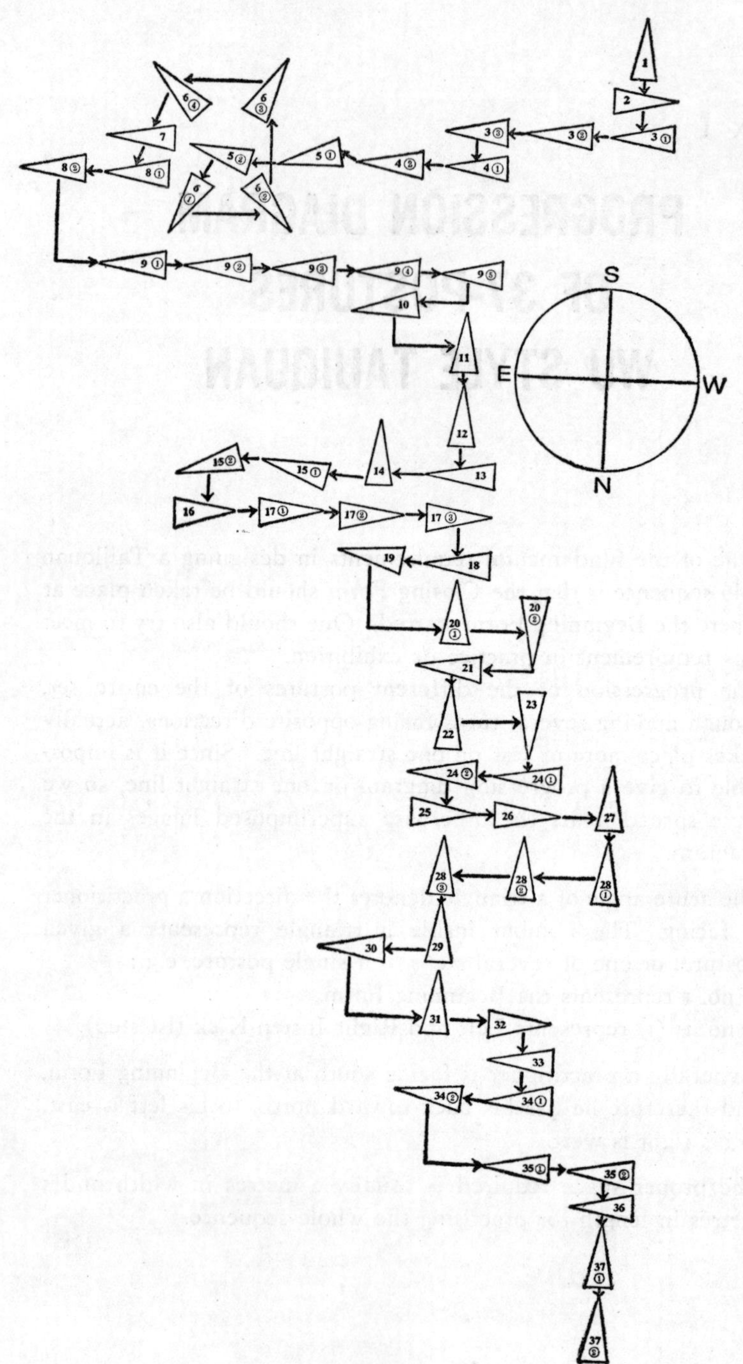

S
E
W
N

Posture Name Represented by the Number within a triangle:

1. Beginning Form
2. Grasp Bird's Tail

3(1). Brush Knee and Twist Step (step one)

3(2). Brush Knee and Twist Step (step two)

3(3). Brush Knee and Twist Step (step three)

4(1). Play the Lute (step one)

4(2). Play the Lute (step two)

5(1). Part the Wild Horse's Mane (step one)

5(2). Part the Wild Horse's Mane (step two)

6(1). Fair Lady Works at Shuttles (step one)

6(2). Fair Lady Works at Shuttles (step two)

6(3). Fair Lady Works at Shuttles (step three)

6(4). Fair Lady Works at Shuttles (step four)

7. Watch with Fist Under Elbow

8(1). Golden Cock Stands on One Leg (step one)

8(2). Golden Cock Stands on One Leg (step two)

9(1). Step Back and Repulse Monkey (step one)

9(2). Step Back and Repulse Monkey (step two)

9(3). Step Back and Repulse Monkey (step three)

9(4). Step Back and Repulse Monkey (step four)

9(5). Step Back and Repulse Monkey (step five)

10. Diagonal Fly

11. Lift Hand

12. Stork Spreads Wings

13. Insert Needle to Sea Bottom

14. Flash the Arms

15(1). Left and Right Separate Instep Kicks (step one)

15(2). Left and Right Separate Instep Kicks (step two)

16. Turn and Strike with Heel

17(1). Step Forward and Punch Down (step one)

17(2). Step Forward and Punch Down (step two)

17(3). Step Forward and Punch Down (step three)

18. Turn Around and Cast Down with Fist and Palm

19. Double Kick

20(1). Left and Right Striking Tiger (step one)

20(2). Left and Right Striking Tiger (step two)

21. Two Fists Blow Ears

22. Dodge and Kick

23. Turn Around and Kick

24(1). Press Face with Palm (step one)

24(2). Press Face with Palm (step two)

25. Cross-form Kick

26. Brush Knee and Punch at Underbelly

27. Front Single Whip

28(1). Wave Hands Like Clouds (step one)

28(2). Wave Hands Like Clouds (step two)

28(3). Wave Hands Like Clouds (step three)

29. Down-pushing Stance

30. Step Forward to Form Seven Stars

31. Step Back and Ride Tiger

32. Turn Around and Press Face with Palm

33. Turn and Kick Horizontally

34(1). Bend Bow to Shoot Tiger (step one)

34(2). Bend Bow to Shoot Tiger (step two)

35(1). Step Back, Deflect, Parry and Punch (step one)

35(2). Step Back, Deflect, Parry and Punch (step two)

36. Seeming Close Up

37(1). Embrace Tiger and Return to Mountain (step one)

37(2). Embrace Tiger and Return to Mountain (step two)

Appendix II

Key to the Foot-weighting Diagram

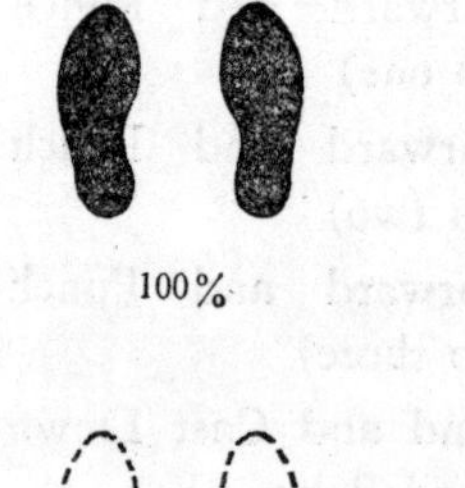

100%

70%

50%

30%

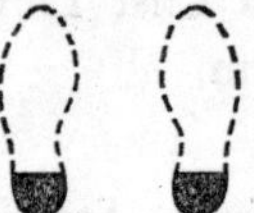

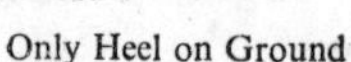

Only Heel on Ground

Only Toe on Ground

Less than 30%

Foot Suspended

Appendix III

Diagram of Vital Points Mentioned in this Book

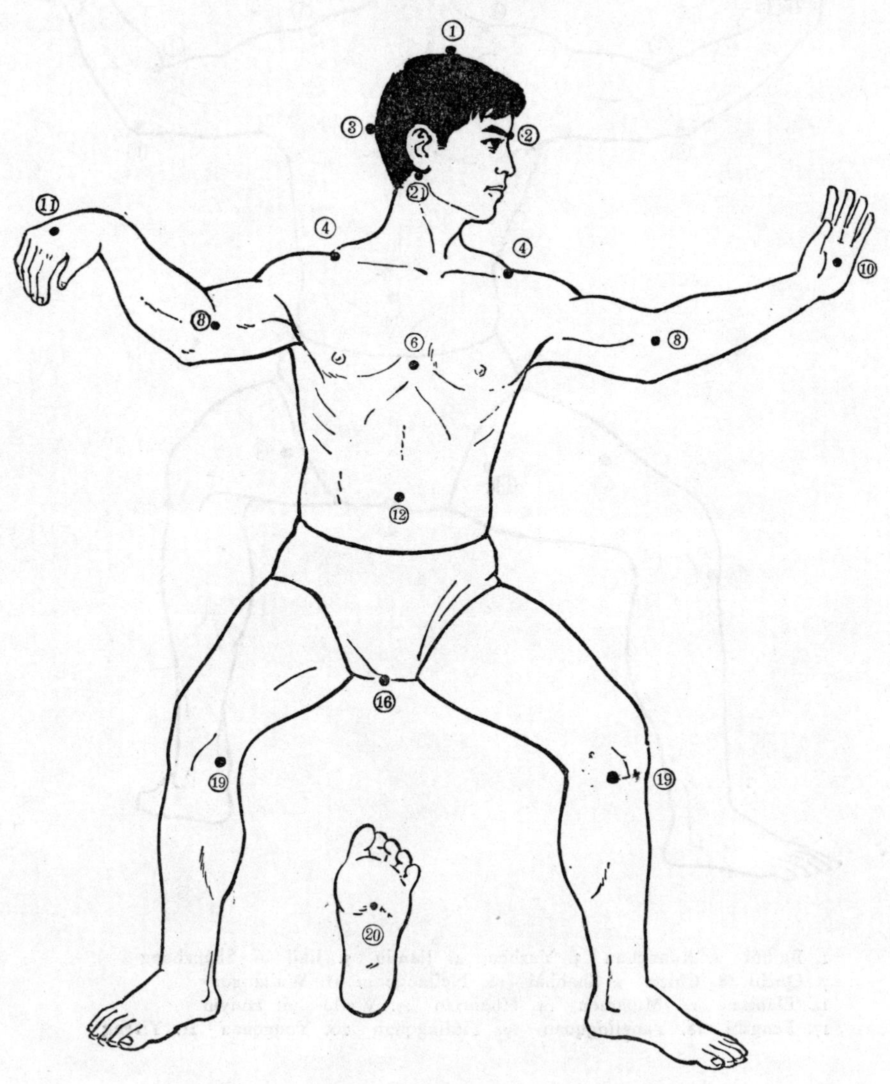

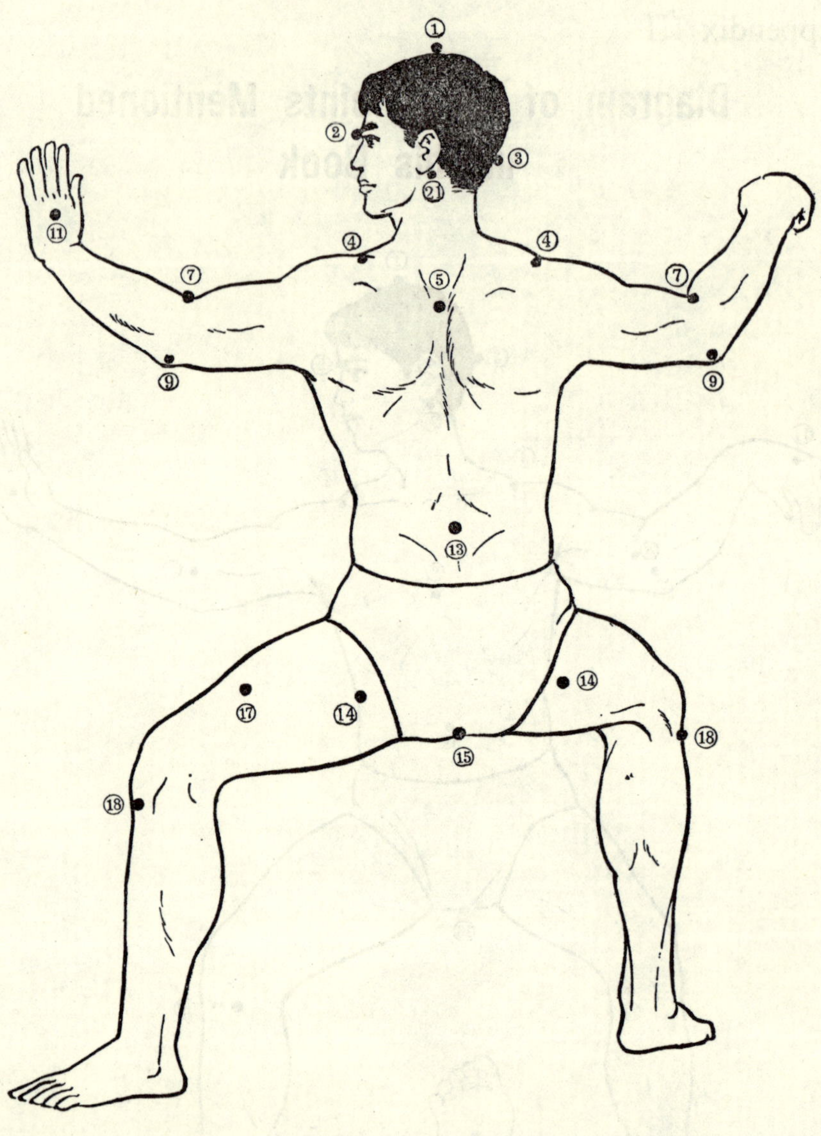

1. Baihui 2. Xuanguan 3. Yuzhen 4. Jianjin 5. Jiaji 6. Shanzhong
7. Quchi 8. Chize 9. Shaohai 10. Neilaogong 11. Wailaogong
12. Dantian 13. Mingmen 14. Huantiao 15. Weilu 16. Huiyin
17. Fengshi 18. Yanglingquan 19. Yinlingquan 20. Yongquan 21. Yifeng